Unsettling Gaza

Unsettling Gaza

Secular Liberalism, Radical Religion, and the Israeli Settlement Project

JOYCE DALSHEIM

OXFORD
UNIVERSITY PRESS

OXFORD
UNIVERSITY PRESS

Oxford University Press, Inc., publishes works that further
Oxford University's objective of excellence
in research, scholarship, and education.

Oxford New York
Auckland Cape Town Dar es Salaam Hong Kong Karachi
Kuala Lumpur Madrid Melbourne Mexico City Nairobi
New Delhi Shanghai Taipei Toronto

With offices in
Argentina Austria Brazil Chile Czech Republic France Greece
Guatemala Hungary Italy Japan Poland Portugal Singapore
South Korea Switzerland Thailand Turkey Ukraine Vietnam

Published by Oxford University Press, Inc.
198 Madison Avenue, New York, New York 10016

www.oup.com

Oxford is a registered trademark of Oxford University Press

Library of Congress Cataloging-in-Publication Data
Dalsheim, Joyce,
Unsettling Gaza : secular liberalism, radical religion, and the Israeli
settlement project / Joyce Dalsheim.
    p. cm.
Includes bibliographical references and index.
ISBN 978-0-19-975120-4 (hardback)
1. Israelis—Gaza Strip—Katif Bloc.
2. Israel—Politics and government—21st century.
3. Judaism and politics—Israel.
4. Religion and politics.
5. Religious Zionism—Israel.
6. Radicalism—Israel.
7. Government, Resistance to—Israel.
8. Arab-Israeli conflict—1993—Peace.
9. Katif Bloc (Gaza Strip) I. Title.
DS110.K316D35 2010
953'.1—dc22   2010011036

1 3 5 7 9 8 6 4 2

Printed in the United States of America
on acid-free paper

To Steve and Olga, for their endless support.
And to Rafi, who makes it all possible.

Preface

"Your fellow is your mirror. If your own face is clean, so will be the image you perceive. But should you look upon your fellow and see a blemish, it is your own imperfection that you are encountering—you are being shown what it is that you must correct within yourself."

—Ba'al Shem Tov

The Ba'al Shem Tov, an eighteenth-century Jewish sage, is credited with these words of wisdom. It is easy to find fault in others, to criticize and thereby differentiate ourselves from those whose beliefs and practices we deplore. But beware, the Ba'al Shem Tov warns; when you find fault with others, it may well be your own imperfections you see. Sigmund Freud, in his theory of the narcissism of minor differences, offers a very similar insight (although he does not credit the earlier sage), suggesting that we often project negative feelings onto others who in fact resemble us. These ideas, their similarities, and the fact that they are traced to both religious and secular sources stand as a metaphor for the story that unfolds in the course of this book. It is a story about settlement in Israel, about antagonism between Israelis, and a story of the discomfort arising through that antagonism.

Because the book emerges from a place of discomfort it has been the kind of work that led some to ask why I was writing it and others to suggest abandoning the project. But throughout the process that eventually led to this volume, family, friends and colleagues provided support and encouragement, as well as the kind of honest criticism that such work requires.

Support for this project came in numerous forms, including generous financial support and invaluable intellectual support from friends and colleagues, many of whom recognized the discomfort revealed in this study as very close and personal, and others who saw it as less so, yet understood the importance of publishing this work for the critical conversation it would spark.

The research for this book was carried out with funding from the Lady Davis Foundation at the Hebrew University in Jerusalem and with a Rockefeller Fellowship at the Joan B. Kroc Institute for International Peace Studies at the University of Notre Dame. I am very grateful for the opportunities afforded me by both of these foundations and for the warm homes and supportive colleagues I found at the Sociology and Anthropology Department and the Truman Institute at Hebrew University, and at the Kroc Institute at Notre Dame.

Numerous colleagues and friends have been very helpful to me throughout this project, providing supportive advice as well as critical readings of early versions of the manuscript.

The first encouraging nods for this project came from my dearly missed friend, Tania Forte (*zichrona l'vracha*), who reminded me that life was short, in a prescient moment long before we knew she would leave us so young. I told Tania of the research project that had been on my mind since about 1995, when then–Prime Minister Yitzhak Rabin was assassinated, revealing a deep rift between left-wing secular and right-wing religious Israeli Jews. It seemed to me then that there was more going on in that apparent rift than met the eye. Tania suggested applying for a Lady Davis Fellowship to carry out this research and not to wait, because "life is too short to put off the projects that inspire us." She read and commented on the research proposal and we celebrated together when the fellowship was awarded. I will always be grateful for her encouragement, wonderful friendship, and challenging intellect.

Once in while a great teacher will share insights that open up new horizons and change one's thinking. In 1995, I was in graduate school taking a class on theory and went in to talk to my professor, Talal Asad, about the paper I had to write for his class. He listened intently and then told me that Foucault had this notion of episteme that might prove helpful, and he sent me off to read *The Archaeology of Knowledge*. That single suggestion made all the difference, and has influenced my thinking ever since. I would like to thank Talal for his insight on that day and for his scholarship in general. Among the many generous colleagues and friends who took the time to read parts of this work were Louise Bethlehem, who offered valuable theoretical insights, shared her friends with me, and offered the support of challenging and brilliant conversations. It is nothing short of a gift to be able to think together with Louise. Jonathan Boyarin was one of my teachers at the New School, and I was very pleased when he agreed to read an early draft of a chapter. Later, he read the entire manuscript and offered an expert critical reading with the kinds of challenges that led to a greatly improved book. His knowledge and attention to detail are invaluable. Jan French became a very close friend when we met at Notre Dame, each one of us working on a manuscript. (She published hers first!) Jan has always been willing to read for me and help me think through this project, offering encouragement with a brilliant sense of humor and the kind of critical feedback that pushed me to expand my explanations, making the work intelligible beyond a narrow audience. Jackie Smith has been very generous with her time and always willing to allow me to learn from her experiences. Besides providing occasional babysitting for my boys and hosting us at wonderful gatherings at her home, Jackie provided important and useful insights into the publishing process, the kinds of things that no one ever tells you but you really need to know. I was very pleased to be invited by Steve Caton—a wonderful mentor—to share my work at a graduate seminar in Anthropology of the Middle East at Harvard University, where I received important feedback at an early stage of this work. Hillel Cohen, a writer and historian who is much too humble, shared his insights on writing and publishing and acted as a cultural translator on several occasions. I am grateful to Dodie Hart for technical assistance, attention to detail, warm friendship and laughter. The anonymous readers at Oxford University Press provided important critical insights, and my editor, Cynthia Read, has been most encouraging throughout this process.

I would like to thank all my colleagues for their time and their input, but I owe a special debt to Gregory Starrett for believing in the value of this project and investing so much of his time and energy. Gregg read entire drafts of the manuscript and provided detailed comments as I worked through the revisions; he offered endless support and encouragement and always insisted that he took pleasure in reading my work, just the kind of intellectual flattery that keeps a scholar going.

Mostly, of course, I owe this book to the people of Gush Katif, the Eshkol Region, and beyond, who opened their hearts and homes to me, shared their stories and experiences, and helped me understand. I hope this book will provide readers with a glimpse into the ethnographic journey that taught me so much.

Finally, I am most grateful to Rafi, Edan, and Ziev for all their patience, support, and the endless wisdom they offered throughout this process. And, of course, to Rusty who is always there for me.

Portions of this book have appeared before and are reprinted here with the gracious permission of the publishers. Portions of chapter 2 appeared as "An/tagonizing Settlers in the Colonial Present of Israel/Palestine" in *Social Analysis* vol. 49, no. 2, pages 122–143, Summer 2005. It is reprinted here with permission from *Social Analysis* and Berghahn Journals. Portions of chapter 9 appeared as "Twice Removed: Mizrahi Settlers in Gush Katif" in *Social Identities*, vol. 14, no. 5, pages 535–551, September 2008, and is reprinted here with permission from *Social Identities* and Taylor and Francis. Portions of chapter 9 appeared as "On Demonized Muslims and Vilified Jews: Between Theory and Politics" in *Comparative Studies in Society and History*, vol. 52, no. 3, pages 591–603, 2010, and is reprinted here with permission from *CSSH* and Cambridge University Press.

Contents

Unsettling Gaza

I

Fundamentally Settlers?

"As far as I'm concerned, we can build a wall around them . . . throw away the key. Let them have their own state as long as they don't interfere with us!"

In the space of Israel/Palestine, one might expect such sentiments of exasperation to be expressed in reference to Palestinian Arabs by a Jewish Israeli, or by a Palestinian Arab in reference to a Jewish Israeli. In fact, the statement above was made by a secular, Jewish, Israeli high school student in reference to religious, Israeli Jews. This young man expressing his aggravation with the ways in which religious Judaism interferes with his secular liberties provides an extreme articulation of the tension between religious and secular Jewish Israelis. That tension recently resurfaced with two dramatic events. In 1995, Israeli Prime Minister Yitzhak Rabin was assassinated by a gunman identified as a nationalist Orthodox Jew (generally associated with the Jewish settler movement), and it was believed that the act was motivated by religious beliefs. In this troubled space where the phrase "the conflict," or "the situation" as it is called in Hebrew, conjures up images of violence between Jews and Arabs, between Israel and neighboring Arab countries, and between Israelis and Palestinians, this grave act of political violence had been perpetrated by one Jew against another. It was a kind of defining moment, leading both to reflection and outrage. Among many secular Jewish Israelis, the response came in the form of a rhetorical question: How could they have done this to us? Another such moment came a decade later with the 2005 disengagement, Israel's unilateral withdrawal and the forcible removal of settlers from their homes in the Gaza Strip and a small part of the West Bank. This time, many in the religious nationalist camp and their supporters asked: How can they do this to us? These two moments can be thought of as crescendos in the tension between the secular and liberal left wing of Israeli politics and the religious and right wing, which is the focus of this book.

This study began in the year prior to the 2005 disengagement, about the time the following letter was published.

An Invitation: "Death to the Settlers"

May 2004

> Dear Residents of the Eshkol Region,
>
> Yesterday I was driving past the Eshkol Regional Council building and was shocked to see the words "death to the settlers" written on the side of a bus shelter.
>
> I am a settler mother, a mother of a family blessed with (many) children. I work hard to raise my children and to support them. Do you want me to die? Why? I was raised to love every person in Israel even if their ideas are different from mine. This is also the way I raise my children. There are 8,000 residents bravely living in Gush Katif, who are surrounded by a million Arabs. The state of Israel lives heroically in the heart of Muslim countries that surround it. The proportion of Jews to Arabs in the Gaza Strip is more or less the same as the number of Jews in Israel compared to the number of Muslims in the Muslim space that surrounds it. Gush Katif was established 34 years ago as a mission by the Labor government. No one has the right to expel us from here. If someone is angry at us because there are many Arabs who live in the Gaza Strip under harsh conditions, then I want to say that the Gush Katif settlements are not responsible (guilty) for that. The conditions of the Arabs were hard before 1967. I invite residents of the Eshkol region, who live so close to me, to come and visit and see Gush Katif, to talk and listen.

We will probably never know the identity of the hand that spray painted the ghostly white lettering on the bus shelter at Eshkol, a region of the Negev bordering the Gaza Strip. The phrase mimics and returns the hate-drenched slogan that often appears following acts of Palestinian resistance against Israel, when right-wing demonstrators shout, carry signs, or spray paint bus shelters with the words "Death to the Arabs!" Something seemed very amiss in the Land of Israel these days. The rift among the people had grown deeper since the fabric of the nation was dramatically torn by the assassination of the prime minister in 1995. The woman from Atzmonah in Gush Katif who wrote this letter expressed a growing concern over a certain lack of unity that had shocked the nation in 1995. There had previously been a widespread sense of confidence about the depth of Jewish social solidarity inside Israel, a certainty of safety among the extended family, as it is often imagined. Yes, there had always been crime that could involve violence, but it had previously been considered unthinkable that one Jew would deliberately raise a hand against another for political purposes.[1] Political violence had been widely perceived as located between Jews and Arabs, Israelis and Palestinians, the state of Israel and neighboring states. Although there have been other incidents of such violence, the perception remained strong. What lies behind the words in this letter, then, can be understood as a story of the Jewish state and a story of the Jewish people.[2] The state of Israel was established to ensure the continuity of the Jewish people, to bring an end to exile and homelessness—in short, to ensure survival. Now, inside that state, an anger and hatred had grown between members of the extended family about how best to continue ensuring survival. For some, it appeared as though that anger and hatred itself could threaten survival by leading to a civil war.

This book is based on ethnographic research carried out among Jewish Israelis on both sides of this conflict, primarily during the year preceding the disengagement. It also draws on earlier fieldwork, later visits, and ongoing contacts following the disengagement. This study finds that the intense antagonism expressed between these groups is located less in their differences than in a *desire to differentiate.* That is not to say that there are no differences between the Left and the Right, the secular and religious, and those opposed versus those in favor of settlement in the occupied territories. Yet focusing on those differences works to conceal the very depth of commonalities that fuels the hatred and intolerance between these groups, commonalities that point to both the conditions of possibility of this apparent conflict and what these sets of discourses and practices enable. The antagonism reinscribes existing categories, setting the boundaries of ways of being, and the limits of public debate. The appearance of incommensurable discourses in conflict conceals continuities and commonalities among these Israelis who are all part of the settler project in Palestine and who are all subject to the disciplining processes of state rationality. The appearance of deep differences and conflict enables settler-colonial practices to continue throughout Israel and the occupied territories while maintaining a sense of moral legitimacy for the Zionist project as a whole through denouncing and delegitimizing religious settlers.

The goals of this book include moving beyond the work that is accomplished through this hegemonic discourse of conflict, taking note of commonalities and continuities, and making room for a closer look at some of what is missed when attention is focused on the antagonism between these variously situated Israelis. There are a number of broader questions emerging from this work that shed light on other instances of conflict at the interface of liberalism with those forms of religiosity often categorized as radical or fundamentalist and on the interface of religion more generally with formations of the secular. Before moving to that broader context, I will return to the local scene of antagonism between neighbors.

This book is concerned with a discourse of conflict, its outcomes, and that which its commanding presence conceals. It is not intended as a holistic description of the population groups involved in this conflict. Indeed, I will have achieved my goal if readers finish this book with lingering questions and a feeling of not fully knowing the people encountered in these pages. This may be frustrating, but it reflects my reluctance to either essentialize differences or deny their meaningfulness to those involved.

Contours of Conflict

The tensions and conflicts between religious and secular Jews in Israel are neither simple nor straightforward. They bear similarities to tensions between religious and secular groups elsewhere but include important aspects that are very specific to the Israeli-Palestinian context. Among the secular in Israel, ultra-Orthodox or Haredi Jews are often despised. They are stereotypically viewed as nonproductive members of the state because of the emphasis they place on religious study. In addition, they are known for actively attempting to impose their belief system by insisting that the Sabbath be protected, for example, by closing places of business and entertainment, thereby interfering with secular liberties. However, those deemed most dangerous in the current political climate are found among nationalist Orthodox often referred to by the misnomer Jewish "fundamentalists."[3] The sets of ideas and practices commonly referred to as religious fundamentalism tend to create a certain sense of anxiety. Fundamentalisms are categorized, analyzed, marginalized, and demonized in both academic and popular spheres (Nagata 2001).[4] So-called Jewish fundamentalism in the space of Israel/Palestine is no exception (Aran 1991,

1997; Lustick 1988, 1993; Neuman 2004; Silberstein 1993; Sivan 1995). The term, in this case, can include a number of forms of right-wing and religious beliefs and practices but is often associated with the settler movement: those religiously motivated nationalists who make their homes in Israeli-occupied Palestine on land conquered by Israel in the June 1967 war and who believe deeply in the value of Jewish presence in the biblical Land of Israel.[5] This includes, more specifically, those who are convinced that Jewish settlement of the Land is a God-given requirement, an obligation that will be fulfilled preceding the coming of the Messiah. Just prior to the disengagement, moderate, left-wing, and secular discourses often referred to those settlers as "the greatest current threat to democracy." Indeed, from these perspectives the settlers are often reviled and ridiculed, and this hatred and derision is considered legitimate in numerous contexts.[6] Religiously motivated settlers are construed not only as dangerous to democracy but also as posing an existential threat to the future of the state of Israel. These depictions continue to emerge in both Israeli and international media.[7] In the popular media and in increasingly popular political pronouncements, right-wing religious settlers are depicted as violent, irrational, and an impediment to the potential for a just resolution to the conflict between Israel and the Palestinians. In particular, their unwillingness to make territorial compromises is considered a major obstacle to peace.[8]

The terms *left-wing* and *secular* also describe a range of positions and practices within Israel. Versions or degrees of secularity, left-wing, and "mainstream" Jewish Israeliness can be found in numerous locations. For the purposes of this study, it is important to understand that the secular kibbutz, in particular, has historically been associated with the Left, with socialist ideology and secularity. For right-wing religiously motivated settlers, the Left and the secular can be seen as posing a great danger to the future of both the People of Israel (meaning Jews both inside and outside the state)[9] and the state of Israel for numerous reasons. In the current political climate, it is what religiously motivated settlers see as the lack of understanding on the part of left-wing or secular Jews of the central importance of the connection between the Jewish people and the (biblical) Land of Israel that is considered most damaging. For these settlers, peace will come when justice has been done, and justice means returning all of the Land of Israel to its rightful owners, those to whom God promised it, the Jewish People.[10]

The debates between Left and Right, secular and religious, and those Israelis living on either side of the pre-1967 border appear as sets of incommensurable discourses, competing narratives about what it means to be Jewish that will determine the future character of the state, or whether the state will have a future. The left-wing discourse is rooted in a progressivist, secular humanism, while right-wing, religiously motivated settlers speak in terms of sanctification, fulfilling the will of God, and redemption. This rupture becomes God's Rule versus Man's Rule, incommensurable from the very grounds upon which each is based, and ways of thinking that are hard-pressed to speak each other's language, each relegating the other to the past and vying to represent the future. These competing narratives took on greater political urgency in 2005, when then Prime Minister Ariel Sharon announced his government's unilateral disengagement plan to dismantle settlements in the Gaza Strip and parts of the West Bank, taking center stage within a broader context of ongoing violence and the continuation of land expropriation from Palestinians both in the occupied territories and inside Israel (Cook 2003; Siegman 2004; Yiftachel 2002, 2006).

Neighboring Communities

The letter of invitation to visit Gush Katif was published in a local newspaper that serves the communities of the Eshkol Region in the northwest portion of the Negev Desert. The Eshkol Region consists primarily of cooperative (*kibbutz*) and semi-cooperative (*moshav*) communities that were first settled in the pre-state (*Yishuv*) era as agricultural cooperatives establishing a Jewish presence in British Mandatory Palestine. Both of these kinds of cooperative communities have changed over time; some have moved away from agriculture to industry, and many are less structured according their founding principles and original ideologies. The kibbutz communities, from which many of the opponents to religious settlements came, are closely associated with the socialist Zionist founders of the state. They were based on Marxist socialist principles of equality—from each according to his abilities, to each according to his needs. These communities placed a very high value on labor itself and on working the land. Kibbutz members shared the fruits of their labor and ran their communities through direct democracy. In this region, as elsewhere, many kibbutz communities struggled to survive as the Israeli economy became increasingly privatized. Many have begun making structural changes for economic reasons. The kibbutz had once been a key symbol of a kind of cultural elite, the highly valued pioneering socialists who settled the land on which the state was later established. The once favored sons of the kibbutz, however, have long since fallen from grace. Since the late 1970s and the decline of the Labor party in Israeli politics, the kibbutz settlements lost the state financial support they had once received. And by the time of this research, the mythical figure of a heroic and virtuous pioneering socialist of the kibbutz was nothing more than a proud symbol of the past. In addition to their internal struggles, the kibbutz communities have also been in a position of competing for resources with settlements across the Green Line.

A number of the communities in the Eshkol Region line the border with the Gaza Strip around the Kissufim Crossing (see figure 1.1). Among the people in the region, who lived so close to the settlements in Gush Katif, it seemed that only a small number had actually visited. Gush Katif was separated from Eshkol by an army checkpoint situated on the Green Line that marked the pre-1967 armistice line (see figure 1.2). In other words, it marked the entrance to Israeli militarily occupied territory. Many Israelis, even those living fifteen minutes away, had never been to Gush Katif. Many refused to cross the border at the checkpoint out of fear for their physical safety. Others

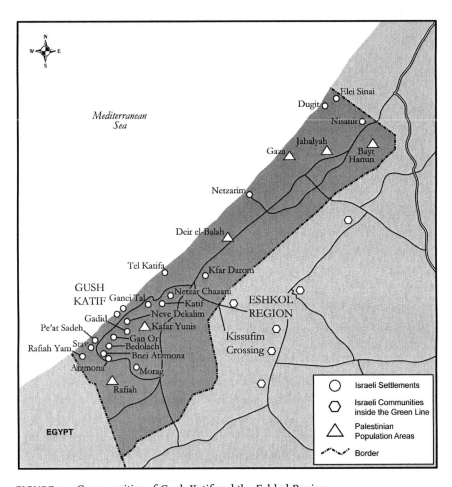

FIGURE 1.1 Communities of Gush Katif and the Eshkol Region.

FIGURE I.2 A quiet time at the checkpoint at the Kissufim crossing. Author photo.

refused on ideological grounds, based on their opposition to the practice of building Jewish settlements in the post-1967 occupied territories. Still others did not cross the border because of the constraints of everyday life. At the same time, there were those Israelis who provided goods and services to the settlements in the Gaza Strip. Doctors, social workers, technicians, and truck drivers all crossed the border regularly. Of course, there were also soldiers in the regular army and those in the reserves who crossed the border carrying out their orders.

Maintaining Borders

Fear has often been harnessed in the struggle between Israelis and Palestinians to maintain the border between these two national groups, especially between those living on either side of the 1949 armistice line, the Green Line. This fear has historically been tied to a deeper existential fear following the Nazi Holocaust, which can easily be rekindled in the present by reports of growing anti-Semitism in Europe and around the world. That fear and anxiety remains deep despite the arguments that such anti-Jewish sentiments and actions are responses to Israeli government policies and practices. But to many, it appears that there is an eternal hatred and that there will always be enemies threatening the continuity of the Jewish people.

The small settlements in the Gaza Strip that were established following the 1967 war had experienced relative quiet in the first decades of their existence. It was only following what has come to be called the Second or *Al-Aqsa Intifada* (uprising) that began in 2000 that these settlements became targets for Palestinian acts of resistance. The specific fear of traveling to these communities, then, came relatively late, but organized opposition to post-1967 settlements arose much earlier in Israeli politics, particularly following the first Palestinian uprising (*Intifada*) against the military occupation in 1987.[11]

The communities of Gush Katif were not perceived to be easily accessible to Israelis inside the Green Line. They were located in places that required driving through, past, or around "hostile territory," places where Palestinians lived. The communities of Gush Katif had become increasingly distant as hostilities in the region increased. Many of those who had lived there since the first days of settlement recalled earlier, quieter times, times when their own relatives were more inclined to visit. Recalling those days, one man explained that he, his family, and the other families who had set up homes in the Gaza Strip had not been "ideologically driven" to move there. Nor had they been labeled "extremists" then. It is true that the first settlements in the Gaza Strip, like those in the West Bank, had been established during the late years of the Labor Party's dominance in Israeli politics, as the letter above declares. Immediately following the 1967 war, there had been a spontaneous move to settle the newly acquired territory by members of the secular kibbutz movement (Shafir and Peled 2002; Zertal and Eldar 2007). Residents of Gush Katif were far more inclined to recall that moment in history than were their kibbutz-dwelling neighbors.

Having found support by successive governments since their establishment, the prospect of impending evacuation was quite shocking to many of the residents. They wondered what had happened, how they suddenly had become extremists and dangerous in the eyes of many Israelis. They wondered why some of their neighbors on the other side of the Green Line were demonstrating against them (see figure 1.3). And being in the position of having to defend their right to go on living in the post-1967 occupied territories, many were eager to host visitors and looking for opportunities to reach out to their estranged extended family.

The letter of invitation and other such appeals did not generate a great deal of empathy among the opposition.[12] Instead, the very symbols used to signify virtue generated increasing antipathy. "I am the mother of a family blessed with many children" signified goodness and positively valued humility to religiously

FIGURE 1.3 Demonstrating against the settlers, in favor of disengagement. The signs call for an end to the occupation, an end to Gush Katif, withdrawal from Gaza, and movement against racism and toward peace. Author photo.

motivated settlers. To the liberal, secular Left, however, it could signify arrogance, selfishness, and a lack of concern for the well-being both of children and of the nation. The final sentence of the letter, about having been "raised to love every person in Israel," signifies part of a moral triad found among religiously motivated settlers who believe in the central significance of the People of Israel (Jews), the Land of Israel, and the Torah of Israel. The more secular, liberal Israelis who favored disengagement had grown weary of this talk about love. Some were quite disgusted by it. They were skeptical and angry, often saying they wanted to have nothing to do with that love, which they saw as an expression of racist attitudes because "every person in Israel" was a deceptive phrase, since settlers meant only Jewish Israelis. This love applied only to other Jews and not to Palestinians, revealing a racism that liberal Israelis wanted no part of. Others reacted to the patronizing, if not insulting, tone they sensed in these expressions of love that accept secular Israeli Jews and their secular nationalism as a temporary and degraded form of Jewishness, lacking in the light of holiness. This degraded form is seen as a necessary or expected aspect of the return of the Jewish People to the Land, but it is also considered a passing phase that is expected to wither away as the People return to the Torah and holiness on the path to redemption.[13] In addition, among the secular and Left, it was argued that this love ultimately required Israelis who oppose the settler project to sacrifice life and limb to protect settlers in the post-1967 occupied territories. Rather than sacrifice themselves for those settlements and the ongoing occupation, according to many skeptics among the Left, it was time to teach those settlers a lesson about their misguided, racist, violent dreams by removing them from their illegal homes.

In the Space of Israel/Palestine

The antagonism between Israeli Jews reflected in the letter can be thought of as a conflict within the broader Israeli-Palestinian conflict. The debates over settlement in post-1967 occupied territories are situated at the heart of a struggle inside Israel over the contours of a potential peace settlement with the Palestinians. The land on which these settlers live is the territory that has been considered in peace negotiations that would establish a Palestinian state on part or all of the post-1967 Israeli occupied territories.

Israel became a state in May 1948, its establishment leading to a war that lasted through 1949. The armistice lines following that war became the internationally recognized borders of the state, known as the Green Line. Following the 1967 war, Israel gained a significant amount of territory that had been under the control of neighboring states. This included the Golan Heights from Syria, which has been annexed to the state of Israel; the West Bank of the Jordan River (also known as Judea and Samaria) and East Jerusalem from Jordan; and the Sinai Peninsula and Gaza Strip from Egypt (see figure 1.4). Israeli settlements have been built in all of the areas gained in the 1967 Six Day War, while Palestinians living in these areas have been subject to military occupation and denied the citizens' rights of Palestinians living inside the Green Line. The Sinai was returned to Egypt as part of a peace agreement in the 1980s, and Israeli settlements there were dismantled. Jordan relinquished control of the West Bank, and in the early 1990s, Israel reached an agreement with the Palestinian Liberation Organization to hand over control of parts of the occupied territories to the Palestinian Authority. Israel withdrew from the Gaza Strip in a unilateral move in 2005, removing its soldiers and dismantling the communities of Gush Katif and two settlements in the northern portion of the strip.

Israeli settlement in the occupied territories has become increasingly contentious, both in the international community and inside Israel itself. On the Israeli socio-political-religious scene, the conflict between Jewish Israelis tends to

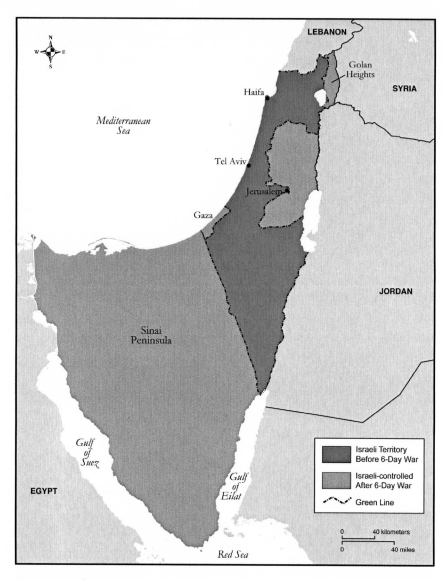

FIGURE 1.4 The Green Line, marking Israeli territory prior to and following the 1967 Six Day War.

be depicted in both popular and academic discourse in sets of binary oppositions: Right-Left, religious-secular, settler-opposed to settlement in post-1967 occupied territories. These complex and overlapping divisions are often conflated to the simple opposition of left-wing secular versus right-wing religious, and are considered a part of what is known locally as the "rift among the people."

The so-called rift among the people became exacerbated following the 1995 assassination of then Prime Minister Yitzhak Rabin. That event brought the split into focus with considerable media attention on the religious community from which the assassin came, and a great deal of collective soul-searching in reaction to the shock of one Jew purposely killing another for political or religious reasons.[14] However, the commonly understood political distinctions between Left and Right, secular and religious have a longer history.

The "Left" of Israeli Zionist politics emerged from the socialist or labor Zionist movement that arose in Europe in response to a growing sense that Jews could never become fully assimilated or fully accepted in Europe.[15] Today, it tends to be associated with a liberal or secular humanism, with the secular kibbutz movement, and with what is known as the "peace camp" in Israel. It generally includes those Israelis who are opposed to the occupation of territories gained in the 1967 war. This Left however, is not necessarily exclusively secular. It includes shades and variations of secularity and religiosity, including some Orthodox Jews,[16] particularly those often called "modern Orthodox" which is another category including variations but is generally viewed as distinctive from Haredi or ultra-Orthodox Jews.[17]

The "Right," on the other hand, which cannot be divorced from modern discourses of liberalism, is historically associated with a more hawkish position, with the Revisionist Zionism of Ze'ev Jabotinsky that later became the Likud party, and with a belief in the right of the Jewish people to establish a state on what is known as "greater Israel" or "the whole of Israel" (*Eretz Israel ha-Shlema*). This position has historically been opposed to relinquishing territory (following the 1967 war) and has often been aligned with more traditional or religious Jews who share a belief in the right of Jews to settle on the ancient biblical Land of Israel.[18] Of course, the Right is not exclusively the domain of the religious and includes versions and shades of religiosity and secularity. In addition, there is an Orthodox Jewish community that rejects modern political Zionism and therefore does not fit into the left-right spectrum of Israeli politics (Rabkin 2006).[19]

Secular, anti- or non-Zionist Jewish Israelis are categorized as the far or radical Left. It is also important to note that ethnicity, class, and other dimensions of social identity further complicate these categories. There are, of course, many nuances, differences, and even seemingly contradictory positions within each category, which will be introduced later in the book.

The Clash

The appearance of stark binary divisions on the Israeli scene echoes broader divisions at the interface of liberalism with religiosity, expressed in debates over secularization and modernity. Numerous scholars have addressed the problematic representation of a binary division between religiosity and the secular. Recently, for example, theologian Martin Marty argued that we need a new model for describing the world that we actually inhabit, which he contends is a complex combination of both the religious and the secular, with religious and secular phenomena occurring at the same time in individuals, in groups, and in societies around the world (Marty 2003). Asad complicates this further by refusing to conflate the secular and religious or to view a historical progression with religion preceding the secular. The secular is not the opposite of religion, Asad contends, yet at the same time, he asks that we consider what politics are promoted by the notion that the world has *no* significant binary divisions (2003:15). The answers to such complexities, it seems to me, can only be approached through careful investigation of historically specific instances.

A number of scholars have most recently expressed concern over representations of Islam in today's heated political context. However, more than a decade ago, anthropologist Susan Harding reflected on academia's difficulty with studying certain groups. Harding was writing about Christian fundamentalists and raised the problem of what she called representing the "repugnant other" (Harding 1991). As much as anthropologists have taken pride in their efforts at cultural relativism and openness to difference, Harding found that there seemed to be a line drawn when it came to the particular difference of those labeled religious fundamentalists. If that line has moved among some anthropologists who have taken an interest in studying and representing (radical or fundamentalist) Islam[20] in the context of a growing distrust, if not outright hatred, directed toward Muslims by many in the West (see Ewing ed. 2008), this tolerance seems to have reached its limit with so-called radical or fundamentalist Jewish settlers.

With emerging global power struggles, and in particular following the defining moment of September 11, a wave of scholarly analyses have been published addressing the interface of liberalism with Islam. There are scholars who see some form of clash of cultures or civilizations (notably Bernard Lewis and Samuel Huntington), which resonates deeply with the appearance of discourse in conflict on the Israeli scene. But a growing number of scholars reject this division and the problematic way in which it results in both homogenizing entire communities and ignoring the relationships between communities. Writing against the idea of a clash of civilizations, Asad (2007) suggests a more nuanced understanding of historical relationships, changes over time, and commonalities between groups that appear in stark contrast. Asad's approach makes it quite impossible to understand current conflicts between religious ways of life (whether they be radical forms of Islam or radical forms of Judaism) and formations of the secular as a clash between hermetically sealed, separate, and static groups of people in the world. Such an approach has proved far more useful in understanding the socio-political-religious scene in Israel that appears as deep differences in beliefs and ways of life. This is not to say that there are no differences between secular and religious Israelis or between the left and right wings of Israeli politics. Instead, it is to ask what continuities and commonalities are hidden in the appearance of deep conflict and what is accomplished through that appearance.

Harding was concerned with the "othering" of Christian fundamentalists and how they were discursively constructed as modernity's other. A very similar discursive pattern can be detected in this case study, where there is an asymmetry between the groups. One group establishes its identity is contrast to the other, and in many ways each is construed as the constitutive outside of the other, marking group boundaries of identity, politics, and ethics. The differences, however, are not equivalent, as religiously motivated settlers are the marked group within the broader Israeli context. They are the others to the unmarked, hegemonic secular.

My concern here moves beyond the mutual othering and the asymmetry to consider what is accomplished through this conflict and what is missed as a result of its centrality. For some readers, the moves I make will seem counterintuitive—questioning that the conflict between the religious Right and secular Left in Israel arises from deep differences. For others, pointing to the continuities beneath this conflict will seem quite obvious. It is my hope that in either case this exercise will shed fresh light on politics and identity among Israelis and on the troubling conflicts in Israel/Palestine, as well as provide both challenges and insight to broader questions at the interface between religiosity and formations of the secular.

The Work of Conflict

Decades have passed since Foucault began warning against easily accepting apparent unities and suggesting that the appearance of disunity is no less a cause for skepticism (1972: 22). That warning continues to resonate, urging the interrogation of such appearances because the ways in which we order, divide, and categorize our sociopolitical world are not innocent.[21] These divisions have very real outcomes, including the formation of categories of identity and politics, delimiting the contours of action and debate in the present, as well as the boundaries within which we might imagine possible futures. Allow me to illustrate some of the continuities beneath the appearance of disunity in question here through a brief reconsideration of responses to the assassination of then Israeli Prime Minister, Yitzhak Rabin on November 4, 1995.

Yigal Amir, a twenty-seven-year-old Jewish Israeli law student confessed to the crime. As reported in the *New York Times* the following day, he said, "I have no regrets. I acted alone and on orders from God" (Schmemann 1995). In the aftermath of the assassination, a debate emerged among Jews in Israel and in the international media. People immediately began taking sides, almost everyone trying to distance themselves from the act of murder. Those who shared Amir's political views denounced his means and attempted to characterize him as insane or an somehow exceptional. In a letter to the editor of the *Jerusalem Post*, one man wrote, "This demented assassin has successfully destroyed much of what the right-wing has accomplished.... Normal right-wing supporters will drift away in fear of being stigmatized . . . what have we Jews done to deserve such maniacs among our brethren?" (Gilor 1995). Those who opposed Amir's political views blamed the Right in Israel, especially the religious Right (Keinon 1995). The anger directed at the religious community was evident in daily life in Israel. For example, it was a common courtesy to give lifts to hitchhiking soldiers. Following the assassination, it was reported that soldiers identified as religious by their crocheted yarmulkes were not being given rides. Religious Jews in Israel and abroad hurried to dissociate themselves from the act of the assassin. The *New York Times* quoted an Orthodox Jew in Borough Park, New York, who said of the act of assassination, "it's not a Jewish way, that's for sure" (Purdy 1995). This was represented as an act by an extremist fundamentalist, quite different from other Orthodox Jews. Even Yigal Amir's own parents reportedly disowned him and removed from their car the bumper sticker proclaiming, "God's Law is Above the Law of Man."[22] As the argument raged, categories of people and politics were being created and contested as usual: left-wing, right-wing, religious, secular, extremist, terrorist, traitor. . . . As each side of this debate attempted to denounce the other, the discourse in conflict continued to inscribe a particular set of taken-for-granted objects, concepts, and meanings constituting the field in which this debate takes on meaning and through which it continues.

In 1995, the immediate political context of the debates between Left and Right, secular and religious included critical questions involved in the peace process, which just prior to the assassination was at its height. Recall the Oslo Accords and the famous handshake between Yasser Arafat and Yitzhak Rabin on the White House lawn in 1993. The Oslo Accords provided the framework through which a "land for peace" resolution to the Israeli-Palestinian conflict would be achieved, resulting in a Palestinian state alongside the state of Israel. The land for peace recipe was then and continues to be supported by much of the left wing of Israeli politics. The land in question included the remaining territories gained by Israel in the 1967 war from Egypt, Jordan, and Syria. Israel began by returning the Sinai Peninsula to Egypt in exchange for peace, which was followed by establishing Palestinian self-rule in parts of the West Bank of the Jordan River and in the Gaza Strip. Among the right wing in Israeli politics, there has been a great deal of opposition to the establishment of Palestinian self-rule and further opposition to territorial compromise. The political debate in Israel was depicted as a struggle over primary values. Thomas Friedman of the *New York Times* constructed a duality in which the Jews of Israel would have to determine which they value more highly, "land or life" (Friedman 1995). David Horovitz of the *Jerusalem Report* echoed this idea, writing that the key dilemma confronting Israel's divided people is "Which do they value more, their democracy or their Biblically promised lands?" (1995: 14). The most acute line of distinction between Left and Right drawn both in the public media and in academic discourse is that between liberal, secular Israeli Jews and the so-called "Jewish fundamentalists." Ian Lustick contends that the ideology of Gush Emunim, then the organizational core of the religious settler movement, "represents a complete reversal of classical Zionist ideology" (1993:111). What emerge then, are two separate, distinct, mutually exclusive, incommensurable discourses: one apparently based on the laws of man, rationality, and democracy, and the other on the laws of God, biblical texts, and sacred interpretations.

At another level, however, we can see that what is being described, categorized, and objectified by the religious and secular, left- and right-wing discourses is more than just the groups in opposition. While each group is othering the other through comments like "this is not the Jewish way" and "this is a radical break from Zionism," both are engaged in constructing the Jewish people and the Jewish nation as a certain kind of unity. (Hence the use of the term *brethren* in the letter to the editor quoted earlier.) At the time, it seemed outrageous to many Israelis that one Jew would murder another Jew for political reasons. Many commented that the assassination would have been easier to comprehend had it been carried out by an Arab. The act offended a deep sense of family or "peoplehood" among Jewish Israelis (Dominguez 1989). The press referred to Amir as "a son of Israel" who ripped apart Israel's soul (Horovitz 1995; Kifner, Goldberg, and Greenberg 1995). One Israeli explained that despite the tremendous political debates, cultural and religious arguments, Israelis are all "*sachbakim.*" This term, ironically a slang term in Hebrew derived from Arabic, is used in the Israeli army and among civilians to denote a very deep level of friendship or camaraderie. It refers to the kind of relationship in which people are convinced they can rely on each other. A young

Israeli man interviewed on American television the day after the assassination said he had always loved his country so much because he always knew that if someone falls down in the street, everyone around would rush to that person's aid. The assassination of Rabin led him to believe that perhaps this was no longer true. This murder by one Jew of another Jew seemed incomprehensible; it was a tragedy within the family and a betrayal of trust. A columnist in the *Jerusalem Report* wrote, "the old social contract which stipulated that, no matter what, we were all Jews together . . . is now dead" (Chafets 1995).

The discourse of conflict between the secular Left and religious Right participates in constructing a deeper unity through objectification of "the Jew" as a particular category of humanity that is distinct from and cannot include "the Arab." The behavior of the assassin was denounced by some, and his system of beliefs by others, but each of the discourses is concerned with creating a kind of homogeneity that constitutes the people of the nation. And inasmuch as they argue over where to draw the line marking the boundaries of the geographical nation-state, both are also participating in reinscribing the underlying concepts of people, territory, and sovereignty.[23]

The conflict between left-wing secular and right-wing religious Jews participates in reconstituting the elements of nationalism—settler nationalism in particular—in the space of Israel/Palestine. Jews did not claim sovereignty in the places they were living in Diaspora. Instead, when they arrived or returned to Palestine in the nineteenth century to realize their right as a people to sovereignty in their homeland, someone else was living there. Settler nationalism clearly provides the conditions of possibility for the conflict between Palestinian Arabs and Israeli Jews. And a number of scholars, beginning with Ella Shohat, have pointed to the Arab-Jewish binary distinction as a powerful and troubling fiction and have worked consistently to undermine that distinction, which, she argues, provides the basis of the modern political Zionist project in Palestine.[24] But, settler nationalism also provides the conditions of possibility for the antagonism between Israeli Jews. This commonality is also in many ways concealed through the appearance of deep antagonism and conflict. Indeed, I will argue, it is precisely this foundational commonality that produces a particular anxiety and actually fuels the antagonism between these groups in conflict. It is the similarities between the two groups that prove so threatening to the very core of Jewish national identity in Israel, particularly to the secular and Left, as religiously motivated settlers in post-1967 occupied territories narrate and enact a version of Zionism in the present that secular and left-wing Zionists insist belongs to the past. This desire to differentiate can be understood as a kind of Freudian narcissism of minor differences and will be elaborated upon in chapter 2.

A number of scholars (and activists) have engaged in deconstructing apparent unities or disunities in Israel/Palestine in order to undermine, if not discard, those categories of identity. This work has mostly targeted the Jewish/Arab divide, as previously noted, but Israeli critical and poststructural scholars also pose a challenge to previous scholarly representations of religious and secular clashes inside Israel. This challenge holds that religious and secular Israeli Jews are tied to each other through mutual necessity and that the appearance of a sharp binary division represents a discursive formation that has served to delimit possible categories of identity, marginalizing and excluding other possibilities. Goodman and Yonah contend that the very centrality of this conflict, the way in which it is represented as "the rift among the people," has the effect of setting the parameters for who can be included in "the people," as well as what can count as "authentic" Judaism, which is so central to citizenship rights in the State of Israel (2004:8). In addition, they argue that the result of this discursive split has served to legitimize a secular hegemony that marginalizes more traditional forms of Judaism that are characteristic of Israeli Jews of Middle Eastern and North African origin (*Mizrahim*). In other words, that discursive split also has racist implications, as it privileges a particular ethnic group of Jews. Amnon Raz-Krakotzkin pushes this idea even further, calling for a rewriting of history from a Mizrahi perspective that would pose a challenge to the categories Arab and Jew underlying Zionism and offer the potential for a binational perspective in Israel/Palestine (Raz-Krakotzkin 2005). I am suggesting that we must interrogate these categories and conflicts and understand the work accomplished through them but not necessarily undermine their integrity or toss them aside. To discard as meaningless that which gives meaning to so many lives seems impractical, if not impossible, but more important, it is a form of violence that contradicts its very rationale. Yet this analysis is more than just an academic exercise. I will elaborate further on this point and its implications in Israel/Palestine, as well as how it speaks to other conflicts between religious and secular formations, in the concluding chapter.

The Scholarly Rift

The representation of hegemonic discourses in conflict—the rift among the people—continues to be reproduced in much of the scholarly work on Israeli society.[25] Some conceptualizations of the settler movement in post-1967 occupied territories, Gush Emunim, held that movement in isolation. This was, at least partially, because of the actual geographical separation, but it was also a result of a taken-for-granted difference between religious settlers and other

Israelis and a scholarly desire to explain those different, exotic, or dangerous others to a largely secular academic audience. These representations might be thought of as resulting from a scholarly desire to differentiate.[26] In so doing, this work re-creates the differences and the divide between a secular, liberal, rational "us" and a religious, radical, or fundamentalist "them." A recent study by Israeli anthropologist Michael Feige reproduces the rift among the people by considering the settler movement in *contrast* to the mainstream peace movement.[27] Feige's study compares the ways in which these two competing sociopolitical movements in Israel construct two places within the space of Israel (Feige 2003): one place by the mainstream, liberal political movement Peace Now and the other by the right-wing, religious followers of Gush Emunim. Feige's book offers a detailed and nuanced analysis of the ways in which each of these movements conceptualizes space and time and the practices through which these competing conceptualizations are constructed. Feige's study of competing conceptualizations or hegemonies within the space of Israeli society and politics also reinscribes these categories of difference, which raises an epistemological question. This is the double problem of what makes these discourses and their attending practices possible, as well as what this apparent conflict actually enables. This, I argue, means remembering the foundations of modern Israeli society and (re)situating the current conflict and its mutually constituting categories—left-wing and secular Jewish Israelis opposed to expanding settlement activity, and right-wing and religious Israeli Jews in favor of current settlement activity—as a struggle between colonizers in a settler-colonial social formation. This conceptualization of the modern political Zionist project is not meant to deny a deeper Jewish historical connection to the Holy Land. Nor does it evaluate the intentions, motivations, or justifications that resulted in migration to Palestine and the establishment of the modern Jewish state. It is a conceptualization that builds on the early work of sociologists of Israel such as Shafir and Peled, as well as on studies of other settler-colonial societies.[28] Rather than investigate competing hegemonies inside the Israeli sociopolitical sphere, I argue that these groups in conflict are better understood as part of the same settler hegemony and that the conflict between these two groups has also enabled settler-colonial practices. There are everyday ways of being Israeli and central organizing features of society, which taken together with certain state practices can be understood as part of a single continuum that is concealed through the appearance of deep differences between beliefs and practices among Israelis on either side of the Green Line and on opposite ends of the political spectrum. That single continuum is most evident from a long-term view that reveals the processes through which Israeli governments have consistently sought the greatest possible territory with the fewest possible Palestinians in order to build a Jewish society that would have demo-graphic, economic, and military strength.[29]

Beginning around the late 1980s, critical Israeli scholars were writing about the historical foundations of the Zionist project in Palestine as a colo-nizing project.[30] Today, however, the notion of colonial rule has largely been associated with post-1967 occupied territories. Thus, ending the occupation is sometimes spoken of as decolonizing Palestine. In that framework, Israel inside the Green Line is a multicultural democracy (not devoid of problems), and the occupied territories are the remnants of colonial rule. But rather than rushing past the past, understanding contemporary Jewish Israeli society as colonial culture in the present, in line with Shafir and Peled's analysis of the foundations of Israeli society, brings into focus both historical connections and current continuities behind what currently appear as discourses and practices in stark contrast. Resituating this conflict within colonialism in the form of settler nationalism in the space of Israel/Palestine sheds a different light on a number of processes taking place on both sides of the Green Line. While settler nationalism should be distinguished both from nationalism as it emerged in Europe and from the decolonizing forms of nationalism emerging in former non-settler colonies (Moran 2002; Wolfe 1999), elements of each of these can also be found in settler forms of nationalism. In the settler nationalisms of Australia and the United States, for example, issues of dispossession haunt the present in the form of guilt, avoidance, and self-justification. In Israel, where settler nationalism continues to be a colonizing nationalism, dispossession is not a haunting ghost from the past. Instead, it characterizes the present.[31] In settler colonies, the settlers come to stay and build their own society, creating a situation in which the local people, as a distinct collective, become superfluous. "Elimination" of members of a previously existing society can take many forms. In some instances, including the case of Australia, assimilation has been considered a form of elimination (Wolfe 1999). In Israel/Palestine, however, the genealogical underpinnings of Jewish identity preclude the possibility of assimilation. Instead of assimilation in Israel, elimination (of a previously existing society) has taken the form of physical, legal, formal, and informal separation and removal. In categorizing the various forms of colonialism, Wolfe wrote most succinctly that the difference between settler-colonialism and other forms of colonialism is quite simply that the settler comes to stay. He writes that "invasion is a structure not an event," such that the designation *settler-colonial* is not only a statement of origins but also a primary structuring characteristic of the society (Wolfe 1999:3, 163). Insisting upon this designa-tion in the contemporary moment with increasing scholarly attention on diaspora and post-territorial identity may seem anachronistic. It may seem anachronistic, that is, except to those people who continue to struggle over a piece of land on which to make their individual and collective home. This designation, with all its negative connotations, is far from the way most Israelis would choose to define themselves. Yet the cleavages and complexities of settler societies can be found in numerous contemporary societies (Stasiulis and Yuval-Davis 1995). More important, this characterization of Israeli society helps clarify the findings of this study. It allows us to understand some of the continuities between Israelis living on both sides of the Green Line and provides insight into the animosity between these groups. Placing the Israeli sociopolitical-religious landscape within the broader lens of settler-colonialism in Israel/Palestine allows one to see dynamics of separation and exclusion between Jewish Israelis and the local Arab population (Greenstein 1995), as well as elimination through various forms of the Judaization of Israel/Palestine (Yiftachel 1999, 2006). What emerges, then, is a society continuing to struggle with the outcomes of its settler origins and ongoing settlement activity broadly construed, even as it struggles to relegate those foundations to the dustbin of the past.

Resituating the discourses in conflict and viewing them from within a single frame calls into question the category *settler* as it emerges from this discourse. In Hebrew, there are two terms denoting *settler*. The noun *mityashev* and its corresponding verb *hityashvut* carry neutral or positive connotations and are generally used in reference to the pioneering socialist settlers in the prestate era. The terms *mitnahel* and *hitnahlut* also refer to settlers and settlement activity, but these terms carry negative connotations as they are used in reference to Jewish settlement in the land occupied by Israel following the 1967 Six-Day War. I use the term *settler* interchangeably (whenever possible) to disturb the separate categories that emerge in popular discourse.

The arguments between settlers that focus on issues of morality and their attending practices, which are carried out, so to speak, on the backs of the Palestinian people, can be understood as emerging from a place of privilege, despite the obvious fact that not all settlers (or migrants or Jews who can trace their ancestry to pre–British Mandatory Palestine) are privileged economically or socially, nor are the benefits and suffering attached to this position distributed equally. Nevertheless, the appearance of a hegemonic discourse of conflict serves to constitute settler identities in the current context. In this way, it is reminiscent of the two factions of whites in the waning days of institutional apartheid in South Africa, as described by Crapanzano (1985). In addition, the apparent split that emerges can be likened to Memmi's (1967) depiction of two kinds of colonizers. In many ways, the left-wing, secular voice in the Israeli/ Palestinian conflict resonates with Memmi's portrait of the "colonizer who refuses," while the right-wing settler movement may be likened to the "colonizer who accepts." Memmi writes: "a colonialist is, after all, only a colonizer who agrees to be a colonizer. By making his position explicit, he seeks to legitimize colonization. This is a more logical attitude than the tormented dance of the colonizer who refuses and continues to live in a colony" (1967:45). Indeed, that "tormented dance" is recognizable among the secular, liberal Left in Israel, who often reluctantly take the role of colonizer while maintaining a moral high ground by justifying their actions as the result of having no other choice. Don Handelman explains that "the rhetoric of 'no choice'—shutting down reflection, dissent, the serious consideration of alternatives—appears like clockwork when crisis looms and the State is perceived as threatened" (2004:13). This kind of rhetorical move allows liberal Israelis to hold on to a sense of morality as they "shoot and cry" (*yorim u'bochim*), expressing sadness and discomfort with certain acts of violence directed toward Palestinians. At the same time, right-wing and religiously motivated settlers seem to display complete confidence in the moral justification of their activities, like the colonizer who accepts. Yet upon closer inspection, we find a far more complicated reality. For example, there is a movement of conscientious objectors growing out of the Israeli Left, refusing to participate in the occupation, refusing to shoot and cry, and moving beyond the idea that there is no choice. In addition, we find that despite outward appearances of great confidence, religiously motivated settlers are continuously involved in introspection and reflection. They are, in fact, not quite as certain as they might first appear. In later chapters, we hear a number of unusual or creative voices among settlers on both sides of the Green Line that indicate different forms of questioning, believing, and living in the troubled space of Israel/Palestine. However, the hegemonic categories through which the Israeli sociopolitical scene is generally understood has the effect of pushing these voices to the margins.

The settler foundations of the modern Zionist project allow us to understand certain continuities and connections in beliefs and practices found among Israeli Jews on both sides of the Green Line, but recalling the settler foundations of the state does not provide a new set of categories to account for the variously situated Israelis encountered in this book. The animosity often expressed between settlers on both sides of the Green Line arises at least partially from a desire to differentiate, but this insight represents a beginning, not a final analysis of how Israelis continue to struggle with the foundation and character of their state. This conflict, in which we find the hegemonic appearance of an intense struggle between a secular liberal state and religious extremism, resonates so powerfully with the representation of a deep divide between some forms of Islam and the so-called West. It is a case that calls into question some of the recent theorizing around that divide, thus speaking to broader, pressing problems. I will say more about the broader implications of this study later in the book, especially in Chapter 9 (see also Dalsheim 2010).

Religious Zionism and Islamism

A number of scholars have pointed to the contradictory ethics contained in liberal and secular humanism, which on the one hand abhors violence on the basis of difference and at the same time engages in violent practices to protect its way of life (Asad 2003, 2007; Brown 2006b; Butler 2008; Mahmood 2006; Povinelli 2001; J. Scott 2007). This includes projects aimed at changing religious forms of life and especially certain practices of Islam. Indeed, within current global political constellations, numerous progressive scholars have come to the defense of the religious group currently most targeted as enemies of the so-called West. But this raises questions about the broader applicability of this theorizing that defends (radical) Islam through a critique of modern liberalism and secularism. Can this kind of theorizing be applied beyond the case of today's targeted, vilified other? If so, what are its implications? This question runs throughout this book, at times explicitly addressed, at other times more subtly considered. In the final chapter, the questions that are raised by this study will be revisited: Are there similar rhetorical patterns directed against religiously motivated Jewish settlers and against Islamists? If the desire to differentiate provides some explanation for the vitriol expressed toward religious settlers, is a similar explanation to be found in the outrage expressed toward radical Muslims? If there are, even among deeply religious believers (those often called radical or fundamentalist), different voices among settlers that could be creatively engaged, are there similar voices among radical Muslims?

There is a degree of discomfort in making these comparisons, which returns to Harding's concerns with the "repugnant other." A number of scholars and political activists, particularly those who identify as left wing, liberal, or progressive, have made compelling arguments to defend Muslims against stereotyping and profiling or to explain the anger resulting from inequalities that have resulted in pious Muslims' (or Islamists') acts of violence. However, similar attempts to explain, understand, or defend the beliefs and practices of Israeli religiously motivated Jewish settlers have not occurred. Indeed, these settlers remain the vilified, repugnant others among the liberal and Left. The critical insights arising from some of the scholarship analyzing contradictions and problematics contained within political liberalism raise questions about the limits and possibilities of liberal democracy, as David Scott suggests in *Refashioning Futures*, where he asserts that it is not enough to deepen and extend liberal democracy, as the radical democrats would have it (1999). The motivation for Scott (and others) lies in the disappointing current political reality in which anticolonial struggles have not achieved their liberating goals. This work seems not only poignant but also appealing when applied to the subaltern. Taking these insights and applying them within a colonial power— that is, inside Israel rather than between Israelis and Palestinians—seems politically risky. But at the same time, this might be precisely the discomfort required to open up a conceptual space from which to rethink the present.

Disturbing Categories

Although my aim is to disturb existing categories, I also have to maintain the labels to a certain extent for the purpose of clarity. Throughout the book, I refer to the left-wing or liberal, bearing in mind that this terminology is insufficient at best and at times misleading. In Israel as elsewhere, a far more complex reality defies such easy categorization. What counts as left and right have shifting meanings and are employed differently by variously situated groups. For example, what is considered the mainstream, middle-class peace movement (Peace Now) by some is the extreme Left for others; those considered radical right-wing fundamentalists by some are traditional observant conservatives in the eyes of others. Those categorized on the political Right are not necessarily religious, nor is the Left necessarily secular. The word *liberal* will be used to distinguish the politically progressive from more radical left-wing positions, thus marking Western, liberal, political ideology more broadly. I will use the term *secular* both as an adjective describing Israeli Jews and as a noun: "the secular." In so doing, it is my intention to invoke the complexity of meaning suggested by Asad (2003), who takes "the secular to be a concept that brings together certain behaviors, knowledges, and sensibilities in modern life." In other words, like "religion" and "religious," the category of the secular should not be taken for granted as one with an obvious or unchanging content.

In referring to religiously motivated settlers, I will sometimes use the term Gush Emunim as a kind of shorthand.[32] Gush Emunim (the Bloc of the Faithful) was the name of the settler movement prior to the establishment and institutionalization of a large number of settlements in the West Bank and Gaza Strip, those areas of the biblical Land of Israel called Judea, Samaria, and Gaza.[33] Once the communities were established in these places with local governing bodies, what is known as the Yesha Council became the political leadership of the settler movement. Yesha is the Hebrew acronym for Judea, Samaria, and Gaza.[34] The Yesha Council remains, even though since August 2005 the physical settlements in the Gaza Strip are gone, and the group of believers faithful to the teachings of the two Rabbis Kook, father and son, as well as the next generation of rabbinical leaders, continues.[35] This book is less concerned with rabbinical/political leadership and more concerned with interpretations among those faithful who lived in the Gaza Strip, although it sometimes includes rabbinical opinions and sometimes moves beyond the Gaza Strip. It seeks to examine both discourses and practices among the faithful and among the skeptical liberals who lived outside the Gaza Strip. To accomplish this, my methods included very deliberate border crossings, as will become clearer in the following section that takes the reader to the field for my first visit to Gush Katif.

Crossing Borders, August 2004: Methods

Shira met me at the checkpoint marking the border between pre-1967 and post-1967 Israel. She had suggested that I park in the lot just outside the army base at the Kissufim crossing, being certain that I would not want to drive my own car into Gush Katif. Nor, she imagined, would I be willing to venture forth into this unknown territory on my own. She was keenly aware that so many Israelis were afraid to enter Gush Katif. Members of her immediate family would no longer visit. It was just the last five years or so, she said, that things had gotten quite bad. The army would surely have to do something more serious to protect the settlements, she thought. On the back of the passenger seat of Shira's car was a bright orange vest worn by emergency medical volunteers. Shira was a nurse and a midwife. She volunteered in her community and might be called to assist in cases of Palestinian attacks against settlers.

This was my first visit to Gush Katif, the first time I had crossed the border. I was hoping for a guided tour, but Shira drove so fast on the road between the checkpoint and her settlement that it was nearly impossible to take in the surroundings that blurred with the speed and the whitewashing sunlight. Why was she driving so fast? I knew I was supposed to be afraid, but was she afraid, too? It seemed to me that a sense of comfort in one's own surroundings would be expressed through a more leisurely pace. A religious settler convinced of the righteousness of settlement—both the right and sacred obligation—would not fearfully drive past Palestinians but linger with self-confidence. (Does a settler ever feel that comfort?) At the very least, I had expected a sense of comfort that I associate with feeling "at home."

I later discovered that Shira's speeding had not broken any laws. Instead, there was a different set of laws on the other side of the border. I knew that Palestinians there lived under military rule, unlike Palestinian citizens of Israel. But I had been certain that even though the territory had never been annexed to the state, Israeli law applied to Israelis living there. On the contrary, as one colleague disparagingly described it, "Israelis in the occupied territories live as though they were in the Wild West!" There are no rules, he said; they simply do as they please. I wondered if that derision did not also contain an element of desire, a desire for a kind of freedom and adventure. There were no police to give out speeding tickets, only border patrols to ensure the safety of Israelis traveling on those roads, to monitor the fence between pre-1967 Israel and the Gaza Strip, and patrol the perimeter of each community inside.

Later in the day, when we left Shira's house on an errand, as a matter of habit I pulled the seat belt around my shoulder and buckled it. Shira told me it wouldn't be necessary to use the seat belt since we were only driving a short distance from the moshav to the main town in Gush Katif, Neve Dekelim.

> "That's OK," I told her, "I'm used to wearing a seat belt, I feel safer
> that way."
> "Actually," she explained, "they recommend not wearing a seat belt
> here."
> "Huh?" It was taking me some time to register that comment.
> "Well, you know, that way if something happens, you'll be able to
> get out of your car and run away more quickly."

"Oh," I thought to myself, "a different set of issues about safety," as the fear rose steadily within me, and I wondered what on earth had brought me here and how quickly I could get out without insulting the people I had come to study. Anthropology and violence, risk, and fear all fall under the category of "fieldwork under fire" (Nordstrom and Robben 1995). But there is the other kind of fire that patrols the borders, not the fear of physical danger but the political and intellectual border patrol.

Anthropology under Fire

Shira invited me into her home and offered me coffee as we adjusted ourselves around her kitchen table for a talk. I had come to find out about Shira and the people living in Gush Katif, but first I had to be interviewed. Shira knew who I was. That is, she could easily place me within the categories and divisions of

Israeli society. She knew I lived on a secular kibbutz, indicating an association with the left wing of Israeli politics, and she wasted no time in clarifying these issues. Among the first questions she asked was "Are you wearing black because you're a Woman in Black?" Women in Black is a political movement opposed to the occupation in the post-1967 territories. It began in 1988 and has since become an international women's peace movement. That might not have been the motivation for my wardrobe choices, but it was true that I had spent many Friday afternoons demonstrating with the Women in Black against the occupation. In fact, I'd been standing with those women since the late 1980s. There was no sense in trying to hide this information from Shira. She might even have seen me at those or other demonstrations and could indeed see me there in the future. I hadn't intended to hide anything, but I also hadn't expected to be confronted so directly and so quickly. If this was my political position, Shira wanted to know what my purpose was in Gush Katif.

I had come to learn, to see what it was we were demonstrating against, I told Shira. I lived only ten minutes away from the crossing at Kissufim, but I had never been here before. Like so many secular or left-wing Israelis, I shared a disdain for the project of settling post-1967 occupied territories and for the settlers themselves, without even knowing them. I shared the ideological conviction of maintaining the clarity of the pre-1967 border by refusing to cross for any purpose other than opposing the occupation. The border had become blurred in other areas around the West Bank, especially in Jerusalem. This was increasing the difficulty of calling for a two-state solution based on the pre-1967 armistice line.

Shira seemed to have taken this as an opportunity to promote the communities of Gush Katif, their purpose and way of life—an opportunity for politicking. She took it upon herself to introduce me to her neighbors and friends and, in the months that followed, often helped me find my way. There were times when I joined Shira and her family when they went to demonstrate against the disengagement plan. It was very strange for me to cross to the other side of the street, to stand with the demonstrators I had demonstrated against. Her family sometimes teased me, vowing to post my picture among the orange flags, banners, and T-shirts opposing disengagement. They would put my picture on the Gush Katif Web site, they chided, and all my left-wing friends would see.

Crossing the border to meet with Palestinians meant getting beyond the fear induced by popular media coverage and military reports. It sometimes meant getting beyond the disapproval of neighbors, colleagues, or friends. In some circles, crossing the border on behalf of the Palestinians to promote their human and civil rights was applauded. This often included the circle of anthropologists. In many ways, it was easier to find the moral justification, to present a self to oneself that seemed appealing, when crossing borders against the occupation than it was to cross borders to meet with Israelis living in the occupied territories, unless one's goal was to demonstrate the role of post-1967 settlers in expansion and occupation. The physical, geographical border pales in comparison to the moral barrier against the idea of getting to know these settlers on their own terms and against placing them in a single theoretical frame with other Israeli settlers. Yet it is precisely this uneasy move that opens up a new conceptual space from which to think about the present in Israel/Palestine and to contemplate possible futures.

The chapters in this book are designed to disturb commonly held social, political, and religious distinctions on the Israeli scene. They are presented in a manner that mirrors a central argument of this book: No single set of oppositions, continuities, or empirical categories adequately frames the debates around settlement.

This book offers a set of interrelated essays based on ethnographic fieldwork carried out among Jewish Israelis living in and around the Gaza Strip and the conflicts between them around the issue of settlement. It is not intended as a holistic description of the lives of Israelis in that area of the country, but rather as an investigation into the hegemonic appearance of conflict and what that appearance conceals—both the work it accomplishes and the ways of believing and living it marginalizes. Chapters 2, 3, and 4 each begin from a point of contention that arose in conversations during fieldwork. While the antagonism between settlers on either side of the Green Line is mutual, there is generally a different ethos at work in each community. The secular Left tends to desire difference and distance from religious settlers, while religious settlers often express a desire to reach out to the secular and Left. This desire is directly related to the teachings of the elder Rabbi Kook, often considered the spiritual founder of the religious settler movement. It might be argued that religious settlers were less comfortable expressing animosity toward the secular and Left in my presence, although they sometimes did so in a directly confrontational manner. Because the book raises questions about the appearance of a binary division that privileges liberal and secular humanism, it addresses points of conflict that tend to be those articulated by the secular Left.

Chapter 2 focuses on the ways in which each of these groups represents itself to itself, so to speak, by comparing field trips for high school students that narrate the past and the present, performing continuity with a younger generation. Settlers in the Gaza Strip represent the present in the occupied territories as a continuation of the socialist Zionist foundations of the state. The secular Left expresses outrage at this representation by religious settlers, as they seek to differentiate between pre-state history and the current occupation in post-1967 territories. This desire to differentiate protects a sense of moral legitimacy, which is threatened by right-wing settler representations of continuity. This, I argue, is the threat that lies at the heart of the antagonism between settlers on both sides of the Green Line, which I analyze using the Freudian concept of a narcissism of minor differences. This desire to differentiate found among the secular and Left is further interrogated in chapters 3 and 4. Chapter 3 considers similarities in the ways in which Israelis on both sides of the Green Line produce their own belonging to the landscape. Chapter 4 considers commonalities around issues of uncertainty, questioning, and skepticism.

The second part of the book moves beyond the arguments and points of conflict that reinscribe the binary division found in the hegemonic appearance of discourse in conflict and beyond the commonalities beneath that appearance. This part of the book centers on ways of believing and acting that tend to be lost, marginalized, or discredited as hegemonic categories of identity are reinscribed. Chapters 5, 6, and 7 introduce some of the lesser known voices among Israeli Jews who tend to be marginalized, ignored, or erased, at least partially because of scholarly and popular representations of the Israeli socio-political-religious scene as sets of distinct binary divisions. Chapter 5 focuses on the ways in which hegemonic representations have concealed the presence of Mizrahim as religious settlers. Chapters 6 and 7 deal in greater depth with some of the deeply religious beliefs among settlers that fall outside common representations of religious settlers. The belief in the coming redemption among religious settlers is often understood to justify various forms of violence. In Chapter 6, we see how this same belief can also lead to nonviolence and inaction. Chapter 7 shows some of the thinking among settlers who follow the teachings of Rabbi Abraham Isaac Kook and their deep faith in the Sovereign of the Universe that allows thinking beyond territorial nationalism. Chapter 8 considers insights, contradictions, and ambiguities among Israeli Jews debating disengagement. Finally, chapter 9 concludes by considering the implications of this study for Israel/Palestine and the questions it raises about conflicts between formations of the secular and the religious in other contexts as it compares theoretical interventions into representations of demonized Muslims to questions of vilified Jews.

2

Disturbing Doubling

Antagonizing Settlers and History in the Present

"Awareness of history . . . enhances communal and national identity, legitimating a people in their own eyes."

—David Lowenthal

"The constitution of identity is an elaborate and deadly serious game of mirrors . . . history is the discourse of identity."

—Jonathan Friedman

Historical narratives are considered essential to the construction of national identity as the naturalness of nations is called into question. As early as 1882, Renan commented on the temporary nature of the nation, as well as the particular content required of a national past: "A heroic past, great men, glory . . . this is the social capital upon which one bases a national idea . . . One loves [the nation] in proportion to the sacrifices to which one has consented, and in proportion to the ills that one has suffered"(Renan 1990:19). Because of the significance of constructing a usable past upon which national identity is based, conflicts between Israeli and Palestinian narrations of the past are not only understandable but also to be expected within the context of two national groups vying for a single piece of territory. But how are we to understand conflicts between Israeli Jews over representing their past? This chapter illustrates the antagonism between Israeli Jews as it is expressed in their tellings of the past. The arguments between the two groups concerning uses of the past serves as a reference from which to demonstrate that the desire, particularly among the secular, to differentiate rather than identify is located in a fear of what today's settler activity reveals about the Zionist project more broadly and what it therefore stands to potentially undermine.

In this chapter, I bring together stories about the collective past told by the secular Left and the religious Right. These are narratives on which collective identities are built, the stories each group tells about itself and passes on to the next generation to instill a sense of pride and impart a particular meaning to the present.[1] The arguments between these groups of settlers concerning uses of the past fuel a great deal of bitterness. Today's settlers in post-1967 territories narrate their present as a continuation of the heroic acts of the pioneering founders of the state, which they see the secular Left in Israel as having abandoned. The left-wing secular are infuriated by what they see as an act of mimicry, which they interpret as a form of abuse of a Zionist past that belongs to them. This past, from their point of view, has been both appropriated and inappropriately reinterpreted by the settlers, leaving the secular Left enraged and frustrated as they watch their pure and heroic heritage being stolen, so to speak, and given a meaning they oppose.

This chapter illustrates how post-1967 narratives told by religiously motivated settlers employ tropes, tales, and metaphors similar to those of the pioneering founders of the state. It also shows the anger provoked by what is experienced by the secular Left as a form of imitation: both mimicking and less than authentic, a poor and improper copy of the original. At the same time, it shows how rhetorical expressions with very different surface appearances can have very similar outcomes in practice.

To illustrate these processes, I present data from two very different high school field trips that I participated in as part of this research. One is a secular left-wing kibbutz high school and the other, a religious high school for girls (*ulpana*). The kibbutz high school students were taken on a trip by their history teachers to learn about and identify with their ancestors, the Jewish immigrants of the second *aliya*, who established the first kibbutz communities in Israel. The *ulpana* students were brought to the communities of Gush Katif to learn about or identify with the religious settlers there. I present the two field trips as an interwoven text, blurring the distinctions between them while drawing attention to similarities and continuities. I also include excerpts from interviews and field notes gathered among kibbutz members, other secular Israelis, and right-wing religious settlers from the communities of Gush Katif in the Gaza Strip.

I should like to draw the reader's attention to the similarities in signs and symbols, the shared cultural meanings that find expression both in material objects and in the choices of words and images by tour guides and teachers in both field trips. These find expression through representations of heroism, life, and living, combined with suffering and death, as well as a certain revered attitude toward displaying the nerve to take risks.

Right-wing and religiously motivated settlers tend to narrate their present as a continuation of the project of the pioneering founders of the state.[2] This is often interpreted and dismissed by the left wing and secular as an inauthentic imitation. The depth of discomfort experienced by the descendants of the Leftist founders of the state seems indicative of an uncanny and disquieting doubling (Freud 1946 (1919)). What is experienced here by the secular is part of the antagonism between settlers in which the *identification* between these two groups proves so threatening (Freud 1961 (1930): 62). Freud suggests that "minor differences" between groups can provoke particularly bitter disputes, and this idea has often been invoked to explain ethnic groups or groups on either sides of national borders who find themselves in situations of conflict.[3] Aggression toward outsiders can be understood as promoting cohesion within each group. But this idea grew out of Freud's earlier insight that "small differences" resulted in virulent hatred precisely because such small differences pose a threat to one's core sense of self, a threat far greater than that posed by those who are extremely different (Freud 1957(1917)). In the case at hand, the struggle between Israeli Jews seems to emerge precisely over such an anxiety at the very core of collective identity. The once dominant secular Zionist narrative appears to be threatened by a competing narrative told and enacted by right-wing religious Zionists. And I would suggest that the desire, particularly among the secular, to differentiate rather than identify may be located in a fear of what this settler activity reveals about the Zionist project more broadly and what it therefore stands to undermine.

The desire to represent contemporary settlement activity as a continuation of the socialist Zionist past becomes very clear on the field trip of a religious girls' high school to the Gush Katif settlements in the Gaza Strip when compared with a secular high school field trip to the places where the first kibbutz communities were established.

Field Trips

A group of eleventh-grade students from a secular kibbutz high school set out with their history teachers to experience the story of the Second Aliya in a way that would not be possible inside the classroom. This field trip was planned by the history teachers, who explained their understanding of the power of taking students out of the classroom for a day. The atmosphere of a field trip—with its aspects of communitas—creates an experience that makes use of the power of collective memory in two ways. First, it serves to emphasize certain content to be remembered. Second, it creates a memorable experience for the participants that contributes to their sense of belonging together as a group.[4] The teachers were convinced that students, who may remember little of the lectures they heard in class, would remember the experience and content of this field trip, and they spoke about choosing the specific destination and content on that basis.

The Second Aliya refers to the wave of Eastern European immigrants who arrived in Palestine in the early twentieth century (1904–1919) and includes those who established the first kibbutzim (plural for kibbutz). These students were being taken on a tour to rediscover their roots, to gain a better under-standing of the lives of their ancestors, and mostly to evoke an emotional attachment to those ancestors. This tour is among the processes by which this heterogeneous group becomes "descendants" of the socialist Zionist foun-ders of the state. Such processes occur in moments when teachers or tour guides telling historical tales slip from the pronoun *they* to *we*, collapsing distances in time and place and erasing the specific, personal, and family his-tories of these students, who include new immigrants from the former Soviet Union and other places, as well as the grandchildren of Middle Eastern and North African Jews, whose past is not that of the socialist Zionist founders of the state (Dalsheim 2004:154–155; Ram 1995b).

Life and Living/Death and Suffering

By far the most moving and memorable part of this trip, according to students and teachers alike, took place at the cemetery of Kibbutz Kinneret on the shores of the Sea of Galilee, where the tour guide's performance seemed to bring the dead to life. The tour guide met the group in the parking lot of the cemetery at Kinneret, a place from which to set the stage and establish the mood before entering the cemetery. This was artfully accomplished by the guide, who made an immediate impression through both his words and his appearance. Amitai Engelman, a middle-aged son of Kibbutz Kinneret, wore a black T-shirt com-memorating eighty years of Kinneret on his polio-twisted torso. The polio vac-cine was not available in Israel when Amitai[5] was afflicted. His body seemed to reflect suffering and fortitude, sacrifice and resilience, foreshadowing the story he was about to tell.

Amitai told the group they were about to enter a "magical world of special people." This place, he said, is a place of heroism. The people who came here never thought of a cemetery, he said; "they were focused on living." A very similar rhetorical move could be heard by the tour guide in Gush Katif, the bloc of settlements in the Gaza Strip where about 8,000 settlers lived, surrounded by more than a million Palestinians living in crowded conditions in villages, cities, and refugee camps. The settlements were surrounded by security fences and constantly guarded by a high military presence. As the busload of *ulpana* girls entered Gush Katif, the school principal handed the microphone over to a local guide. Mordecai, a teacher at the *ulpana* and a resident of Gush Katif, began by saying, "It is my intention to talk to you about life and living, but here on the left you see a memorial for Tali and the girls [her daughters] who were shot and killed on this road by Arabs."[6]

In the cemetery at Kinneret, Amitai established his authority to tell the tale of the founders by relating that he had fought in the 1967 Six Day War. That war ended in a great victory for Israel, and it is the event that captured the territory currently occupied by today's settlers. The end of the Six Day War is remembered as a period of jubilation and valorization of soldiers. Even those Israelis who advocate returning to the pre-1967 borders remember the joy of visiting the Old City of Jerusalem or playing on tanks as school children celebrating the victory with their parents. In Gush Katif, Mordecai established his authority by pointing to his own house as we drove past tanks and armed soldiers through the streets of Kfar Darom. Amitai was a warrior; Mordecai continued to live the danger of the front lines. Amitai spoke of war and death, with a great sigh, and said it was difficult for him to enter the cemetery—though he has guided tours there for years. He told the group of kibbutzniks that he still doesn't know how to deal with this place, what to make of it, expressing a deeply felt ambivalence that appealed to the sensibilities of these students and teachers, that "tormented dance" of which Memmi speaks.[7] Right-wing and religious settlers deride this self-admonishing as a kind of psychological defect associated with living in Diaspora (*galut*) that should be overcome now that the Jews have returned and are sovereign in their homeland. In Gush Katif, there seemed to be far less ambivalence. Among those settlers, it was this apparent certainty of the holy mission of the settlement project that seemed most appealing to its constituents and offensive to the opposition.[8]

As the group entered the cemetery at Kinneret, the guide said he would try to "speak the language and the spirit of the pioneers" who had been here. Indeed, the group witnessed a performance that seemed to make the gravestones speak, make the buried come to life. Amitai's performance aroused emotions in everyone and brought some listeners to tears as the stories he told became their stories through personal details that evoked a sense of identification. He told us of the people who were buried here as though he had known each one personally. The pain, the suffering endured, the struggle, and the tragedy were all reflected in Amitai's own twisted body. For Mordecai, there was no need to bring history to life. He was himself representative of "today's pioneers" in Gush Emunim (settler movement) terminology, and in his daily reality, suffering and death were well known. The film shown at the museum in Kfar Darom depicted that suffering as evidence of bravery and steadfastness. The website for Gush Katif continuously reiterated this collective disposition. For example, during the Hanukah holiday in 2004, a notice on the website read, "Yigal Kirshendeft, whose son was wounded by mortar fire continues to hand out warm doughnuts to IDF soldiers."[9] The preceding notice reported on the mortar fire that had struck less than an hour before. According to these representations, the settlers in Gush Katif remained in their homes, on this territory, against all odds, just like the pioneers of the Second Aliya.

Naïve, Arrogant, Crazy, Chutzpah

Amitai described the pioneers as "naïve and arrogant" for thinking they could succeed in their pioneering effort. Naïve and *arrogant* are strong and critical words, but Amitai was combining realism with admiration and gratitude. This naïveté is not foolishness. It is the innocence that allowed the youthful pioneers to take risks, which ultimately resulted in founding the state of Israel. The use of arrogance in this case echoes a deep and widely shared value among many Israelis. It is a kind of chutzpah, which in this usage connotes a positive form of arrogance. It refers to having both the nerve and the sense of assuredness to take certain risks. In a conversation with a settler from Gush Katif, this cultural value was once again invoked. Waiting in a left-turn lane after returning from a nationwide demonstration in favor of settlement activity, the convoy of cars and minibuses returning to Gush Katif overtook the road. Many of the settlers driving home passed on the right, cut us off, and took the left turn while we waited. Such behavior might be expected to provoke anger, but our driver, Motti, knew the other drivers who were cutting him off. He laughed and called out, "Hey, that's Moshe, look how crazy he is!" When I asked him about this wild driving, his initial answer seemed aimed at appeasing my cultural sensibilities when he said that indeed it is problematic, and that in Europe and the United States drivers are much politer. But after a moment's reflection, he added with a naughty smile that this kind of behavior is chutzpah, and it is precisely that Israeli chutzpah that "has gotten us to where we are today. It is the kind of behavior that won us our state and that makes us among the best in the world in technological advancements." This way of behaving continues in the occupied territories, where settlements can be illegally established and where, sometimes, settlers have been known to take the law into their own hands. These kinds of behaviors are deeply intertwined with Israeli constellations of masculinity, and it may be that on some level the hatred and anger displayed by some left-wing, secular Israelis conceals a certain admiration or desire to be able to behave in these wild ways themselves, defying the law and taking risks with a sense of self-righteousness. However, these emotions are also couched in an anger that can be understood as directed at the ways in which today's settlers are seen to be taking what does not belong to them. On the surface, what they are taking is land that does not belong to them, land belonging to Palestinians. But the anger evoked is a result of a different theft. It is the very moral justification of the nation-state that is being pulled out from underneath, unsettling the very foundations of legitimacy. This provokes a defensiveness against what today's settler activity reveals about the Zionist project, further submerging the issue of land expropriation or any discussion of the Palestinian right of return. The settlers are reacted to as though they were stealing the pure and noble story of socialist Zionist settlers and giving it a meaning that the liberal Left considers a perversion of the original intentions of the pioneering founders of the state. This anger is intensified because today's settlement activity has been sanctioned and supported with state resources for decades.[10] This creates a double sense of anger since it means that left-wing, liberal taxpayers who serve their compulsory army duty and send their children to the army as well are in effect protecting and supporting settlement activities that they believe to be immoral and dangerous both to their children and to the future of the state.[11]

The notion of heroism is expressed in the secular narrative as a kind of craziness. "Those pioneering socialists were insane," the history teacher tells his students. They were insane for coming here and living in such harsh conditions, crazy for staying and enduring. But it is precisely this kind of craziness—here a term of endearment—that is deeply admired. These sentiments do not extend to today's settlers on the other side of the Green Line, who are also depicted as insane. Their behavior, which the settlers themselves represent as so similar to and a continuation of the pioneering acts of the socialist Zionist ancestors, is often despised by today's kibbutzniks and other Leftists. The settlers' "insanity" is characterized as irrational in its messianism and immoral in its practices. In addition, it is considered a set of ideas and practices that belongs to the past and prevents progress. Just prior to the withdrawal from the Gaza Strip, one kibbutz member told me, "If we were living there today—which of course we wouldn't be—but if we were, we would not behave the way they do. We would treat our Arab neighbors with dignity and respect and everything would look different." For this man, separating himself from the settlers involves an invocation of essentializing difference. This is interesting for two reasons. First, the newer, revisionist history of the founding years of the state that has been challenging Zionist mythology since the late 1980s reveals precisely the kinds of acts from which this kibbutznik wants to distance himself.[12] Second, among many left-wing Israelis, it is not unusual to find expressions of empathy for Palestinian acts of violence that are explained in terms of identification and context. Palestinian suicide bombings, for example, are seen to represent the acts of desperation of a people without a state and an army. But neither the acts nor the suffering of settlers evoke much empathy, and there is no attempt to appreciate today's settlement within the context of their own worldview. Instead, this activity is dangerous and unnecessary in the eyes of the left-wing secular. The limits of liberal tolerance in this case cannot be easily reduced to the imposition of a secular worldview on religious others, although the rhetoric of delegitimization is comparable to that used in the process of creating distance from or delegitimizing certain practices of Islam. The critique of these other Jews does not seem to interfere with the values of liberal humanism. That is, there is no sense of discomfort at expressing a lack of toleration in this case.[13] At least partially, I would suggest, this assuredness can be understood as a kind of cultural intimacy, that sense of insiderness that is a powerful place from which to critique.[14] It is very much like arguments within a family, and such is precisely the representation today's settlers put forth of their relationship to the secular.

Natural Disaster/No Choice

At the cemetery at Kinneret, Amitai, the tour guide, moved forward through the gravestones and spoke of the difference between *falahim* and *ekarim*. *Falahim* work the land but do not own it, he said. "These pioneers were *ekarim*," he explained. "They lived on land that did not belong to them. We also live in a place that is not ours," he said. "What can you do?" he asked rhetorically. "We entered a movie theater without a ticket, what can you do?" At this moment "they," the pioneering socialists, are gently folded into "we" as Amitai makes a reflexive move that both reveals a critical consciousness—we took something that wasn't ours—and at the same time, by acknowledging this problematic past also absolves the collective self as he asks, "What can you do?" This common Hebrew rhetorical tag question is not a question at all. It is a way of saying that there is nothing to be done, a phrase that continues to resonate with security-related discourses of "no choice" in Israeli policy-making regarding

Palestinians. That rhetoric of "no choice" shuts down reflection, dissent, or serious consideration of alternatives (Handelman 2004:13). Among the secular, liberal, and those concerned with politically correct behavior, the rhetoric of no choice can go a long way toward justifying unseemly government policies and actions. It is a rhetorical move that provides a moral alibi located in intentions rather than actions.[15] For example, a left-wing secular woman living on a kibbutz expressed her sorrow at the construction of the separation barrier, or wall between Israelis and Palestinians, the ongoing logic of separation that has been creating havoc in the daily lives of many Palestinians who are cut off from their means of making a living and from each other as territory is expropriated.[16] This woman explained that she found the wall "unfortunate," not the way she would choose to live. However, she said, "in today's reality, we have no choice. This is the best way of protecting ourselves from terrorists at the moment." For this population group, the notion of no choice is often accompanied by a deep and heartfelt sigh, indicating a moral dilemma in which actions must be carried out, even though the left-wing liberal would like to be able to do otherwise. Among the right-wing and religious settlers, a very different rhetoric that appears quite far from politically correct has the same effect. A settler in Gush Katif explained that the situation could best be understood as a kind of natural disaster. "This is what I tell my wife," he explained. "In some parts of the world, they have hurricanes, earthquakes, or volcanoes. There is nothing you can do about it except to remain steadfast. This," he continued, "is our natural disaster," referring to Palestinian acts of violence against Jewish Israelis, whether in the occupied territories or inside the Green Line. Both discourses naturalize the situation, reducing the extent of Israeli reflection on responsibility and limiting possibilities of change by announcing that this is just the way things are—an act of God, beyond our control. Both can be understood as techniques that enable waiting for some kind of evolutionary progress that will improve the situation while maintaining particular forms of domination.[17]

Childhood and Innocence

Amitai moved on through the cemetery as he led the group to a set of graves dated 1913 and told his audience that the pioneers thought these would be the last victims of war. "How naïve," he remarked, as he stepped toward a tiny gravestone where an infant was buried, and spoke of the many deaths of children and the frustration of the pioneers as "children fall like flies." The death and suffering of children and the loss of innocent lives paint a picture of tragedy but at the same time resonate with notions of continuity, of having to preserve that for which these lives were lost. This was one of the powerful messages the tour guide and teachers wanted to impart to the high school students: the idea that "we" have the responsibility to continue the project that the pioneering founders began. "We" are indebted to these ancestors, as one of the history teachers on the kibbutz school field trip remarked. "They were crazy, but thank goodness they were crazy. Otherwise we would not have the state we have today." And it is the responsibility of the next generation to carry on fulfilling the Zionist dream. Today in Gush Katif, the suffering of children who have lost their limbs, their parents, or their lives is central to the narrative of heroism and steadfastness told by settlers. The children are presented as themselves being brave in a move that differs from and is deeply disturbing to a left-wing secular sensibility. Leftists are often heard proclaiming that today's settlers can do as they please, risk their lives if that's what they want to do. But settlers are deeply criticized on two levels for involving children. First, they are criticized for involving their own children, who are seen as innocent victims of ideological zeal. Second and more pointedly, the settlers are seen as responsible for the suffering of "our" children, the children of the secular and liberal who, at the tender age of eighteen, are sent off as soldiers to protect the illegal, dangerous, unnecessary, and insane activity of settlers. A kibbutz member who had been demonstrating against the settlements in Gush Katif, which are situated just across the Green Line from his kibbutz, explained that it was the suffering of the children that moved him to take to the streets. There is a well-known story about the Cohen family in Gush Katif whose children were maimed when a bomb exploded under their school bus. One of the Cohen girls lost both her legs, and the children spent months in rehabilitation. What was inconceivable for this kibbutznik and many other left-wing liberals was that the family continued living in Gush Katif. "This is where I draw the line," David told me. "They simply must get those children out of there. Why should those children have to suffer for their parents' crazy ideology? That ideology is over, and those children will end up hating their parents." Other secular left-wing Israelis speak about not wanting to sacrifice the lives or the moral integrity of their own children who are sent as soldiers to protect settlers. In these cases, it seems that morality ends at the Green Line. For the settlers themselves, these arguments are meaningless. Life and death, explains a woman on the film shown in the museum at Kfar Darom, are in the hands of God, and the settlers see themselves as sent on a holy mission to do God's work. In another film clip, Mrs. Cohen herself speaks about the suffering of her children and continuing to live in Gush Katif. She speaks about the cruelty of "Arab terrorists who placed the bomb beneath the school bus" and asks how it is possible to imagine "rewarding such barbarous acts by giving those terrorists the settlements," her home.

The tour guide at Kinneret cemetery moves rhetorically back in time as he recalls the early days of kibbutz, the "almighty" women who cared for children then, and the prestige and authority the community bestowed on them. He tells the story of Amalia, the first daughter of Kinneret, as the group gathers around her small grave. The pioneers did not have the means to cure her of illness, which is something that cannot be said for today's settlers. Today's settlers, according to the Left, *do* have other choices. A number of small and unmarked graves at the Kinneret cemetery speak of hurried burials. Amitai said people were buried in haste to prevent the spread of disease. The picture emerging from these tales is one of hardship and struggle, awakening a sense of respect for these ancestors, if not admiration. The tour guide sums up his own emotions. "I feel like this is Mt. Sinai, where the Torah [of kibbutz] came from."[18]

Continuity or Mimicry?

At the Museum of the Land and the Torah in Kfar Darom in Gush Katif, the narrative presented is also aimed at awakening a sense of respect and admiration. In Kfar Darom, the girls from the *ulpana* in a nearby town outside Gush Katif are shown a movie that tells a pioneering tale of Kfar Darom. For the settlers of Gush Katif, it was very important to establish the legitimacy of their location, which was constantly called into question in mainstream discourse because their communities were built outside the pre-1967 borders.[19]

The movie begins with a very brief reference to biblical times, a sentence about Abraham and Isaac walking this land. However, the central emphasis of this film is to make a direct connection between this settlement and those of the pre-state era. In this way, the history of today's community in Kfar Darom is narrated as having precisely the same historical roots as pioneering socialist Zionism. In the corner of the room where the film is being shown, there is a display of early agricultural equipment, with the very same wooden pitchforks found in kibbutz museums and, outside in the garden, the very same plows. Tamar Katriel (1997) has documented the performances of tour guides in kibbutz museums commemorating pioneering socialism. It is uncanny how the photos in her book could easily be replaced by photos taken in 2004 at the museum in Kfar Darom (see figure 2.1).

Kfar Darom, the movie explains, was one of the eleven settlements established on the eve of Yom Kippur in 1946. This is the history of a number of secular kibbutzim in the same region but inside the Green Line. The movie tells of the heroism of the first people who came to Kfar Darom in 1946 and how they fought to hold their ground under attack by Egyptian forces. The original

FIGURE 2.1 Images of pitchforks and other agricultural equipment from the museums at Kfar Darom (L) and Yifat (R). L: author photo. R: courtesy of Tamar Katriel.

community did not last the war and was abandoned in a matter of months. The community that exists today was founded in 1990, but in 1996 it celebrated its fiftieth anniversary, once again narrating continuity with the secular Zionist project.

Establishing settlements clandestinely, under cover of darkness to evade detection by the British then in control of Mandatory Palestine, is a central motif of the Zionist narrative.[20] Jews were not permitted to build new communities during certain time periods before the establishment of the state. There was, however, a law stating that a building with a roof could not be destroyed. So, the Zionist pioneers would work through the night and by daybreak have built a crude structure with a roof that allowed them to remain.

Later settlers in the West Bank and Gaza Strip saw their activity as a continuation of the pioneering settlements. For them, today's kibbutz dwellers had abandoned the project, betraying the true intentions of the Zionist ancestors (Ron 2001:238). Post-1967 settlements have also often been set up under cover of darkness. The difference is that these outposts are established clandestinely to avoid detection by the Israeli government. This difference is seen as more ironic than significant in the eyes of settlers, but for left-wing liberals, this is the difference that counts. For left-wing Zionists, illegal settlements built after the founding of the state in 1948 on territory that has not been recognized as

Israel by the international community is no longer Zionism. Indeed, it is counter to the very spirit of Zionism—the very limits of mimicry.

Today's religiously motivated right-wing settlers continue to believe in the central importance of establishing a Jewish presence in what they define as the biblical Land of Israel, which, according to some interpretations, extends far beyond the current boundaries of the state.[21] It is their belief that they must seize any opportunity to fulfill the will of God and establish both a Jewish presence and sovereignty on this land. Their activities often began illegally, but they often succeeded in obtaining subsequent government approval. On the tour of Gush Katif in November 2004, after the approval of the disengagement plan to evacuate these settlements, the tour guide took the group to show them the new construction going on as settlements were expanded and outposts continued to be set up. The tour went to a row of trailers set up on the beachfront with a wire fence in the sand to separate these dwellings from the Palestinian fishing village alongside. The teachers accompanying the girls from the *ulpana* looked upon that row of trailers and exclaimed with joyous emotion, "These are the pioneers of today!" (See figure 2.2.)

FIGURE 2.2 Looking at the row of trailers on the beach. Author photo.

Israeli Zionists who view themselves as descendants of the socialist pioneers or as carrying on in the same spirit are outraged by any comparison between settlement then and the ongoing settlement that began after 1967 across the Green Line. "The difference is the state and the army," I have been told on numerous occasions. The tanks around which our tour bus had to navigate to enter the museum at Kfar Darom signify that difference (see figures 2.3 and 2.4).

The goal of the modern Zionist project to establish a homeland—a sovereign Jewish state—has been achieved. "That was Zionism," left-wing kibbutz members explain. "What settlers are doing today is not Zionism," as David from a secular kibbutz near the Green Line told me. "That ideology is over" it belongs to the past.

For liberal, secular Zionists, the pre-1967 border is crucial. If that border is not recognized, the entire Zionist project may be undermined. Recognizing international law rather than God's law is central to maintaining the legitimacy and the existence of the current state. If the idea of the pre-1967 border (the 1949 armistice line) is erased, and if Israeli presence beyond that line is

FIGURE 2.3 Driving out of the museum, past an army post in Kfar Darom. Author photo.

FIGURE 2.4 Tanks in front of a separation barrier in Kfar Darom. Author photo.

illegitimate, then the legitimacy of the state itself may be called into question. If there is no difference between the two sides of the Green Line, one of which includes the internationally recognized state and the other that is called "occupied territories," then the state of Israel itself can be called an occupation, which some anti-Israeli constituencies have called it. If the Green Line does not represent a crucial difference, then a deep existential anxiety arises.

A young woman, Hadass, who married into life on a secular kibbutz in the Eshkol Region, explained her concerns over this problem. It is not that she believes there is a *qualitative* difference between this or that side of the Green Line, nor does David, quoted previously, believe so. He told me he would have been quite pleased if the state was bigger. It just didn't turn out that way. Neither Hadass nor David can speak of their God-given right to this land, as religiously motivated settlers do. They see the right of the state of Israel to exist as based in historical necessity and international recognition. In her heart of hearts, Hadass did not like the idea of dismantling settlements. However, she recognized the importance of the pre-1967 border and decided to support the disengagement plan. For if internationally recognized borders are considered arbitrary, then what gives legitimacy to the state of Israel? If settlement within current state boundaries is equivalent to that beyond the Green Line, then Hadass says, "I have no right to be here at all." This, it seems, is the underlying fear—a deep anxiety that the entire Zionist project may be called into question. The fear that Jewish presence and sovereignty on this territory stands to lose its moral and rational legitimacy in the eyes of the international community may be the driving force behind the hatred aimed at post-1967 religiously motivated and right-wing settlers. This is the anxiety underlying the desire to differentiate, that narcissism of minor differences that finds expression in the appearance of deep differences and conflict between settlers on both sides of the Green Line.

Representations of the past contribute to establishing collective identity and the relationship between a collectivity and a particular piece of territory. But that relationship is also constituted in the present through everyday practices and habits, as will be seen in the next chapter.

3

Producing Absence and Habits of Blinding Vision

"[The settlements of Gush Katif are] obviously temporary. You just have to go there once to see how they are set up, like an unnatural imposition in the middle of all those Palestinians. You just have to see them and you'll understand right away why they have to get out of there."

—Activist calling for the removal of
settlers from the Gaza Strip

"The Land of Israel, the People of Israel, the Torah of Israel. Together these make up a unity, a wholeness. It is like a living being, a living body. . . . Removing any part—being removed from this land—is like the removal of a limb."

—Resident of Neve Dekelim in Gush Katif

The Jewish settlements of the Gaza Strip were often disparagingly described by their opponents in spatial and visual terms using biological or physiological metaphors. Gush Katif was said to be an "artificial transplant" in the midst of a large Palestinian population. It was described as an "unnatural" and unsustainable imposition on the landscape—clearly out of place, clearly temporary. At the same time, religiously motivated settlers spoke of unity and wholeness and also employed biological or physiological allusions, such that leaving the land was even likened to amputation.[1]

Critical scholars have long questioned the apparently natural relationship of any "people" to a particular place. The seemingly timeless existence of nations results from very specific processes, including building roads to connect populations in remote areas and compulsory education teaching a single language and disseminating shared culture (Gellner 1981; Weber 1976) and the advent of the printing press, which allowed people to become "imagined communities" with a sense of common purpose among people who would never meet each other (Anderson 1983). The constructed nature of a "natural" relationship between such a people and a particular territory has been shown to be accomplished through the use of mapping as a visual technique and through rhetorical metaphors that liken human groups to rooted trees, for example (Malkki 1997). These constructed connections are not only solidified but also elevated as morally righteous or superior through historical narratives that create a usable past and traditions that bring people together as "a people" through both collective memory and forgetting.[2] In addition to producing and naturalizing relationships between people and place, the spaces in which people live also shape them, as processes of identity take place in time and space and include the ways people identify in relation to interpretations of their surroundings.[3] In other words, people make landscapes, design and build their surroundings, and those surroundings in turn make or shape people (Bender 1993; Bender and Winer 2001; Bourdieu 1977; Boyarin 1994). Here, in Israel/Palestine, where struggles for territory and intense conflict over the relationship between people and place are ongoing processes between Israelis and Palestinians, it seems strange to find such antinomy between Israeli Jews questioning each other's beliefs or representations of their historical ties or natural relationship to the Land.[4] Yet, each group sees their interpretation of that relationship to the territory both as the morally correct interpretation and as providing the key to the future.

As in the previous chapter, the antagonism surrounding a relationship to the land and ways of living in and on the land seems to be located in a desire to differentiate. The left wing and secular expressed criticism of the settlements of Gush Katif, while the settlers defended their natural and historical relationship to the Gaza Strip. The contours of this argument become part of an ongoing narration connecting the present to the past, continuations of the arguments over historical representations visited in the previous chapter. Here again, categories of conflict are reinscribed, redefining differences that conceal continuities in the ways communities on *both* sides of the Green Line have produced relationships to the land, and the ways in which both have participated in producing the relative absence of Palestinians from the land.

People, Territory, Sovereignty

For left-wing, liberal, and secular Israelis, their right to have a state in Israel is based on a history of the Jews as a persecuted people and the internationally recognized right of nations to self-rule. Their understanding of this right also includes the historical relationship of the Jewish people to the ancient Land of Israel. Many secular and liberal Israelis share the belief held by religious Jews that because this particular piece of territory is the ancient, biblical homeland of the Jews, they have the right to make it their state. However, they understand the relationship between the people and the territory to be historical rather than sacred, and this leaves room for territorial compromise. While defending the right of the Jewish People to the space of Israel, many insist that extending the border beyond the Green Line denies the right of the Palestinian people to have a state. That right, they say, must be recognized because it, too, is a moral imperative and because it is a step on the path to peace. From this perspective, territorial expansion is a sign of greed, of wanting more than you need and of lacking the willingness to compromise. It is also considered dangerous. Thus, compromise is the pragmatic path to avoid direct provocation and ongoing conflict with Palestinians.

Pronouncements by the secular Left, such as calling Gush Katif an "unnatural imposition on the landscape," are interpreted by the religious Right as taking sides with anti-Israeli if not anti-Semitic voices that claim that the Jewish state in its entirety is an unnatural, foreign imposition and that it, too, will come to an end. For religiously motivated settlers, denying the relationship between Jews and the Gaza Strip is equivalent to denying the relationship between Jews and Tel Aviv, if not Jerusalem, or any other place in the country. It undermines the legitimacy of the Jewish state. A profound sense of precariousness, of existential danger, seems to underlie both points of view. This is an existential anxiety founded on the belief of security in sovereignty that harks back to an earlier anxiety of Jews in Europe (Arendt 2003 (1951))—an anxiety that is deeply embedded in Israeli collective memory.[5] In both cases, it rests firmly on the concept of sovereign citizenship in the nation-state, and both express fears of losing the security associated with that sovereignty while each finds fault with the other.

Despite the expressed antipathy and the desire to differentiate, the practices through which Jewish settlers in the Gaza Strip produced a connection between themselves and the land where they made their homes were, in many ways, congruous with practices in other parts of Israel, including communities in the Negev on the other side of the Green Line from the Gaza Strip. I should like to begin considering that congruity by taking a closer look at the settle-ments of Gush Katif, now no longer there, that were often described as artifi-cially or unnaturally imposed on the landscape; raising some questions about those qualifiers; and then moving on to communities inside the Green Line, while bearing in mind what is by now an anthropological certitude that "all associations of place, people, and culture are social and historical creations to be explained" (Gupta and Ferguson 1997:4). In this chapter, I will compare techniques of (collective) self-representation and production in relation to both people and space among the settlers of Gush Katif and those who live in Jewish settlements inside the Green Line. I use the word *production* here deliberately, emphasizing the conscious effort at self-staging that becomes subconscious in the form of habit memory. This is not to say that I consider these representa-tions less than "authentic" but to point to the active work involved in creating collective selves as connected to the land and how that activity melts into habits of everyday ways of seeing and being in the world. There is labor that has gone into creating and interpreting the landscape. To recognize that work is to con-sider the ways in which people understand and engage with the material world around them, which is always contingent and always in process, potentially conflicted, untidy, and uneasy (Bender 1993; Bender and Winer 2001:3).

To consider the techniques of self-representation and production between people and place is to make more visible that which lies beneath "the non-transparency of society" (Chakrabarty 2002:46). These are the ways in which the past, both recent and distant, becomes part of people in ways that are not immediately evident, through embodied memories and through cultural training of the senses.[6] Much has been written on the processes of imagining collective identity, particularly national identity, through spatiality (Alonso 1994; Crain 1990; Gupta and Ferguson 1997; Hansen and Stepputat 2001; Radcliffe and Westwood 1996; Zerubavel 1995). Here I am pointing to an intra-national conflict over such imaginings and the work involved in learning cul-tural interpretations of the landscape. I begin with ways of seeing, with the cultural training of vision in Gush Katif.

Envisioning Gush Katif between the Sand Dunes

One of the ways in which settlers of Gush Katif represented themselves and their deep relationship to their communities was through the use of films. Films were produced largely to engender empathy among people who might never visit the area, but they were also used as an introduction for those who did come and stopped by the visitors' center at the museum in Kfar Darom.

A major role of that museum was to narrate the ancient relationship between the Jews and this particular piece of land.

The permanent exhibit at the museum in Kfar Darom began with biblical quotations referring to Jewish ancestors walking on this land. It continued through Diaspora and destruction in the Holocaust, and ended with return to the Holy Land and the establishment of the state. This was a more localized version of the national narrative that is illustrated in museum displays elsewhere in the country, explained in greater detail in schoolbooks, and canonized in the Israeli Declaration of Independence. The declaration, partially quoted here, invokes both the ancient connection of the Jewish People to the Land of Israel and international recognition of their right to establish a state on that territory. It also participates in producing the absence of Palestinians as it links the ancient past with the present, leaving out hundreds of years in between when Arabs made their homes in Palestine and most Jews lived in Diaspora.

> The Land of Israel was the birthplace of the Jewish people. Here their spiritual, religious and political identity was shaped. Here they first attained to statehood, created cultural values of national and universal significance and gave to the world the eternal Book of Books.

> After being forcibly exiled from their land, the people kept faith with it throughout their dispersion and never ceased to pray and hope for their return to it and for the restoration in it of their political freedom.

> ... In the year 5657 (1897), at the summons of the spiritual father of the Jewish State, Theodore Herzl, the First Zionist Congress convened and proclaimed the right of the Jewish people to national rebirth in its own country.

> This right was recognized in the Balfour Declaration of the 2nd November, 1917, and re-affirmed in the Mandate of the League of Nations which, in particular, gave international sanction to the historic connection between the Jewish people and Eretz-Israel and to the right of the Jewish people to rebuild its National Home.

> The catastrophe which recently befell the Jewish people—the massacre of millions of Jews in Europe—was another clear demonstration of the urgency of solving the problem of its homelessness by re-establishing in Eretz-Israel the Jewish State,

which would open the gates of the homeland wide to every Jew and confer upon the Jewish people the status of a fully privileged member of the community of nations.

Survivors of the Nazi holocaust in Europe, as well as Jews from other parts of the world, continued to migrate to Eretz-Israel, undaunted by difficulties, restrictions and dangers, and never ceased to assert their right to a life of dignity, freedom and honest toil in their national homeland.

. . .

On the 29th November, 1947, the United Nations General Assembly passed a resolution calling for the establishment of a Jewish State in Eretz-Israel; the General Assembly required the inhabitants of Eretz-Israel to take such steps as were necessary on their part for the implementation of that resolution. This recognition by the United Nations of the right of the Jewish people to establish their State is irrevocable.

This right is the natural right of the Jewish people to be masters of their own fate, like all other nations, in their own sovereign State.

The museum in Kfar Darom repeated the familiar national story of flourishing Jewish life in the ancient homeland, exile, dispersion, persecution, and finally the triumph of return. In Kfar Darom, however, there was a specific emphasis placed on the biblical relationship of the Jewish people to the area of the Gaza Strip, a relationship that is disputed by secular and liberal Israelis. The exhibit in Kfar Darom ended with a display showcasing the modern technological advances employed by farmers in Gush Katif to produce kosher food as required by Jewish law, a sign that the People were once again flourishing, having reconnected with their Land. This reflected pride in the accomplishments of the settlers combined with a sense that God was clearly pleased with the work his People were doing. Part of the visit to the museum included viewing short films about the communities, including one called *Between the Sand Dunes*. This film and others like it were also taken to other parts of the country to generate support for the communities of Gush Katif. It provides a typical depiction of how Gaza settlers described themselves and their project and how they hoped others would also come to view them. The film, like the museum, invoked well-established tropes, which among the secular are used in reference to the past and were thought of as belonging in the past, images and imaginings that should not be invoked in the present.

For example, *Land of Promise* is a film produced in 1935, prior to the establishment of the state, to promote the return of the Jewish people to the land of
Israel. That film showcases the pre-state Jewish community of Palestine, fea-
turing hardworking pioneers and refugees from Europe who build the nation
and cultivate the land. The similarities between these films are quite striking,
but when such similar images were employed by Gush Katif filmmakers,
secular and left-wing Israelis were infuriated. Not only were these tropes—like
the idea of an empty land or the notion of bringing civilization by "making the
desert bloom"—used by some Leftists to describe the past but they also have
been widely criticized and revised by newer, revisionist scholarship. That scholarship (often associated with post-Zionism) remains controversial and disputed,
and it, too, is part of the conflict between the Left and the Right, the secular and
the religious.[7] However, the work of undoing myths of the Zionist past has also
reached the mainstream. New history textbooks that were written for public
schools in the 1990s[8] and the television series *Tekumah*[9] are indications of how
that revised history became more widely known, particularly during the years
of the Oslo peace talks (Dalsheim 2003, 2007).

Between the Sand Dunes is a production of the religious settler community,
a representation that has been carefully constructed and edited. Importantly, it
was one of the productions shown to the girls from the *ulpana*, whose visit to
the communities of Gush Katif we followed in chapter 2. This was a depiction
chosen by adult educators with images and scenes that evoke a specific positive self-image, one that creates a sense of comfort, solidarity, or "home"
among like-minded viewers. The very same images provoke outrage among
those opposed to the settlement project in Gaza and the West Bank. The gap
in emotional responses to the sights portrayed in this film is an indication of
the cultural training of the senses. Reading the landscape, like reading any
text, involves interpretations that are based in previous training, learning, and
reading experiences (Starrett 2003). Interpretations are intertextual, drawing
on previous knowledge and codes and falling back on learned narratives. Variously situated groups read their own moral superiority into these representations as they create and re-create their identities in the process. Religious
settlers identify positively, seeing themselves as hardworking, pious people
carrying out the work of God against all odds. Secular and liberal viewers
express outrage and identify as diametrically opposed.

Between the Sand Dunes depicts life in the settlements of Gush Katif,
focusing on the beautiful seaside landscape, the crimson sunsets, and rows of
palm trees. It emphasizes the industrious settlers who worked hard developing
agriculture in the arid and nonarable sand dunes, showing vast expanses of
greenhouses. The film tells of the special techniques of planting and raising

vegetables and flowers in the sands of the Gaza area. It zooms in with close-ups of the innocent faces of young children, with their large, deep brown eyes and endearing smiles. All the while a melodious song in the background lends an atmosphere coinciding with the innocence in those eyes. A voice sings, "Here is a strip of land that kisses the waves. Here, where people live with love, and in their hearts there is hope. . . . Here in the Land of Israel!"

There is one short scene of horror and burning. This was an incident in which Palestinians from the surrounding area had attacked the settlers. Otherwise, there were no Palestinians in sight, no large brown eyes of Palestinian children or men and women at work. Their presence, the enormous population, so much greater than the Jewish population of Gaza, was hidden from view. Indeed, the settlements were built in such a way as to largely occlude any vision of the Palestinian towns, cities, and refugee camps that actually surrounded those settlements.[10]

For example, when I spoke to Rachel, a young woman from the largest settlement, Neve Dekelim, I asked her, "Where is Khan Yunis?" This nineteen-year-old mother had been born and raised in Neve Dekelim and expressed a deep love of both the people and the place. She knew the layout of the community with intimate familiarity. While I was aware that Khan Yunis was adjacent to Neve Dekelim, pressed right up against it, I was not sure exactly where the two places met, and I wondered about the ideas of people like Rachel, who were born into existing settlements and raised there. Mortar fire was known to fly over the barriers from Khan Yunis and land in the schoolyard at Neve Dekelim, but from inside the settlement, one just could not see the Palestinian town or the refugee camp. "Where?" I asked this young woman. "Where is Khan Yunis?"

Rachel was with her nine-month-old son and her mother when our conversation began. Her mother recalled earlier days, when she and others would drive over to Khan Yunis to do their shopping before there was a commercial center in Neve Dekelim. Her mother spoke of taking driving lessons in Khan Yunis, of walking through the market with friends, and of leaving their children in the care of Palestinian women who had market stalls. She spoke nostalgically about feeling comfortable and safe. Passage between the Jewish settlements and Palestinian towns and refugee camps was now blocked and barricaded, and one had to make a special effort to see Khan Yunis. In the months preceding disengagement, it became increasingly difficult.

Rachel offered to take a short ride with me and show me Khan Yunis. Her mother stayed with the baby while Rachel and I drove to the industrial zone of Neve Dekelim. It would be impossible to cross into Khan Yunis; the military would not allow us past the checkpoint. But from the industrial zone of Rachel's hometown, we might be able to see Khan Yunis. Rachel said that she had not been to that section of town in more than a month and was quite surprised to find a brand-new electronic fence with a gate guarded by a young soldier. It had not always been so difficult to get around Neve Dekelim, and it was a shame, Rachel said, unfortunate that these fences and barriers were now necessary for protection. The buildings at the edge of the industrial zone were flanked by a ten-meter-high separation wall. We drove to the top of the hill and got out of the car. Just beyond the soldiers and their watchtower, one could strain to see the houses of Khan Yunis.[11]

Walls and actual physical separation are not necessary to occlude vision. There are also habits of seeing that blind: bodily habits of looking beyond, of not noticing, not encountering, or not counting as fully part of humanity. These habits of seeing or not seeing, it seems to me, can be understood within an expanded notion of Connerton's theorizing of the role of habit-memory within social or collective memory. "There is a class of memories that consists in our having the capacity to reproduce a certain performance," Connerton writes of how we remember to ride a bicycle or how to read (Connerton 1989). He explains that this kind of memory works through the body. Connerton is interested in how this bodily memory works in national rituals and commemorative ceremonies and how this kind of memory creates society as its members perform collective memory. It seems to me that such memory is also at work in everyday ways of noticing, not noticing, and interpreting the surroundings. Very much like the physicality involved in memory when riding a bicycle or reading, there is also physicality involved in screening the surroundings. One must first be taught what to notice, what is important to see, and how to understand what one sees—like learning to read, discerning the meaningful markings of the very landscape of one's environs. This learning is forgotten in productions and reproductions later performed.

On the road to Gush Katif stands a Palestinian flour mill (see figure 3.1), a factory which, by the time I began visiting, was no longer used to grind wheat. The roof had been transformed with camouflage netting into an Israeli military outlook point. On my first visit that I recount in chapter 1, when Shira picked me up at the roadblock marking the edge of military occupation, we whizzed past the flour mill. Shira, whom I had thought of as my local guide, was conspicuously silent about the surroundings until we arrived at Jewish Gaza. I pointed left and right and asked what we were driving past. She responded with a tone that indicated something between indifference, annoyance, and disbelief at my questions. As we sped by, she said something like, "What!? Don't you know?!? Those are the Arabs." Who precisely, the names of the places they lived, none of that would be part of the tour to Gush Katif. These people and

FIGURE 3.1 Palestinian flour mill on the road to Gush Katif. Author photo.

their homes were a part of the landscape, but a troubling part, a danger and a hindrance.

The flour mill struck me because it stood alone along the barren road, a rather large structure unencumbered by any fencing or planted greenery. It stood out in its sandy surroundings, not easily ignored. Shira's responses to my questions as we drove by might be considered my first lesson in reading this landscape. I was admonished for even noticing it. The flour mill lesson was reinforced on another occasion when I traveled with Shira and her family to an anti-disengagement demonstration in Jerusalem. As we approached the city, Shira's husband decided to stop at a well-known bakery on the outskirts of town to purchase some kosher cakes and cookies. The bakery was located in an industrial area adjacent to a flour mill. Shira's eight-year-old son turned toward his father and said, "Look, Abba [Dad], just like the one on our road." His father laughed nervously and then turned to me and said, "My son still has a lot to learn." Then turning to the boy, he said, "No, it is not the same at all." The boy apparently was not supposed to notice the mill on the road to Gush Katif; neither was he to find Palestinian industry comparable to Jewish industry.

Shirat Ha-Yam, the Song of the Sea, was a neighborhood or outpost of Neve Dekelim consisting of a row of trailers along the beach. To get there, one drove past the Palestinians of the Muassi. They were not hidden from view by walls or a bypass route, and although some settlers expressed concern that their numbers were growing, few expressed fear. Muassi, according to the settlers of

Gush Katif, refers to the kind of agriculture practiced by those Palestinians. Underground water is used to irrigate the land. These Palestinians were described by some settlers as very like Bedouin; they were seen as nomadic or temporary, primitive and dirty, and not posing any real threat. This depiction echoes back in time to early Zionist explorers, decades prior to the establishment of the state, who scorned the fellaheen who permanently inhabited the land they desired in comparison to the more positively valued Bedouin, who were seen as transient.[12] It also reverberates with the recent past, when the Bedouin were considered something like "friendly natives." For decades, they were either largely ignored or prized for their exotic culture, which was preserved in Israeli museums. The Bedouin, who sometimes serve in the Israeli military, had not been considered threatening in the same way as other local Arabs.[13]

In the Negev, deep inside the internationally recognized boundaries of Israel, there is another road. This road is not guarded by soldiers, nor is one required to pass a military checkpoint to enter this road. One simply turns at the traffic light at the Shoket Junction and begins the winding ascent toward the Jewish town of Arad at the top of the hill that overlooks the Dead Sea. The road to Arad is a beautiful desert pathway, where morning and evening rays of sun reveal magnificent hues in the sandy soil. But the road to Arad is also lined with Bedouin towns and villages. Some of those communities were established by the Israeli state to sendentarize the semi-nomadic Bedouin. Many of the people who live along this road have not been interested in leaving their land to move into those recognized towns and villages, which have been likened to Indian reservations in the United States. Those towns are often plagued by social ills, including high unemployment, crime, and violence. A teacher at one of the schools there told me he had no intention of moving to a town like that and didn't care how often the Israeli government sent crews to knock down parts of his family's home. He would continue to rebuild and they would continue to demolish until one day the government granted his extended family recognition as a village.

Some of the residents of Arad describe this road as dirty, foul-smelling, and unpleasant. Some complain of the dangerous ways their Arab neighbors drive or of the Bedouin thieves who live there. The residents along the road to Arad are not erased. Instead, they are quite visible and seen as a menace or nuisance, perhaps wished away, except by the handful of Jewish residents who have formed coalitions with their Bedouin neighbors, together struggling for equal rights.[14] Many of the trailers on the seashore at Shirat Ha-Yam in Gush Katif had windows or sliding glass doors facing the Mediterranean. From inside those dwellings, one could easily look out to an empty and beautiful sea, a view undisturbed by such menacing surroundings.

The settler nationalist myth of an empty landscape, well known in Zionist ideology, resonates with other settler nationalisms. It began as a tale of a land without a people for a people without land that was transformed into processes of emptying the land physically, through the legal status of individuals or property, metaphorically, or through the erasure of memory and history (Dalsheim 2004). In the settler imaginary of Australia, the legal term *terra nullius*, empty land, was the central legitimizing idea for Australian colonization. Produced as an empty land, the British could settle Australia without treaty agreements with indigenous peoples. Aboriginality, Moran writes, was perceived as an absence (Moran 2002). Australian settler nationalism, he explains, was carried out with the thorough cultural exclusion of the indigenous. The fundamental resource was land and not labor or other goods. Thus nineteenth-century Australian politics was dominated by questions of how to divide up the land among settlers, as well as arguments among them over the form of society that would emerge, like the arguments among Israeli settlers on both sides of the Green Line about the character and future of the Israeli state.

The indigenous in Australia, as in other settler societies, stood in the way of the colonial enterprise: economically, practically, and symbolically. The desire to get rid of them was seen in its most naked form in the massive land-clearing operations from the early 1820s and for the rest of the nineteenth century as the colonial frontier spread. To supply Britain's industrial revolution with wool products, vast land tracts were expropriated from the Aborigines. "This structuring of relations and desire, with its messy combination of anger, hatred, murder, rape, moral doubt and ambiguity profoundly shattered the emergent Australian settler national consciousness" (Moran 2002:1020). Aborigines, seen as a "rural pest" with detrimental impact on pastoralism, had to be "cleared" from the land, Moran writes. But, he continues, they also stood in the way in a *cultural sense* because establishing settlers' relationship to the land was integral to the development of their national identity.

Among Israelis, those opposed to post-1967 settlement activity often relate to the development or cultivation of such a relationship between Israelis and the land as a thing of the past, much like we saw in chapter 2. For example, a kibbutz member and high school history teacher explained that Israel should by now be "a confident nation," rather than one that is "still concerned with establishing itself;" the stage of nation building and establishing a relationship to the land has passed. For many others, the relationship is obvious, taken for granted; it has already been established, and a willingness to part with some of the territory is often considered a mature and responsible attitude. The relationship between people and place, the sense of ownership is necessarily deeply embedded in Israeli consciousness. If it were not, how could Israelis speak about exchanging land for peace as part of negotiations with neighboring states and with Palestinians toward a two-state solution? To speak about exchanging land for peace, Israelis must believe the land is theirs to give away. Israelis who aspire to a more cosmopolitan lifestyle require moving beyond the cultivation of a relationship to the national territory (Newman and Ram 2004). However, the processes of producing ownership and belonging are ongoing, and it seems quite clear that conquering, transforming, and the processes of producing a sense of belonging to and ownership of the landscape have been central to the processes of Zionism, as it is in settler nationalisms more generally.

A number of practices are common to both secular and religious settlers in the space of Israel/Palestine—practical, ideological, and discursive continuities, as well as state practices that cannot be easily divided between the secular and religious, nor easily divided between the Left and Right of politics. These practices of transforming the landscape, working the land, and planting on it, as well as marking the landscape with commemorative sites and graveyards,[15] conspire with construction and architecture to erase, conceal, or avoid Palestinian presence.[16] But that erasure is never quite complete, remaining a haunting presence.[17]

Planting trees; farming; building infrastructure, roadways, and housing; and raising ancient archeological structures to modern constructs all contribute to creating the relationship Jews and Jewish Israelis have to this place.[18] At once transforming space and at the same time through that transformation a relationship is produced that is both intimate and sacred. There are processes that have become part of state policy, which for decades has been driven by the need to maintain an Israeli state with the most territory possible and the fewest "Arabs" on that territory (Masalha 2000; Yiftachel 2006). In current political parlance, this is often called keeping Israel both democratic and Jewish, although many would argue that such policy results in an Israel that is neither. It is a simple matter of statistics and demographics that adds up to the problem that might arise of maintaining a Jewish state and a democracy without a Jewish majority that might mean the end of either the state as a Jewish state or the end of democracy. This had led to controversies over the definition of Jewishness and to policies encouraging immigration of some population groups while removing others. According to Wolfe (1999), settler colonial societies display a "logic of elimination" because at base these societies contain a central struggle over land. This is different from other forms of colonialism that primarily sought profit through the exploitation of labor and other resources. This is not to say that settlers do not exploit the local labor force, but when the settlers come to stay, the struggle for land is primary and the natives become superfluous. They are a hindrance and over time through state policies are subjected to various forms of "elimination." In Australia, Wolfe writes, the final stage of this process is assimilation. In Israel, it has not been assimilation, but rather processes of separation between population groups, expropriation of land and other rights,[19] accompanied by a struggle over production and representation of ownership and belonging.

The Land of Israel, the People of Israel, the Torah of Israel

Between the Sand Dunes, the video of Gush Katif, never shows the fences, the guard posts, the walls, or the soldiers. In short, it habitually forgot the force by which those settlements existed. One might argue that Israelis more broadly are no longer aware of the extent of militarization by which they live, as this, too, has become so much a part of everyday life, part of Israeli habit-memory, a simple matter of how one goes through life. But in the film about the settlements of Gush Katif, the force seems to have been forgotten specifically to emphasize the important relationship between the Jews and the Land given to them by the Lord. The land is spoken of as a sacred land, but it is through the relationship between the Jewish people and that land that its sacred quality is revealed (or produced). In other words, it might be argued that this segment of the Jewish population in Israel produces its belonging to the land, its native status, through this revelation.

In a meeting between religious settlers and secular kibbutz dwellers just months prior to the disengagement, religiously motivated settlers tried to explain their understanding of the relationship between the Jewish People, the Land, and the Lord. These were professional educators who had been meeting since 1995 in an effort to heal the "rift among the people" that came to the fore with the assassination of then Prime Minister Rabin. The deeply faithful settlers at this meeting spoke of how the land lay barren until touched by a Jewish presence, explaining that the land responds to the Jews and comes to life. Blossoms appear on the trees, and vines bring forth fruit. The land becomes bountiful. The Land of Israel, according to the educators making the presentation, did not and would not respond to Arab attempts at cultivation in the same way it does to Jewish stewardship; instead, it rejected their presence, "spitting them out" and off the land. The presentation included a short film that these educators usually showed in their schools, apparently both appealing and emotionally moving to the senses of a culturally trained audience. The presenters chose this film, convinced that liberal and left-wing viewers would come to understand not only how these religious settlers feel about the Land of Israel but also something of the relationship between all Jewish people and the Land. The teachings of Rabbi Abraham Isaac Kook, the first chief Rabbi in the pre-state Yishuv, are considered foundational to the theology of the contemporary settler movement. Rabbi Kook wrote passionately about the relationship between the Jewish People and the Land of Israel. His words echo throughout the beliefs of today's religious settlers.

> Eretz Israel [the Land of Israel] is not something apart from the soul of the Jewish people; it is no mere national possession, serving as a means of unifying our people and buttressing its material, or even its spiritual survival. Eretz Israel is part of the very essence of our nationhood; it is bound organically to its very life and inner being. Human reason, even at its most sublime cannot begin to understand the unique holiness of Eretz Israel. . . . What Eretz Israel means to the Jews can be felt only through the Spirit of the Lord which is in our people as a whole. . . . Deep in the heart of every Jew, in its purest and holiest recesses, there blazes the fire of Israel . . . the Jew's undying love for Eretz Israel—the Land of Holiness, the Land of God—in which all of the Divine commandments are realized in their perfect form.[20]

In addition to his teachings on the Land of Israel, Rabbi A. I. Kook is equally well known for his thoughts on the role of secular Jews in the return to the Land. Kook saw secular Zionism as integral to the return that is part of the process leading to redemption. This idea provided a bridge between secular and religious Jews in the Israeli context. The presenters of the film depicting the Land responding to Jewish presence were reaching out to the secular in a way that follows the theology of Rabbi Kook. But many of the liberal, secular, and left-wing Israelis at that meeting were infuriated by what they heard and saw. "This is such a racist point of view," they said, asking how these settlers could possibly claim that the land responds in a special manner to Israeli Jews and that it does not respond favorably as if trying to remove, or spit out, non-Jews. Such ideas, liberals shouted, were not only absurd; they were offensive in their racist portrayals that neglected a great deal of historically significant context. Yet, all this furor seemed to contain a certain irony, that same disturbing doubling encountered in chapter 2, since the notion of "making the desert bloom" is so deeply ingrained in Zionist ideology. Indeed, historically, it was the socialist Zionist founders of the kibbutz who settled the land, cultivated, planted, irrigated, and made the desert bloom. The idea of physical labor and working the land was central to early socialist Zionist teachings. Working the land would bring about a true national revival as Diaspora Jews re-created themselves through building their own country and tilling their own soil. A. D. Gordon, who lived his final days on an early kibbutz of the labor-Zionist movement, wrote of the central importance of returning to the land. The Jewish people would experience a rebirth precisely through the physical labor of working the land. They were a people, Gordon wrote, who had been cut off from nature and from the kind of labor that binds a people to its soil and to its national culture (Gordon in Hertzberg 1959:369–385).

Many Israeli kibbutz members feel a very powerful and intimate connection to the landscape and the very soil they, their parents, and grandparents have tilled. And it is not uncommon to hear Israeli city dwellers express an emotional connection to the spaces of the country. Although there are many Israelis who take great pleasure in traveling abroad and others who have moved away from Israel, many still express a deep sense of connection. One city dweller told me of his intense discomfort at leaving the country. His discomfort was not based on an ideological belief, either secular or religious, unlike those who believe that only in Israel can one be fully Jewish or that the only chance for Jewish survival is through national sovereignty. Instead, it was a physical discomfort at being out of his place. He said it was as though his "feet did not actually touch the ground." This physical metaphor of distance described the sensibility that compelled him to continue making his home in Israel and compelled him to political activism toward living with Palestinians without domination. Others have spoken about feeling less whole outside Israel, not completely themselves. Perhaps the more secular among Israelis would not speak of the sacred response of the land to their presence, but relationships to the land and landscape are cultivated over time in everyday ways that become intimate and bodily.

Are these processes of producing belonging comparable to those that occur in other settler and colonial societies? Gasteyer and Flora write of colonizers' perceptions of both humans and the landscape they occupy, arguing that the need to control both form the basis of many past and current colonization projects (2000). They argue that the processes of colonization and settlement rely on a belief in dominating nature, which is rooted in Enlightenment ideals of self-realization and emancipation.[21] Here, religiously motivated settlers do not produce their relationship to the land as one of domination, as earlier settlers might have. Rather, it is represented as a spiritual symbiosis between the supernatural in the Holy Land (*Eretz Ha Kodesh*), a kind of light or force that is nurtured and nurturing in its relation to the holy people. In fact, some among the younger generation of religiously motivated settlers have criticized their elders for becoming too materialistic rather than living in spiritual and ecological harmony with the Land.

The processes involved in becoming attached to the land in the Gaza Strip created a sense of ancient belonging. Following the disengagement, settlers who were removed from the Gaza Strip expressed a deep longing to return to that territory, longing for the very landscape in ways that echo the ancient yearnings of the Jewish people to return to the Holy Land and to Jerusalem expressed through daily prayer. By some accounts, the land of the Gaza Strip was never home to ancient Israelites. An archeologist who lived on a kibbutz inside the Green Line not far from the Gaza Strip was adamant about this. He insisted that there was no historical evidence of ancient Jewish civilization in the Gaza Strip, and he argued that even the geographical features of the landscape exhibited a natural boundary between the sands of Gaza and the Western Negev. That was the land of the Philistines, he argued, and yet religious settlers read their removal from Gaza as another chapter of sacred text, another example of exile that will be followed by return. Gaza was promised to the People of Israel by the Lord: "I will set your borders from the Sea of the Reeds (Gulf of Eilat) to the Sea of Philistia (Mediterranean Sea off the coast of Philistia, approximately today's Gaza Strip), and from the wilderness to the Euphrates" (Exodus 23:31). These promised borders are found elsewhere in the text and represent a promise yet to be fulfilled. Thus, religious settlers of Gaza may question the extent to which they and the rest of the People of Israel (the collective international Jewish community) have or have not succeeded in fulfilling commandments such that removal can be read as a form of divine collective punishment. Having made their homes in the Gaza Strip and having transformed the landscape, they now yearn for that place and vow to remember it until they can return. One hears in this avowal an ancient and transgenerational yearning. The secular and Left will read this as a completely new yearning that attaches itself to familiar narratives and ancient teachings, a yearning that can easily be imagined spanning to future generations as it becomes incorporated into the ancient tale of the wandering Jew. Within the understandings of religiously motivated settlers, what happens now is part of the whole unity of the history of the Jewish People as recalled in biblical text. In this case, the Jew remains in the ancient homeland, yet some religiously motivated settlers portray the disengagement as expulsion or as living in Diaspora.

In a phone conversation with a settler removed from the Gaza Strip several months after the disengagement, I mentioned that I was pleased to be able to speak with this man, pleased that I had caught him "at home." "You did not find me at home," the response came. "I do not have a home." All right, I said, "but your home is the Land of Israel, is it not? So you are at home there," I said, referring both to the country and to his temporary accommodations. He said little except to thank me for the thought, in which he took comfort.

For religious settlers, the Gaza Strip became an integral part of the Land of the People of Israel, the arguments about its actual biblical status not withstanding. Their understanding of the meaning of Promised Land does not coincide with the interpretations of secular archeology.[22] In addition to its religious significance, its newly founded places were often named in ways that might not reveal their location but were meaningful within the Jewish national project. For example, the small outpost on the Mediterranean Sea called Shirat Ha-Yam, The Song of the Sea, conjures up the natural beauty of the place as it recalls the psalm in Exodus (15:1–21). The Song of the Sea is celebratory of God's defeat of Egypt as Moses and the Israelites are miraculously rescued from the pharaoh's army. According to the biblical tale, this happened at the Red Sea, not the Mediterranean. Many of the towns in the Gaza Strip were given names that reflect the beauty of nature in the area. This is common to Israeli communities more generally as it is to popular, Modern Hebrew personal names like Tamar, the fruit of the date tree, or Ilan, the mighty oak. The settlements of Gaza perpetuated Israeli practices of naming towns by Hebraizing the Arabic name, reinstating biblical names, or by naming a town after a tree, flower, or the landscape. Such it was that the largest settlement in Gaza was called Neve Dekelim, the Oasis of Palms. Another town was called Ganei Tal, the Dew Gardens, and another Gan Or, Garden of Light. Just across the border inside the Green Line were the communities of Nirim (Plowed Fields), Ofakim (Horizons), and Sede Nitzan (the Budding Fields).

W. J. T. Mitchell (2000) writes of the paradoxical relationship that emerges when the landscape itself is worshipped. The very idea of holy land, or the Promised Land, becomes a form of idolatry, Mitchell argues, which then leads to violation of the most sacred of commandments, most sacred because idolatry is a sin against God himself. But if Mitchell aims at undoing messianic belief from within those beliefs, his efforts are comparable to similarly failed efforts among the Israeli secular, liberal, and Left. Indeed, this notion of worshipping the land has been the topic of bitter debate between the religious and secular in Israel. Among both secular and religious Jews are those who interpret text differently and are determined to convince religiously motivated Zionists that *land* is nothing more than *matter* and that "the Promised Land" should be understood metaphorically. The ground on which we make our homes, they argue, is material and not spiritual, which means that it cannot be sacred and certainly not more highly valued than human life. These ways of thinking enable migration, as well as territorial compromise. In addition to the disagreements religious settlers have with this argument, it causes a kind of conundrum for the secular. For if the land, this particular piece of real estate, is not the Promised Land or if the Promised Land should be understood metaphorically, why should the Jews make their homeland here and not elsewhere?[23]

Qualitative differences between the ways in which people produce belonging on this or that side of the Green Line may be relatively minor, but the importance of differentiating between each side of the pre-1967 border has taken on an increasing urgency for the secular and liberal Left, suggesting what Shenhav has called a "fetishism of the Green Line" (Shenhav 2006).[24] In other words, maintaining deep differences between the liberal Left and religiously motivated settlers contributes to the idea that the existence and expansion of settlements in post-1967 occupied territories has "utterly transformed Israel."[25] It participates in a kind of nostalgia for a more morally pure Israel that is imagined as having existed prior to 1967—an image that a number of historians and political scientists have been questioning.[26]

For liberal, secular, and left-wing Israelis, their own moral standing and that of the entire Zionist project are at stake in maintaining these differences, for if settlement within current state boundaries is analogous or even equivalent to that beyond the Green Line, then the moral legitimacy of the entire Zionist project may be called into question in the eyes of the international community, rekindling an existential fear for the security and survival of the Jewish people. At the same time, for religiously motivated settlers, differentiating from that liberal, secular idea, which contends that territory is not sacred, and elevating their religious understanding of its importance to the Zionist project and the continuity of the Jewish people are absolutely imperative. Again, this suggests that the antagonism reflected in this conflict can be traced to those minor differences that Freud suggested could be so threatening to the very core of identity.

The following chapters move beyond this antagonism, which continues to inscribe binary differences, to reveal some of the variations and nuances that are missed when we focus on this hegemonic discourse of conflict.

4

Disciplining Doubt

Expressing Uncertainty in Gush Katif

"How can they be so sure of themselves all the time? Don't they ever question what their rabbis say? What are they so happy about anyway? Don't they realize that settling here was wrong and that they are about to be removed?!?!"

—Secular protestor in favor of disengagement

Fundamentally Certain?

Left-wing, secular Israeli Jews say they can't stand the settlers' self-righteousness. They question their apparent certainty and are annoyed by settler sensibilities. Emotional expression can be used to determine belonging and commonality or to distinguish differences. The settlers' apparent certainty and their happiness were both approached by secular, left-wing opponents as indications of their difference from liberal Israelis.

A common image I often encountered throughout my fieldwork among mainstream, liberal, left-wing Israelis voicing opposition to the settler project was a picture of the self-righteous religious settler: an image of *certainty* regarding their path in life, a sense of self-assuredness that many among the liberal left found disturbing. This chapter interrogates that seeming certainty as a window on the larger issue of the problematic interface of liberalism and certain structures of belief. Proposing that this population may not be quite as certain as portrayed, this chapter explores processes of questioning among religious settlers in Gush Katif, as well as the disciplining that prevented this questioning from being heard by a broader audience. These processes of questioning took the form of intimate conversations between believers and their God as people of faith worked through the meanings of events that challenged their beliefs. A closer look at this uncertainty and questioning provides insight into the processes by which openings may occur, transformative interstices, among a people who are often considered rigid, inflexible, nonreflective, and uncritical.

Religious settlers and those commonly referred to as fundamentalists more generally are often construed as people who are not open to critical reflection but rely instead on the authority of their spiritual leaders. It is widely believed that such people of faith do not consistently or carefully examine or question their actions and practices because they are committed to a way of life and are certain of the righteousness of their path. This seemingly counterintuitive certainty is irritating to many liberal Israelis and was highlighted as a source of animosity between secular liberals and religious settlers that offends liberal sensibilities.

Beyond the irritation or resentment, it was noted by liberal and secular opponents of religiously motivated settlers that uncertainty, or the quality of being open to persuasion, is a central value necessary for Israeli democracy. Such a system, they explained, requires the free exchange of ideas. Without a certain amount of openness to other ideas, the argument goes, democracy would become stagnant, if not altogether impossible. A deep-seated belief in the possibility of change through what is considered rational debate and suasion in the public sphere led to a sense of fear that the seeming certainty, as expressed by some religiously motivated settlers, might pose a threat to the very future of Israeli democracy.[1] This apparent certainty then becomes one of the ways in which religiously motivated settlers appear irrational in liberal eyes.[2] This interpretation of irrationality can also be understood as part of the disciplining processes found at the interface of liberalism and this form of religion that falls beyond the limits of tolerance because it is considered threatening to the social order.[3] In this case, the existence of a transcendent power that determines human affairs seems to undermine the autonomous subject and the belief in individual agency such that the sense of certainty among religiously motivated settlers in such a power appears to threaten very basic ideas among secular liberal Israelis, if not their very ways of life.

Certainty and Skepticism

The religious Right, both in Israel and elsewhere, are often depicted as inflexible and lacking openness to alternative ideas. The religious participants in the settler movement, like other political-theological movements, are considered hostile to alternative explanations or arguments that are not based in their belief in the path to redemption. They rely on faith and are certain of their beliefs. Indeed, uncertainty on their part might be interpreted as a sign of lacking faith. Such stereotypes lead liberal and secular Israelis to express a sense of disturbance at the religious, right-wing settler movement. They are concerned that the sense of certainty they find among by this group may actually pose a threat to the very future of democracy. How, they ask, can modern people be partners in a democratic system with a group that espouses an intense certainty in its ideas, a group that cannot be open to other opinions or persuaded to change?

But just how certain are religious settlers? To what extent are they willing to ask questions or raise criticism? What issues are open for debate? And by the same token, how skeptical are the liberals? How open are they to other ideas? Secular liberal subjects in modern democratic systems are concerned with maintaining certain freedoms. The maxim requires the most possible freedom for individuals and groups as long as those liberties do not interfere with the liberties of others. This is clearly applied in Israel when the secular feel their rights limited by religious impositions like closing places of business or public transportation on the Sabbath. But is this maxim reciprocal? What happens when secular freedoms interfere with the religious? What happens when working or playing music interferes with the right to observe the Sabbath?[4] And far more profoundly, what happens when secular decisions about trading land for peace interfere with what some religious Jews construe as their right and obligation to hasten the coming of the Messiah by living according to their interpretation of sacred texts? Clearly, the expectation of not interfering with the lives of others or accepting those others without attempting to contain or change their way of life is not reciprocal.

Conflicts in other contemporary societies similarly appear between religious and secular communities. In the United States, secular and (Christian) religious groups struggle over women's rights to choose to terminate a pregnancy and over the rights of gay couples to marry. In Europe, most recently, the interface of liberalism with religiosity has been most contentious in the case of Muslims, where controversy over public expressions of faith and questions of citizenship rights have attracted a great deal of international attention. While these cases are clearly not identical to problems of secular and religious Jews in Israel, there is room for comparison. Impressions of religiously motivated Jews found among the secular in Israel tend to essentialize the differences between secular and religious Jews, imagining religious settlers as a homogeneous, static, irrational group. The data considered in this chapter reveal a far more complex reality. If religiously motivated settlers are not quite as certain as they appear, perhaps similar uncertainties can be found among those called fundamentalist or radical religious groups elsewhere. While a serious consideration of the question of possible comparisons is beyond the scope of this book, it is worthwhile to keep in mind as we turn to the processes of questioning I found among religious settlers in Gush Katif that challenge liberal presumptions about faith and certainty.

The following section explores processes of questioning among religious settlers of the Gaza Strip, revealing a dimension of life that is not well known among the secular and left wing in Israel. Revealing these processes displays something of what might be learned by following the lead of anthropologist Susan Harding in dealing with those the liberal and often secular academy tend to relate to as "repugnant cultural others" (Harding 1991), those sometimes considered radical religionists or fundamentalists. That sense of repugnance reveals an anxiety among the secular. Ashis Nandy has suggested an anxiety found among secularists who worry and are "haunted by the question 'What will be my place in a nonsecular . . . world?'" (Nandy 2007:109). This trepidation and other discomforts can lead secular and liberal humanists to turn away, even leading those who purportedly support a system of toleration for difference to withhold tolerance.

Faith, Uncertainty, and Fulfilling the Will of God

Among the religious Jews in this study, a constant questioning and level of uncertainty was quite simply part of everyday life. Indeed, reflection, evaluation, and continually probing the extent to which one is succeeding in fulfilling the will of God may be seen as part and parcel of some forms of religious practice, a matter of habit.[5] This process consists in the ways in which the religious govern their own behavior, based on ongoing interpretations of scripture and the consequences of daily life. Yet within these constraints, there is also room for the kinds of reflection that have the potential to lead toward change. Beyond quotidian ways of being, the crisis arising among settlers in the occupied territories around the issue of impending disengagement pushed the edges of reflection and evaluation further as it opened a window on a particular kind of uncertainty.

This process of questioning has gone widely unnoticed, as popular media coverage often ignored or was not privy to this aspect of events. Instead, settlers and their political leaders were depicted as absolutely certain of the righteousness of their settlement activity in the areas slated for evacuation. This was the picture the political leadership among religious settlers strove to present. It was a kind of self-disciplining based on estimations of what would be most effective for the anti-disengagement cause. On many television talk show appearances, settler spokespersons would appeal to the sensibilities of a broader audience. They couched their arguments in terms of security, for example, arguing that removing the settlements would not lead to a reduction in terrorist attacks. They bolstered their arguments with quotes from intelligence and military sources that predicted an increase in attacks. They explained to the general public that the front line of the conflict would simply move closer to where viewers lived, which in retrospect turned out to be true. In the popular media, humanitarian appeals were made, as settlers spoke of being removed from the homes they had built and lived in for decades. In other words, on the popular public scene, the settler movement relied on what are generally considered secular arguments to garner support for its cause. This can be seen as a kind of self-disciplining, or an example of how power can work in what might be considered the mainstream public sphere, the kinds of discourses that can be spoken and the kind of discourses that can be heard.[6]

In addition to these heartfelt pleas, among the settlers themselves there was an understanding that it was crucial to remain steadfast, continuing to justify their settlement activity while waiting for a miracle.[7] Many of the settlers of Gush Katif believed that if they did their part in the struggle to hold on to what they consider to be Holy Land, promised by God to the Jewish People, then the Lord would work a miracle on their behalf, and the evacuation would quite simply never take place. There were many who experienced a profound sense of disbelief in the very possibility that they could be removed from their homes and communities, where some had been living for nearly three decades. One young woman who had lived her entire life in Gush Katif asked rhetorically, echoing the sentiments of many others while driving through her home town of Neve Dekelim, if it was "possible even to imagine that these streets, these houses, these sidewalks would suddenly be gone." Such an eventuality seemed absurd, if not unimaginable at the time. While a number of practically minded settlers began making plans to deal with the aftermath of disengagement, there were also those who held out for a miracle until the very moment the soldiers came knocking at their doors. They did not pack their belongings or make any arrangements for living elsewhere. They quite simply refused to participate in what they saw as an undemocratic act, an immoral act, and an act that was contrary to the will of God. It was their conviction to remain. This would prove their devotion, and such devotion would be rewarded by a miraculous act of God, an act that would turn the entire scenario on its head. The miracle, as we now know, never arrived.

Among the secular and liberal Israeli Jews in this study were those who were convinced that the settlers who did not make practical arrangements were simply religious fanatics or political hard-liners who were couching their politics in religious rhetoric. Some spoke of the increased trauma that would likely ensue if the settlers failed to accept the situation and make the necessary practical arrangements; sometimes they blamed parents for not taking the proper steps to prepare their children. Others commented that the settlers were knowingly and purposely creating a tragedy where none existed by politically exploiting the situation. While it certainly is true that political strategy was involved in the decisions made prior to the disengagement, there was more involved than politics couched in religious rhetoric. The failure, inability, or lack of motivation to understand this reveals something about the interaction between liberal ways of thinking and religious beliefs and practices. Indeed, it may be an indication of the limits of recognition, tolerance, and explanation expressed by these Israelis. It may also be an indication of the contradictory ethics contained within a liberal humanism that claims tolerance as a virtue (Brown 2006a) while withholding tolerance in specific cases to protect a way of life (Walzer 1997).[8]

Waiting for a Miracle

In both sacred and secular temporality, time is not necessarily experienced as exclusively linear. Among the faithful Jews in Gush Katif, time was experienced as cyclical or as a spiral relationship between past and present. Each year and each season, the past is repeated yet changed as the faithful move closer and closer in their relationship to God, watching the divine plan unfold and bringing redemption nearer. The rabbi of a girls' high school (*ulpana*) in Neve Dekelim, speaking at a Purim event prior to the disengagement, reminded his audience that "what happened then is in fact now." The story of Esther, retold on the holiday of Purim, tells a tale in which all logic in the world turns upside down. One can no longer distinguish good from evil, as reason is turned on its head. "This," the rabbi said, was "precisely what was happening now." The disengagement plan was devoid of all logic, the world had turned upside down, and nothing made sense when a Jewish government would consider removing Jews from the Land of Israel. Just as there had been a miracle in the story of

Esther in which the Jews were saved by an ironic twist in the tale, so there would be a miracle now, and once again the Jews would be saved. "There is no difference," the rabbi explained, "then is now. And anyone who does not understand this is sorely mistaken." Historical or political narratives that are constrained by the contours of linear temporality cannot contain the ideas expressed by this rabbi, and the behavior of those settlers who did not make practical arrangements for their removal from the land could then only be interpreted through a limited lens as either irrational or purposely defiant.[9] Many Israelis express ideas about patterns, the tendency of history to repeat itself, and the ways in which history will work out contradictions in human social systems. For example, consider the Marxist thought on which kibbutz communities were founded and its cyclical or dialectical notion of progress as the contradictions of capitalism are worked out through time. Consider also the students in chapter 2 on the kibbutz history tour who were encouraged to identify with their ancestors, to feel like them. On another occasion, I accompanied a group of kibbutz students to a museum that not only tells the story of a pre-state underground military organization (the Palmach), but is set up to make visitors feel like the people then by taking part in the actions as they literally walk through a movie about the Palmach in which they become characters (Dalsheim 2004). Both these cases illustrate ways in which the secular also relates to the past as if then was perpetually now. Yet, the rabbi's prediction of repeated patterns—then *is* now—seemed absurd to many left-wing and secular Israelis.

Despite the rabbi's predictions, Purim passed without the hoped-for miracle. Then Passover came and went in the same way. Had God abandoned his people? Would this tremendous disappointment lead to a crisis of faith? Indeed, there were many who predicted that just such a crisis would follow the disengagement. This prediction was based on a logical rationalism that seems incapable of comprehending, listening to, or recognizing this kind of belief. Yet it might also be understood as part of the desire to differentiate.

If the settlers believed they were carrying out God's will by settling the Land of Israel, which they see as a crucial step leading to redemption, the disengagement, the secular argued, would surely prove them wrong. If God would allow their removal from the Land, there must have been some mistake in their practices, beliefs, or interpretations. The disengagement, it was predicted by outsiders, would result in a crisis of faith. In fact, there was no such crisis. The turn of events was reinterpreted. Perhaps this was a setback, a test of their faith. It might be sign from God that something had been missing in their practices. The disengagement was deeply disappointing, but it never led to a loss of faith. Instead, there were many accounts of *increasing* faith in the face of impending crisis. I should like to be clear about the sense of crisis and increasing faith. Faith in God remained strong and even strengthened, reflecting a kind of certainty of worldview, not so different from secular certainties about human agency and their disbelief in the role of the supernatural in human history. However, despite this faith, among the deep believers in Gush Katif were many who began to question the interpretations offered by their rabbis. Faith in God remained at the same time as questioning of rabbis' interpretations and disputes over recommendations for actions increased. The growing disagreements with religious leaders led to renewed debates among the nationalist religious that continued after the disengagement. In addition, an uncertainty about their own actions and how they had been leading their lives became more measurable preceding the disengagement. Many people in Gush Katif wondered what the disengagement might mean. If it did occur, what sign was God sending to his faithful?

This increasing faith in the face of impending disaster is not unique to the settlers of Gush Katif but seems to be a wider characteristic of messianic movements more generally that have been shown to remain faithful even when prophecy seemingly fails. Sociologists of religion have debated the causes for such resilient faith, based on the notion that it is an unreasonable, illogical response. Festinger's theory of cognitive dissonance (Festinger, Riecken, and Schachter 1956), which was among the earliest attempts to explain this reaction to failed prophecy, has been convincingly criticized on empirical and theoretical grounds (Dawson 1999). But more recent studies reveal more nuanced responses among the religious. For example, Simon Dein studied the case of Lubavitcher Jews in New York who expected their spiritual leader to be revealed as the Messiah. He found that the responses in the Lubavitch community to the death of their rebbe (religious leader) were varied, as members reasoned through the events in pursuit of understanding (Dein 2001). Like the Lubavitchers, the faithful in Gush Katif also worked through the events without blindly following the teachings of a particular religious authority.[10] Indeed, there were numerous arguments between religious leaders and between rabbis and their followers. The website of Gush Katif (www.Katif.net) even published letters of students questioning their rabbis' interpretations of sacred text as it was seen to apply to the current situation, including arguments over conscientious objection and other debates about the correct way to proceed in the given circumstances. One young man told me that the rabbi who led his yeshiva was counseling against conscientious objection, basing his argument in textual interpretation. This young man strongly disagreed and believed it was the duty of the faithful serving in the Israeli Defense Forces to refuse orders to remove settlers from their homes. He sent his rebuttal, which he justified with textual interpretation in the manner he had learned in Yeshiva, to the Gush Katif website, where it became part of ongoing debate about how best to proceed, what message God was sending, and how text could be interpreted to provide guidance during this troubling time.

The sense that increasing faith in the face of failed prophecy is unreasonable or counterintuitive and requires psychological explanation emerges from a value-laden discourse that cannot place these behaviors within the belief systems of the actors, as it denies faith itself. One woman from Kfar Darom used an engaging metaphor to explain the idea that God is known to work in ways that humans cannot always understand, an explanation of her faith. She said, "We should consider the universe a huge tapestry in the process of being embroidered. On one side there is a beautiful picture emerging, colors combine and images are clear. On the other side of the tapestry are all the loose threads, the ends and knots that may appear tangled and in disarray but are necessary to the beautiful picture on the other side. G-d can see the big picture, but humans find themselves on the other side of the tapestry. From here, it is much more difficult to make sense of patterns, to envision the image emerging. Yet, this is why we must place our faith in the kindness and wisdom of the ruler of the universe."

There were those among the religious settlers who reported experiencing a higher level of spirituality in the face of their imminent removal from the territory. Even as the first settlers were being evacuated, others gathered together in prayer and song and felt their faith growing deeper. One woman explained that it was as though "the outer, superficial layers were peeling away as we moved closer and closer to the light." This is a well-known metaphor often heard among religiously motivated settlers. It can be traced to the teachings of Rabbi A.I. Kook, who wrote extensively about the "light" or illuminations of holiness (Bokser 1978). The idea of a seed with superficial layers peeling away and decaying so as to enrich the soil that provides the environment for the inner seed to grow was sometimes used to describe materiality by the faithful in Gush Katif. It was also employed to criticize (yet find meaning for) secular ways of life that were predicted to peel away and decay, feeding the inner seed of living life according to the Torah. Thus, the secular rule of Israel was sometimes referred to as rotten or rotting precisely because elected leaders were not people of faith, so their rule would inevitably disintegrate as the truth was revealed.

Those who experienced higher levels of spirituality said the days before the disengagement were a "time to focus on what is truly important." This focus was accompanied by a great deal of questioning and many expressions of uncertainty regarding what had previously been taken as the righteous path. The following section provides a closer look at this uncertainty and questioning, offering some insight into the processes by which openings may occur leading toward change among a people who are often considered rigid and inflexible, as well as nonreflective or uncritical.

The kind of questioning found here does not quite coincide with the requirements of debate in a secular, liberal democracy. It is not the questioning directed at public officials, which also took place. It is not a criticism of the government or of public support for policy or in any way a debate among citizens. Perhaps it is not always what is called rational debate that is the catalyst for change, even in democratic systems that are premised on this notion. In this case, it was a particular kind of faith-based questioning that held the potential to lead this part of the population to consider alternatives. This kind of questioning poses a serious challenge to a relationship between liberalism and religious structures of belief. Political liberalism often includes claims of tolerance or acceptance of differences and plurality but is hard-pressed to recognize certain forms of religiosity and the ways of thinking and behaving found among certain religious groups, including the case described here. At the same time, of course, religiously motivated settlers are hard-pressed to recognize broader goals, interests, and definitions of community within the broader national group.

Women's Prayers for Gush Katif

One place where this kind of questioning was most strongly expressed during my fieldwork in the communities of Gush Katif was at public prayer sessions, particularly among the women.[11] There are different religious requirements of men and women, and the synagogue is generally a masculine domain. Men lead the prayers, and men and women are seated separately, with the women behind a physical divider (*mechitza*). The event described in this section was only for women. They led the prayers and filled the entire synagogue.

As the disengagement moved closer and political means to prevent its implementation were exhausted, the settlers of Gush Katif and their supporters in the religious community turned increasingly toward prayer. There were some religious settlers who did not believe in the value of political maneuvering or mass demonstrations. All those acts, they said, were superficial—the outer layers that peel away. The place to concentrate their efforts should be between the People and their Lord.

Many public prayer sessions were called by leading rabbis throughout the country. One such meeting was attended by thousands in Gush Katif and included study sessions and prayers led by a former chief rabbi of Israel. A prayer session that received far less attention in the popular media was in some ways far more meaningful. This was a collective public prayer session for the women held in the main synagogue of the largest settlement in Gush Katif, Neve Dekelim. The call to prayer for the safety of Gush Katif came from the spiritual leadership of the community and was attended by women from various settlements representing a range of beliefs and practices. The meeting opened with communal readings of prayers written by a leading rabbi of the settlements, but as the meeting progressed, more and more women raised their own voices, expressing personal concerns. The prayers prepared by the rabbi asked God to intervene in specific ways, to prevent the destruction of Gush Katif, to keep specifically named enemies away. However, the individual prayers of women were far more modest. These were personal, intimate conversations between believers and God.

In the summer of 2005, just two months prior to evacuation, I attended a prayer session for the women. This event was important because, as one woman explained, it gave "public voice to many private concerns." It was felt to be a "source of comfort despite the extreme anguish displayed, simply because it provided reassurance that no one was alone with these deep-seated anxieties."

One of the most moving prayers that day was spoken by a young woman, the mother of three small children, who lived in a trailer on the beach in one of the newer settlements. This young woman was known in the community to be deeply spiritual. She has written and published poetry that expresses her passionate beliefs, and her words rang out through the synagogue that day, although they were interspersed with intense sobbing. Impassioned emotions brought the entire crowd to tears as this young woman, Ruth, beseeched her God to show his people the way. This prayer and others like it did not ask the Lord to perform specific acts. It did not even appeal for the communities to be spared. Instead, it sought clarification. The words of the prayer were profoundly personal. "Dear God," Ruth called out, "Father," she said, using the Hebrew word *Abba*, an informal term that children use to refer to their father, something like saying "Daddy." "Abba, please," she pleaded, "explain to us for we are confused. We do not understand. We believed, we were certain that we were fulfilling your will by living in this place and being industrious and creating a beautiful, prosperous community from which to serve you. But now, everything is unclear. We are confused and no longer certain. Please explain to us what is happening."[12] The impending removal of these settlers from the communities in the Gaza Strip, then, was interpreted as a particular and complicated sign from God, a sign that something had gone wrong. These prayers were not directed at the Israeli government or the Palestinian people, as some of the more formal prayers were. They did not call on the Lord to show Prime

Minister Ariel Sharon the error of his ways. No, if the disengagement was to go forth, that meant that it must be God's will. And if it was indeed God's will, all that remained was to try to understand His meaning. What were these faithful servants supposed to learn? Had they done something wrong? Were they not truly leading righteous lives? Or not righteous enough? "Please G-d," the women implored, "help us to understand."

In the days and weeks that followed, a number of possible interpretations were offered. One woman, Dahlia, suggested that this was God "screaming in our ears." He was screaming, she thought, because perhaps they hadn't been listening. But what was he trying to say? This woman was not prepared, nor did she feel compelled to provide a definitive answer. Instead, she insisted that the first thing to do was to stop and listen. For Dahlia, the turning point, the moment when the people of Gush Katif should have stopped to listen, came in May 2004, when a young, pregnant mother, Tali Hatuel, and her three daughters were shot and killed by Palestinian gunfire on the road to Gush Katif. That, she said, was so tragic and senseless that surely it was a powerful message from God. Dahlia explained that the settlers had a prescribed set of responses. Whenever there was an attack against them or an outpost dismantled, they always replied by renewing their strength and conviction. These automatic responses coincide with broader Israeli trends. It had long ago become a kind of norm in hegemonic Israeli culture that strength meant steadfastness and that war, violence, conflict, or international condemnation would not deter the nation.[13] The idea was to remain strong in the face of adversity, never to retreat. This norm has been losing saliency among various Israelis for numerous reasons. Here, in Gush Katif, Dahlia was expressing doubts. She began thinking that perhaps this was not the best response; perhaps God had grown weary of trying to get a different message across. Now he was screaming in their ears, and so many, she said, particularly the men and male leadership, continued along that prescribed path. Many of the settlers of Gush Katif were determined to remain strong. Just as those who had survived Palestinian attacks or lost loved ones vowed never to leave the communities of Gush Katif, so they faced their own government's decision and would not capitulate. They vowed to continue to build, to bring more settlers to the area, to expand existing settlements, and to never, never back down.

Left-wing and secular Israelis, on the other hand, had expressed a certainty based on their beliefs in enduring regularities of human behavior and the ensuing predictability of politics. They were certain that the settlements of Gush Katif were not only morally reprehensible but also practically unsustainable and would inevitably have to be removed. These ideas led me to ask a settler woman named Hagar a question that many secular and left-wing Israelis asked rhetorically rather than directly of religious settlers. Had I not been working with the people of Gush Katif for nearly a year, I imagine it would have been impossible to raise such a question. I asked if perhaps the message contained in the impending disengagement was that the settlers should never have come here in the first place. Surely this is what many among the left-wing and secular believed. These were illegal settlements, areas never annexed to the state of Israel. In addition, here were about eight or nine thousand Israeli Jews living among more than a million Palestinians existing in overcrowded and impoverished conditions. The entire situation, many liberal Israelis would say, was "unnatural and unsustainable." It should have been clear from the very beginning that this was the wrong thing to do. Was there any room for the deep believers in Gush Katif to consider these arguments? Could it be that this was the message from God?

Hagar, like so many others I have spoken with, was convinced that the answer was a resounding "no!" She likened the situation to the times of the ancient temple in Jerusalem. "When the temple fell," she asked, "did anyone think that meant that it should never have been built?" Of course not was her answer. Of course, she reasoned, settling in Gush Katif and building these communities had been the right thing to do. Hagar and others explained that the Jewish communities in Gush Katif were no different from any other community in Israel. In fact, they often pointed out, the precise areas in which they lived had never been inhabited by Palestinians. Their settlement in these areas had never required expulsion. The same could not be said for so many places inside the Green Line, where Jewish communities were established on the ruins of Palestinian villages (Khalidi 1992). Hagar concluded that if settling Gush Katif was wrong, then the whole of the Zionist project must be wrong, and such a thing was unthinkable.

As I have argued in previous chapters, it is precisely this conclusion that underlies the desire to differentiate between constellations of identity in Israel: the Left and the Right, the secular and religious, and those opposed versus those in favor of ongoing settlement beyond the Green Line. If the settlements beyond the Green Line can be seen as a continuation of the settler project in Palestine that led to the establishment of the state of Israel, and if the current settlement project is morally reprehensible, then recognizing continuity and similarities among the populations on both sides of the Green Line might undermine the very moral justification of the nation-state.

The Land Responds

Hagar had every reason to believe that settling this area was the right thing to do. "Look how beautiful this place is," she remarked. "Look at how successful we have been." The ability of farmers to grow vegetables in the sandy soil that everyone thought would always remain barren was often referred to as a sign from God that this was the right thing to do. This, the people of Gush Katif often explained, was the sanctified land responding to a Jewish presence. The communities had grown and prospered. Clearly, they said, this was a sign that God was pleased and they were being rewarded. In fact, the people of Gush Katif often spoke of the many miracles they had witnessed, how the Lord had protected them. Even though an enemy population surrounded them, they said, it was not until the 1990s that the first settler was killed by those enemies. God was protecting them through His many miracles. Sometimes when mortar fire fell in one of the communities and no one sustained injuries, people commented on the miracle that had occurred. This representation seemed to forget the enormous force and armed presence that made their project possible. The number of Israeli Defense Force troops who worked to defend the settlements and the consistent support by governments from both Labor and Likud appear through this representation to be divinely ordained.[14]

Still, Hagar was willing to modify. It *had* clearly been right to settle the communities of Gush Katif. But perhaps now it was time to do something else, she reasoned. This is an interesting parallel to some of the thinking among more secular and liberal Israelis, who voice their belief that past actions were necessary to establish the state but that now it is time to embark on a different course. Those Israelis who call for an end to the post-1967 occupation view settlement in these territories as excessive and fundamentally different from settlement inside the pre-1967 borders. They often argue that the violence that occurred as part of the Zionist project in Palestine had been necessary to establish the state, but now things are quite different. Now there is a well-established, internationally recognized state that stands to be undermined by ongoing settlement in the occupied territories.

From Hagar's point of view, it was also time to begin wondering if something might be missing from the settlement project. Perhaps, she thought, she and members of her community had not done a good enough job in reaching out to the secular community. Religiously motivated nationalists, unlike the ultra-Orthodox, have been very concerned with their relationship to secular Jews. It is a defining characteristic of the movement traceable to the teachings of the elder Rabbi Kook (Aran 1997; Hertzberg 1959; Lustick 1988). They have been interested in being in contact, in explaining, and in garnering support for their project among the secular. They had become quite adept over the years at living in ways that complemented secular Israeli values. For example, the nationalist religious have taken great pride in serving in the Israeli armed forces. This was significantly valued in the eyes of the secular because ultra-Orthodox

Jews have historically found ways of being exempt from compulsory duty. There are Orthodox Jews who protect the state through prayer, and prayer is understood as more important than fighting in the army. There are also ultra-Orthodox Jews who do not accept the very existence of the state of Israel, arguing that human intervention in this process in wrong and only the coming of the Messiah should bring Jewish sovereignty, only an act of God (Rabkin 2006). The secular, who must serve in the army, harbor a great deal of animosity toward the ultra-Orthodox, whom they often describe as parasites. Many among the ultra-Orthodox were not able to support their large families. Men often studied religious texts rather than working in secular trades. Such Orthodox Israeli Jews have often been perceived as a community that takes from the state while making no contributions to it. There are, among the secular, those who have always been infuriated at what they saw as having to both protect these others and pay their way. The nationalist Orthodox, on the other hand, had been far more palatable to the secular. These were people who, like the settlers of Gush Katif, served in the armed forces, often in elite units. They are also people who are recognized as working hard for a living, a trait that is highly valued among the more secular public, particularly among secular, left-wing kibbutz members. The historical relationship between the nationalist religious and the secular had been quite good. These two groups had found quite a bit of common ground and shared values, especially in relationship to the state. The nationalist Orthodox were not necessarily considered extreme because, while they practiced Orthodox beliefs, they never forced their views on others, unlike the ultra-Orthodox, for example, who have been known to pelt rocks at secular Jews who do not keep the Sabbath. Even the issue of settlement in the occupied territories did not immediately sway widespread public opinion. After all, plenty of more secular Israelis had moved to such settlements themselves.

If the relationship between religious settlers and the rest of the Israeli Jewish community had been strong, then the question arises as to why there was not more support for those opposing the disengagement. At the numerous, large demonstrations organized in opposition to the disengagement, there seemed always to be the same glaring fact: Settlers came out to support settlers. I distinctly remember the disappointment expressed by Avi at the Human Chain demonstration, where people joined hands from Gush Katif to Jerusalem in opposition to the disengagement plan (see figure 4.1). He looked around at the sea of people and asked, "Where is the average Israeli, where are the people (amcha), the supporters of the Likud who are not religious or not settlers? Why haven't the masses come out to support us?" As time went by, that situation did not change. The masses, the people of Israel, did not come out to support the settlers. The demonstrations were always very large and very

FIGURE 4.1 Gathering at the human chain demonstration in opposition to the disengagement. Author photo.

impressive, but it was always the same population group. Reflecting on their situation as they beseeched the Lord to help them understand, some settlers concluded that "if we had done enough to reach out, they would never have been able to do this to us. They would never even have been able to consider it." This was a common answer among the settlers, although often mixed with resentment. Many took responsibility upon themselves for remaining too isolated and failing to establish the kinds of relationships with the secular majority of Israelis that might have prevented what was for them this tragic outcome. Yet others could not imagine what they could possibly have done differently. Many worked outside the settlements among the secular and liberal. They and their children served in the armed forces with other Israelis. Many became bitter and felt betrayed, adding to the sense of a split among the Jewish people in Israel.

Hagar, echoing the voices of religious leaders, expressed her strong commitment to the people of Israel. She, like so many, experienced the time preceding disengagement as one of renewed and deepening faith. It was Hagar's belief that this, along with many of the troubles in the state, was a sign that it was time to rewrite and renew the Torah of Israel. It was time, she contended, for the religious and the secular to work together to think again about what kind of state this should be. What was the meaning of having a Jewish state, after all? What should the character of such a place be? Hagar was quite critical and believed that the secular seemed to have lost their way, again echoing more prominent voices. Settlers in Gush Katif often asked of the secular, "What values do they live by? What do they teach their children?" The secular were often reprimanded for being interested only in material things, in accumulation and in consumption. "They are interested in having a good time," Michal remarked. "That is why their children often leave the country. If they think they can do better elsewhere, they will just leave. They will go to America." This, it was thought, was a result of eroding Jewish values and of a basic fault among the secular and liberal. These Jewish Israelis simply did not understand the importance of the Land of Israel for the very survival and future of the Jewish people. Emunah thought this meant it was time to renew the Torah[15] and to "rethink the ways in which the Jewish People would live in the Land of Israel and to rethink it together." Hagar saw the communities of Gush Katif as setting an example, a model community of Jewish life in Israel. (One cannot help but notice the parallel to earlier beliefs about the secular kibbutz.) These communities were crime free and drug free. They were tight-knit communities based on respect and cooperation. A great emphasis was placed on education, and the youth were considered, even among the secular and liberal who encountered them personally, to be "very fine young people." The residents of Gush Katif were known to be good, decent, hardworking people—often contrasted to settlers in other places. Their communities flourished, the landscape was beautiful, and the landscaping well manicured and clean. Still, Hagar, Emunah, and others like them were willing to concede that this way of life might not be the one that all the people of Israel would choose, but in any case they thought it was time to enter into this conversation. Groups began meeting with secular Israelis precisely to engage in such a conversation. In these meetings, liberal and secular Israelis also expressed anxiety over the future of the state and concern that young people were not returning to the communities—particularly kibbutz communities—established by their parents' generation.

Other residents of Gush Katif proposed alternative but related answers. For example, some reasoned that the problem had to do with concentrating all their energy on fulfilling the mitzvah of settling the land.[16] Perhaps their commitment to this religious duty had resulted in their neglecting other equally important commandments. The three central components for these faithful Jews, as we have seen, are the Land of Israel, the People of Israel, and the Torah of Israel.[17] The Rav Moshe, a teacher at an elementary school in Gush Katif and lecturer at Bar Ilan University, had explained that each of these three were of equal importance and none could take precedence over another. Secular and liberal Israelis opposed to settlement often criticized religious settlers for worshipping the land and bestowing on it more value than life itself. While many religiously motivated settlers could not accept that criticism, here in Gush Katif, many began wondering if their actions had not placed too much emphasis on the Land and not enough on the People and the Torah.

Another possible interpretation focused on intentions rather than practices. It was suggested that this was a time for introspection. It was a time for people to ask themselves why they were living in Gush Katif. Was this truly an expression of faith, or did it have more to do with the lower cost of living and beautiful seaside landscape? Had the people of Gush Katif become complacent, as their brethren in the West Bank often insinuated? Perhaps life had become too easy, causing them to lose sight of what was truly important. Again, the metaphor of peeling back the layers to arrive at the core (*garin*), the truth, was employed to describe the sense that this was a deeply spiritual time of movement toward the coming redemption.

Still others were willing to consider the possibility of a more basic problem with the settlement project. While I never heard anyone openly express such doubts, sometimes people confided their inner concerns. Usually, they reassured themselves that settling the Land had been the right thing to do, but that now it was time to take stock again. There was a suggestion that the question was not one of whether to settle the Land, but how to go about doing so. In some cases, this returned to the idea of intentions and the extent to which settlement activity could be seen as an expression of faith rather than the outcome of desire for a higher quality of life.

This kind of searching for an answer and for the truth continued after the disengagement as well. One woman expressed her thoughts in a letter to God on the occasion of the Jewish New Year about a month after the disengagement. She wrote of her desire to become closer to the Lord but also expressed her sense of disorientation. Her letter opened with these words:

Dear *Abba*,

Ever since you sacrificed my home and expelled me, my family, and community from the place in which we so desired to serve you, and so deeply believed that we were carrying out your will, I feel that I have lost my way.

Feeling disoriented interfered with daily life. Driving to her new place of residence, this woman said she sometimes felt out of place, the maps seemed turned around, and she would find herself lost on the road. But rather than consider this a simple matter of readjustment, this woman felt it was an indication of a deeper problem, a moment requiring spiritual clarity. She sent this letter to a community newsletter, making her sentiments public, and others found they had similar experiences. This woman clearly relates to the withdrawal from the Gaza Strip as an act of God, who is ultimately responsible for all that transpires in the world. Her sense of being lost reminds us that she and others in her community had felt far more certain. Or perhaps complacent and comfortable is a better description. The people of Gush Katif, like most people whose lives are not in turmoil, had felt a greater sense of comfort in their known surroundings. In short, they felt at home. And within that feeling of home and relative comfort, they had also been quite sure that they were on the right and righteous path, that they were fulfilling God's will.

For many, all this suddenly became unclear, as a sense of having lost their way became mixed with many other emotions surrounding the possibility of disengagement. For others, the sense of uncertainty was not at all sudden but part of longer ongoing processes of questioning. In both cases, a previous sense of being on the right path was sustained by the success of the communities, which was taken to be a positive and encouraging sign from God. Things had been going so well in the Jewish settlements of Gush Katif. The people living there had come to a dry, barren, sandy uncultivated land. Nothing grew there. One woman recalled that it was so barren when she first arrived with her family that there were not even any insects to be found. The environment seemed quite uninhabitable. Over time, the residents built greenhouses and developed an advanced method of agriculture using the available sand. They built a factory that cleansed and packaged their vegetables and sold unblemished, immaculate (Glatt Kosher) vegetables both in the country and for export to Europe. They had become very successful and began raising houseplants and orchids as well. The communities grew and prospered, a result that seemed to be God telling his people they were doing the right things and living according to his will. These are the signs that signal the sacred relationship between the Land and the Jewish people, processes interpreted by the faithful to indicate not only the sacred quality of the land but also the righteousness of their living on that land. Indeed, they interpreted their prosperity and the bountiful agricultural yields as a result of the Lord's pleasure at the Jewish presence on the Land. In a certain sense, this interpretation finds parallels in completely secular interpretations of the success of the Zionist project, of coming to what was considered an empty and barren land and making the desert bloom. Indeed, it rings familiar with other settler societies, echoing ideas, for example, in early colonial America where settlers at the Massachusetts Bay Colony also interpreted bountiful crops as positive signs from God as they built their City on the Hill.

Some settlers in Gush Katif questioning their path were willing to go so far as to consider their relationship with the Palestinians (using the word *Arabs* rather than *Palestinians* in most cases). Some explained that perhaps they had not learned enough from their secular counterparts, the liberal humanists, who were constantly expressing concern for the human and civil rights of Palestinians. This again returns to the teachings of Rabbi Kook, stressing the importance of the unity of the Jewish people, which was sometimes taken to mean that the different Jewish communities had a responsibility to learn from each other to become whole. Perhaps they had left too much of this work to other Israelis while they focused on the Land. Almost inevitably, conversations about Palestinians led to the same formulaic answer. For the observant Jew, I was often told, things are very clear. The Jews are the rightful owners of the Land of Israel. It is their right and obligation to live in the Land of Israel and to be sovereign there. The Palestinians in their midst, on the other hand, are guests. And there are very specific requirements in Jewish law regarding how one must treat a guest. A guest must be treated well, welcomed into one's home, cared for, and sustained. This might be interpreted in terms of human rights as opposed to civil rights. The guest should be treated well but never given charge of the home, that is, never allowed to become sovereign. Of course, this is also dependent on religious interpretations of the behavior of the guest. Palestinian acts have been interpreted in ways that move them from the category of guest to that of enemy. That, of course, changes everything.

Among the people who came to support the residents of Gush Katif as the disengagement grew closer were certain settlers from areas of the West Bank or other places in the country who openly expressed their hatred of "Arabs" and their belief that all Arabs should be removed from the Greater Land of Israel by any means possible. I often heard more moderate expressions from residents of Gush Katif, who pointed to their positive relationships with Palestinians from Gaza in the past and in the present. For these people living in Gush Katif, the Palestinians were "welcome to stay." They were welcome, that is, if they obeyed the laws of Israel and accepted the Jews as the rightful rulers. They could remain as guests and would be treated well. One woman explained metaphorically: "If you have a guest, you treat him well. You tend to his needs and provide food and shelter." This, she explained, was one's duty according to the Torah. "But," she remarked emphatically, "you do not give him your house. Not even your porch!" Perhaps, some thought, they had not given enough attention to this issue, which could be connected to the issue of reaching out to the secular. The idea was that the secular humanist concern for the well-being of

Palestinians and a general concern for human rights were things that the religious nationalist community could learn from their secular brethren. Once again, it was considered a matter of strengthening the ties within the People of Israel and again criticizing themselves for perhaps putting too much emphasis on the Land of Israel. However, even those who thought that more should be done to improve the conditions in which Palestinians live almost inevitably were not willing to accept the idea that Palestinians, too, had the right to sovereignty.

On the fringes of settler society are some who have moved one step further in their thinking. These are those rare and often unaccepted opinions among the majority of religiously motivated settlers. These are believers who think that if the Lord put the Jews in this land together with the Palestinians, it must have been for some purpose. So, they reason, clearly the two peoples were not meant to fight over this holy land. Instead, they were intended to learn from each other and to live together. This, it is explained, was God's will. This kind of thinking seemed to emerge as a next step following some of the deep questioning we have already seen and will be discussed in greater detail in chapter 6. Those who expressed these ideas spoke about the violence between Jewish Israelis and Palestinians that led to loss and suffering as indicative of having strayed from the righteous path. That kind of violence, it was argued, is an indication of fear that results from not trusting in God. Those espousing these ideas looked for ways of moving others in this direction. They welcomed the questioning that became so pronounced during the crisis of disengagement, although they, too, felt the removal from this land was a devastating tragedy. This kind of thinking holds potential to imagine an alternative future in ways one might not expect to find among religiously motivated settlers.

Uncertainty

This chapter began by noting a discomfort among many secular and left-wing Israelis at the sense of certainty expressed by religiously motivated settlers. This apparent certainty is taken as one indication of irrationality or unreasonable behavior, an appearance that participates in reinscribing a hegemonic discursive formation of conflict through binary oppositions: Left versus Right, secular versus religious, opposed to occupation versus in favor of *Eretz Israel ha Shlema*, with the addition of rational versus irrational. The debates between Left and Right, secular and religious, and those Israelis living on either side of the pre-1967 border appear as sets of incommensurable discourses, competing narratives about what it means to be Jewish and Israeli that will determine the future character of the state or whether the state will have a future. The left-wing discourse rooted in a progressivist, secular humanism and the right-wing, religious settlers who speak in terms of sanctification, fulfilling the will of God, and redemption are two life worlds that are experienced as antithetical.

Chapters 2 and 3 focused on similarities and continuities that belie the deep divide that appears through these powerful binary distinctions. Continuing to disturb those binary distinctions, this chapter illustrates some of what might be learned when we move beyond that divide, disturbing binary divisions to reveal a more nuanced reality. It focused on a range of ideas expressed among religiously motivated settlers in Gush Katif that show processes of questioning that were not often heard in popular or mainstream representations.[18] This is due, at least in part, to the tendency to demonize and marginalize religiously motivated settlers. Some among their opponents contend that these settlers do not represent Zionism or Judaism, which supports the idea that the existence and expansion of settlements in post-1967 occupied territories have "utterly transformed Israel."[19] It participates in a kind of nostalgia for a more morally pure Israel that is imagined as having existed prior to 1967, an image that a number of historians and political scientists have been questioning.[20]

It is *not* my contention that there are no differences between the Left and the Right, the secular and religious, or those opposed to the occupation in post-1967 territories and those in favor of expansion, nor do I argue that there are no differences between pre- and post-1967 Israel, and this chapter provides greater insight into what might be learned by moving beyond those differences, which is further explored in the following chapters.

5

Twice Removed

Mizrahim in Gush Katif

"I met a settler in the occupied territories who spoke as though he'd just left Brooklyn. He was talking about how dangerous it was to live there and I thought, man that accent does not help your case."

—Pro-Palestinian activist from the United States

"I know there were Mizrahim in Gush Katif, but they were different. They were not there for ideological reasons. . . . They would move if you gave them enough compensation."

—Left-wing Israeli opposed to settlement in the occupied territories

Among liberal Israelis opposed to the occupation and settlement of post-1967 territories and among scholars and activists in the international community, one often encounters a particular stereotypical impression of "the settler" as not only a radical, right-wing, religious fundamentalist but also, specifically, of Ashkenazi (European Jewish) descent and often Anglophone origin. While this book focuses on religiously motivated settlers, it is important to note that the people living in the settlements in post-1967 Israeli-occupied territories include a variety of believers and nonbelievers, ethnic groups, political affiliations, and people from numerous places of origin, and the residents of Gush Katif were no exception. My purpose here is not to recount the variation and nuances of the population of Israeli Jews in the occupied territories, but rather to interrogate a particular silence or absence resulting from this stereotypical image of the settler.[1] This chapter will consider the discursive processes through which the absence of Mizrahim[2] (Israeli Jews from the Middle East and North Africa) in the occupied territories is produced while asking what is at stake in engaging with their presence in that location. Chapter 3 considered processes of producing the absence of Palestinians throughout Israel and the occupied territories. The title of this chapter refers to a double removal, in part because Mizrahim have been subject to erasures throughout the history of Israel in ways that seem even deeper than the discursive absence of Palestinians, who are recognized, even if sometimes only as enemies. Fanon famously wrote about this extremely problematic form of "recognition" when he recalls an incident of being recognized on a bus by a little white girl. It is not that he goes unnoticed, but the girl at once calls out to her mother that she sees this black man and at the same time begins to cry out in fear. He has been recognized, not ignored, but in the same moment of recognition he is also defined as both different and dangerous (Fanon 1967:111–112). This is the kind of recognition often found in Israeli narratives with regard to Palestinians. But the Mizrahim are different. They are not considered enemy others but have historically been subject to the kinds of erasure produced through the demands of assimilation, in this case to an Ashkenazi hegemony.

In the late 1980s and early 1990s, scholars in anthropology and cultural studies began turning a critical eye on the issue of Jews from the Middle East and Arab countries in Israel (then referred to under the label Sephardic, later Mizrahim and Arab-Jews). In 1988, Ella Shohat published a groundbreaking article depicting these Jews as the other victims of the Zionist project (Shohat 1988).[3] Two years later, Smadar Lavie published an ethnography that struggled with the ambiguities of Mizrahi identity, the double positioning as both occupier and occupied (1990, 1992) or, to put it differently, both colonizer and colonized.[4] Yet today we find little if any scholarly attention focused on this ambiguity where it is perhaps most acute,[5] in the settlements across the Green Line in post-1967 Israeli occupied territory. Instead, and understandably, some of the most critical of Israeli social theorists focus their concern on the history and ongoing discrimination against Mizrahim, including income and educational gaps and the location of Jews from the Middle East and North Africa in peripheral development towns.[6] This critical scholarship, like much postcolonial scholarship, is largely confined to a reworking of the past (Pels 1997), and a strange silence remains about the ongoing ambivalence of this positioning in its current complexity. The scholarly silence around the problematic presence of Mizrahi settlers echoes the lack of attention given to Mizrahim in the occupied territories in the media and popular press in Israel.

This chapter raises a set of questions about the hegemonic representation of the Israeli socio-political-religious scene regarding Mizrahim who lived in the settlements of Gush Katif in the Gaza Strip who can be thought of as twice removed: first, quite literally from their homes and livelihoods in the occupied territories and second, from hegemonic representations of political struggles within the Israeli Jewish polity. My concern with these representations is less with the marginalizing and silencing effects than with the ways in which they participate in inscribing groups with cultural value that are produced as contesting moral communities. As we have seen, this appears as a somewhat homogenized portrayal of settlers in the occupied territories against those in favor of ending the occupation and establishing a Palestinian state. Those Israeli Jews who identify as opposing the occupation tend to also identify with a left-wing political agenda that supports social welfare, including government funding for depressed areas like the development towns where many Mizrahim are located. Thus, I suggest that engaging more fully with the Mizrahi presence in the occupied territories contains the potential to undermine this divided landscape of morality.

Landscape of Morality

The hegemonic discourse of conflict that is a central concern of this book conceals or marginalizes certain positions and nuances of identity while producing the appearance of two sets of competing moral communities among Israelis, each found on opposite sides of the Green Line and each viewing the other as lacking in values or as morally reprehensible. The previous chapter explored some of these nuances through a focus on the various ways religiously motivated settlers in Gush Katif interpreted their situation and expressed their uncertainty. This chapter considers ethnic (or racial) and class differences among religious settlers in Gush Katif.

Recognizing the presence of Mizrahim as settlers in post-1967 occupied territories unsettles facile moral distinctions. For the liberal Israeli Left, Mizrahim tend to be categorized as part of a weak population group who have experienced discrimination and are in need of social welfare programs and other forms of government assistance. Many argue that if the state did not allocate so much funding to the settlement project in the occupied territories, more could be spent on employment, education, and other forms of assistance that are sorely needed in the peripheral towns and poor urban neighborhoods where many Mizrahim live. In other words, the moral disdain found among many liberal Israelis for settlers in the occupied territories has a distinctly ethnic/racial component in the stereotypical image of the Ashkenazi settler, an image that fits more easily in opposition to a liberal (also often Ashkenazi) construction of self.

It is not surprising to find that the arguments and antagonism between variously situated groups of Israelis take place on the backs of Palestinians, so to speak, as they are removed from the conversation—spoken of and spoken for—while being physically and imaginatively removed from the landscape through historical narratives and representations, as well as everyday practices and habits, as we saw in chapter 3.[7] And the silencing or removal of Mizrahim *as* Arab-Jews has been theorized. Shohat has written extensively about the ways in which Eurocentric and Zionist scholarship historically removed Arab-Jews as such from the story of Israel and how this has obscured the relationship between Mizrahim and Palestinians (Shohat 1988, 2003).[8] But how can the discursive removal of Mizrahim specifically from post-1967 Israeli occupied territories and particularly the Gaza settlements be understood?

The most outspoken religiously motivated settlers and those often depicted in both scholarly writing and the popular press tend to be of Ashkenazi origin. It is not uncommon to hear North American accents, for example, among militant activists, loud voices often with abundant resources, which of course denote a particular kind of privilege that only adds to the animosity among the secular, liberal Left toward post-1967 settlers, making those settlers easier to despise. But among the settlers in the communities of Gush Katif were a significant number of Mizrahim. Gush Katif consisted of about eighteen communities and between seven and nine thousand residents.[9] Synagogues serving the Mizrahi population were found in almost every community. In Neve Dekelim, the largest population center, where more than 2,500 people lived, there were at least two synagogues serving different subgroups of the Mizrahi population. The Mizrahim of Gush Katif were people who often came from traditional religious backgrounds and for whom living in the occupied territories provided an opportunity to improve their standard of living, as it did for those of Ashkenazi descent.[10] There were families who moved out of the development towns of the Negev and elsewhere, places known for high rates of unemployment and other attending social and economic problems, peripheral places that did not offer many opportunities to their residents and comparable in many ways to U.S. inner cities. Khazzoom (2005) has dubbed these towns "outer cities" and documented the founding racism that resulted in the overrepresentation of Mizrahim in these towns.

The double removal of Mizrahim from Gush Katif raises an important set of questions. First, what are the processes through which this removal was produced? Second, how does the presence of Mizrahim who are ideologically and/or practically committed to living in Eretz Israel, which includes the occu-pied territories, unsettle commonly held hegemonic representations?[11] Shohat has demonstrated the ways in which the complexities of the Mizrahi question unsettle power-laden and destructive binary oppositions—East/West, Arab/Jew, Savagery/Civilization—disturbing if not providing a key to the very undoing of master narratives of nationalism and Zionism (Shohat 2003). After all, if the Zionist settler-colonial project requires Judaizing and therefore de-Arabizing the territory based on the idea of Jewish return to the homeland, the Mizrahi presence as both Arab and Jew presents a significant ideological problem. Creating a homogeneous settler-immigrant population (see Shafir 1989a: xiii) might explain much of the violence experienced by Mizrahim (Shohat 1988), including the attempt at erasure of their identities to assimilate them to the dominant Ashkenazi culture. But this does not sufficiently account for the particular silence or absence in the case at hand. As a result of critical scholarship and political activism, the Mizrahim are no longer absent as an ethnic group in the same ways they have been in the past. Now there is a more recent yet well-established binary distinction hiding their presence: that which tends to associate post-1967 settlement with Ashkenazi Jews and development towns with Mizrahi Jews.[12]

The absence of Mizrahim from academic representations of post-1967 occupied territories is perhaps most striking in the work of geographer Oren Yiftachel. While other scholars concerned with Mizrahim deal with historical narratives, cultural representations, and ongoing forms of discrimination,[13] Yiftachel has worked consistently to present a macroanalysis redefining the system of power dynamics in the space of Israel/Palestine that depends specif-ically on the geographical location of Mizrahim. Yiftachel begins with an analysis of the settler-colonial roots of Israeli society and moves on to reveal a structured social system in Israel and the occupied territories. This system, which Yiftachel calls an "ethnocracy," enhances rule by and for a specific ethnic group in which ethnicity dominates citizenship (Yiftachel 1999). Israeli eth-nocracy privileges the sector of Israeli Jews of Ashkenazi descent over Mizrahim, whose settlement in peripheral, low-status, and segregated localities created the structural conditions that help explain the persistent disparities between Ashkenazi and Mizrahi Jews (Yiftachel 1998), while Palestinians remain at the very bottom of this geographic-socioeconomic power structure.

My purpose in focusing on Yiftachel's research is not so much to dispute his general thesis of ethnocracy, which I find quite compelling, but rather to ask how it is that a geographer who is necessarily concerned about location and for whom ethnic origin is a crucial factor has ignored the presence of Mizrahim *as settlers* in the occupied territories? In his most recent book, in many ways the culmination of more than a decade of research, Yiftachel maps the various population groups within the space of Israel/Palestine (Yiftachel 2006). Contrary to my experience on the ground, Yiftachel does not report on Mizrahim as having lived in the settlements of the Gaza Strip. One map shows all the development towns in Israel in 2003 (Yiftachel 2006:215). Two such towns appear in the West Bank but none in the Gaza Strip. These two towns are categorized as "development towns," not "settlements," even though they are located beyond the Green Line. This representation is quite puzzling. Why can't Mizrahim be seen as settlers when they live in the occupied territories? Is this vision itself an outcome of ethnocracy? What does this particular blindness accomplish? What might be at stake in removing the blinders? To engage with these questions, I would like to begin by bringing into a focus the story of Moshe, a man of Yemeni descent who lived in an agricultural community (*moshav*) in Gush Katif.

"Not for Ideological Reasons": Making It in Gush Katif

Moshe, the father of five and a farmer in Gush Katif, faced many financial challenges, yet despite his trouble making ends meet, he explains that a combination of faith rewarded by an act of God enabled him to build a large home in Gush Katif. We met at his greenhouses in the late spring of 2005 and spoke while Palestinian women day laborers from Khan Yunis took a break for tea. Moshe conversed amiably with the women in an Arabic he had learned growing up. His parents came to Israel from Yemen and spoke Arabic at home. In his childhood, embarrassed by his Arab roots, he would answer only in Hebrew. But he picked up the basics, he said, that allowed him to converse easily with Palestinian Arabs. The women laughed and joked with Moshe, sharing stories about their children and his. They had known each other for many years now, and, he said, they were worried about the impending disengagement. If Jewish agriculture left the Gaza Strip, so would their meager jobs.

Moshe, like other farmers, was able to succeed in Gush Katif partly because of the low wages he could pay Palestinian laborers. These Palestinian workers from Khan Yunis received fifty shekels, a little more than ten dollars at the time, for an eight-hour day of physical labor in the greenhouses. Imported labor from Thailand was more expensive, Moshe told me. Most of the kibbutz communities inside the Green Line were then employing workers from Thailand, China, and other places instead of Palestinians. So did many of the other employers in Gush Katif. Moshe continued to employ Palestinians. "Thai workers must be paid minimum wage, and they won't stay unless you let them earn overtime." Still, Moshe told me, "everyone wants at least five Thai workers because their work is much more precise and professional, there is much less waste. Sometimes a Thai worker will be in charge of a group of Palestinians," he explained.

We wandered through the greenhouses, and Moshe showed me how the tomato vines grow up out of the sand and wind their way skyward around strings attached to the greenhouse ceiling. This way, the tomatoes don't touch the ground or each other. They remain clean, are free of insects, and will not rot. Four older Palestinian women from Khan Yunis were sitting on overturned buckets in the greenhouse drinking their tea, and a man from Khan Yunis made small cups of bitter coffee for Moshe and for me. All the while, as we spoke, the sound of automatic gunfire could be heard in the not too distant background.

> "What is that?" I asked him.
> "Oh," he said, "that's just the time of the day."
> "What!"

> "That's what we hear every morning. There are certain hours, like between and 8 and 10:30 in the morning, then again in the late afternoon. Those are the times of the day when a lot of people are out, children are making their way to school, and adults go off to work. These are the hours when they try to hit us," he said. "That's usually when mortar shells or missiles are fired."

> "But what is that sound that we hear?"
> "That's the gunfire of our soldiers."
> "What are they shooting at?"

"Well," Moshe explained, "they spot a [Palestinian] gunman and aim at him. Or, you know, there is an area there, a strip, which is a closed zone. Any movement there at all, and they shoot, like that eight-year-old Palestinian girl that was killed? You know, when they were checking to see that she was dead? Any movement in that zone . . . and they shoot."

This was followed by a long pause until I asked, "How do your workers get here from there?"

"There's an hour or two in the morning when they're allowed to pass," Moshe explained. "But they have to go through all kinds of inspection. They can't bring anything with them, and they can't have metal at all on their bodies, not even the zipper on their pants. But there's a solution to that now. Now they have buttons."

He spoke matter-of-factly, an employer discussing the constraints under which this agricultural work takes place, the problems of production and profitability. Sensing the seeming callousness of his words, Moshe then explained that he was not insensitive toward his workers, nor does he treat them with disdain. He defended himself and other farmers in Gush Katif, who as settlers in the occupied territories are often depicted as anti-Arab racists because of the ideology they espouse and because of violent acts against Palestinians.[14]

"They think we are settlers who hate Arabs," he told me, referring to those Israelis opposed to settlement in the occupied territories who supported the disengagement plan. Moshe spoke from within the hegemonic Zionist discourse that maintains a division between Arabs and Jews. He spoke about the positive relationship between these distinct groups, saying, "But you see, that's not true. You see how well we get along. There is full cooperation among the simple people (*amcha*). If we could only get rid of the heads [leaders]—on both sides—people would get along just fine. Everyone knows his place; it's the way of nature."

"The way of nature," he said, echoing a well-known Orientalist (Said 1978) phrase that was very likely once used to describe the labor of his parents or relatives from Yemen. These Yemenis, who were indeed Arabs, but Jewish Arabs, were brought to Israel to replace local Arab labor (Shafir 1989b).

This Yemeni owner of a large number of greenhouses, who paid his Palestinian workers fifty shekels a day, told me that he came to Gush Katif twenty-two years earlier seeking quality of life. It was not for ideological reasons, he said. "Not for ideological reasons" was a common refrain, repeated by many of the settlers in the Gaza Strip. It was their way of saying to those who oppose settlement for purposes of expansion that they are good people and no different from anyone else. They are just people trying to make a living, striving to make a good life for their families. "Not for ideological reasons" was a way of differentiating oneself from those who came because settling the land was a mitzvah, a requirement of pious Jews that would hasten the coming redemption.[15] Or those who came because expanding the state of Israel was the right thing to do to ensure the security and longevity of the Jewish state. At the same time, "not for ideological reasons" was also a phrase repeated by liberal Israelis opposed to these settlements. Here it was used dismissively, if not patronizingly, to say, these are not the settlers with whom we have a problem. These are people who moved for economic reasons, which can be easily understood within a liberal rationalism. It also meant that such people were not expected to be problematic in the same way as those ideologically committed to settlement. These people, it was presumed, would leave the settlements without a fight. "Not for ideological reasons" created a fine line of difference for those who took advantage of an opportunity but at the same time never believed that living in Gush Katif constituted a moral problem. Fifty shekels a day—about ten dollars at the time—is more than the twenty that Palestinians might be paid if they could find work in Khan Yunis, which was nearly impossible. And increased closures meant fewer and fewer Palestinians were crossing into Israeli settlements or over the Green Line to work.

Moshe had five children, ten rooms, and a house that measured three hundred square meters, quite large by Israeli standards, all of which brought him great pride. It is unlikely that he would have been able to achieve this had he stayed inside the internationally recognized borders of Israel, where real estate is very expensive and the laws of minimum wage are enforced.[16] Like so many other Israeli Jews of Middle Eastern origin, Moshe's parents had been settled in a town in a peripheral region of the country during the 1950s (Khazzoom 2005; Shafir 1989b). The Yemenis in particular were first brought to the state to provide Jewish rather than Arab labor to build the state (Shafir 1989b). Jewish labor, known as *Avodah Ivrit*, was an important part of the settler struggle with the local population. The Yemenis and other Mizrahim and their children might become settlers (or occupiers), but their history, according to Shohat, can also be told as that of victims of the Zionist project (Shohat 1988). Certainly, Moshe did not speak of himself in the terms used by some Mizrahi scholars. He did not speak of himself as a victim of Zionism or as both occupier and occupied. Indeed, Moshe spoke of the importance of living in the Land of Israel (*Eretz Israel*). He would never leave, not even for a vacation—no, especially not for a vacation! "One can only truly live according to the mitzvot required of pious Jews *in Eretz Israel* [the Land of Israel]," Moshe explained, and travel abroad could only be justified if it, too, fulfilled a mitzvah, one that took precedence over the requirement of living in the Land.

Many of the development towns in the Negev, like Ofakim and Yeruham or Sederot, that were originally populated by Mizrahim have remained places known for high unemployment rates. These are places where jobs are hard to find, and people remain entrenched in chronic unemployment, poor educational opportunities, and symbolic "blackness." Moving to Gush Katif for Moshe, and for many others, led to a better life. It was "not ideological" in that sense. Real estate there had practically been given away to early settlers. Taxes remained low, and cheap labor provided by local Palestinians was readily available. Living in Gush Katif meant better schools, life without the fear of daily crime within the community, and a place where people do not lock their doors. It meant communally organized assistance to prevent poverty and support for neighbors in times of need. In fact, these were model communities where traditional Jews could easily keep the Sabbath and raise children according to their values and beliefs with a feeling of security in the broadest sense of that term.

They were, of course, also model communities built on the land conquered by Israel in the 1967 war. They were built on land never annexed to Israel where Palestinians lived under military occupation and a different set of laws than those inside the internationally recognized borders of Israel. This is the land that many hoped (and still hope) might one day become part of a Palestinian state and part of a future of peace between Israel and the Palestinians.

Near the Gaza Strip but inside the Green Line are a number of kibbutz communities, some of which had been struggling economically of late. These communities, established by the socialist Zionist founders of the state, some prior to 1948, were primarily populated by the descendants of these highly idealized pioneers and often associated with the liberal, secular left, as we saw in chapters 1 and 2.[17] The members of those communities also wanted to make a good life for their families and, like many other liberal and secular Israelis, often harbored anger against the people of Gush Katif and other settlers living in the West Bank because of the large governmental expenditures allocated to the occupied territories for infrastructure and security.[18] The economic troubles of these kibbutz communities had resulted in certain structural changes. To generate income, some communities had begun renting out housing units and taking external children into their daycare centers and kindergartens. A noticeable increase in Mizrahim accompanied this change, which was not always an easy transition for the more veteran kibbutz members. In some places, non-members who rented housing had more spending money available, causing some animosity. In other cases, cultural differences became a source of discomfort. One woman told me that outsiders who brought their children to kibbutz daycare had been requesting changes. These were often Mizrahim from traditionally observant backgrounds. They had asked for kosher food or that a mezuzah be placed on the doorposts. Tzipi, a longtime kibbutz member of Ashkenazi descent, reported on this with indignation. This was her home, she said, her place of comfort. It was a place that was established specifically by Jewish immigrants seeking the freedom to be Jewish in any way they please. And this meant freedom from religious constraints.

Moshe told me the story of how he built his house in Gush Katif: how he didn't really have the money, but faith and fate made it happen. His brother (who also lived in the moshav in Gush Katif) gave him a loan as an act of grace (*chesed*) without interest and told him to pray.[19] And so he prayed, and at about that time, he was fired from his job as the director of youth programs at the local council. Being fired might not have been what Moshe prayed for, but God works in wondrous ways. Moshe received 80,000 shekels in severance pay and was able to double the size of his house. He smiled as he recounted this tale, the story of a modern miracle and a sign from God of the righteousness of his project. That severance pay came from public coffers as his job was with the local council of Gush Katif, which had been supported by national government funding. Liberal and secular Israelis were furious that their tax money went to support the settlement project in the occupied territories. Many argue that the government should spend its money inside the Green Line improving social conditions, education, and welfare. But what would have become of Moshe (and others like him) if he had stayed inside the internationally recognized borders of Israel?

Stunned Disbelief

Rachel, a young Ashkenazi woman who grew up in one of the more affluent agricultural communities of Gush Katif, told a story about labor and the disappearance of Palestinian faces from the settlements. She told me about her father, who also owned greenhouses and raised vegetables. There was "an Arab who worked for him for fifteen years," she said. "And then one day they found an explosive device hidden under the seat" in her father's car. "It was that worker, after all those years!" who placed the bomb. Her father fired all the workers from Khan Yunis and began employing laborers from Thailand instead.

The tenor of Rachel's story was one of stunned disbelief. The question for Rachel was "How could your trusted employee turn on you like that?" For the settlers of Gush Katif, a second moment of stunned disbelief came on their removal from the occupied territories. The question then was "How can a Jew expel a Jew?" revealing the sense of disillusionment at a break in the unspoken ties considered family ties within the nation (Anderson 1983). Recall the same sense of stunned disbelief at the same breach of agreement that was felt among secular and liberal Israelis in 1995, when then Prime Minister Rabin was assassinated by a member of the religious nationalist community. As we saw in chapter 1, their question, too, was "How can a Jew turn on another Jew?" There are layers and layers of stunned disbelief that can be read as the ways in which cultural value is produced, the ways in which people produce themselves as moral beings, moral communities, one against the other.[20]

Chakrabarty writes about the quality of stunned disbelief in narratives recalling the partition of India (2002:115–137). These narratives are emblematic of an important difference between history and memory, Chakrabarty explains. The stunned disbelief expressed at behaviors exhibited by neighbors—Muslims against Hindus—does not seek explanation, as historical inquiry should. Instead, it remains the unexplained, unjust, or immoral acts of transgression by an other. In the context of the struggles in Israel/Palestine, these expressions of stunned disbelief are similarly rhetorical. That is, they ask, "How could you [they] do this to us?" without seeking an answer but rather proclaiming a moral position. These expressions, then, participate in reinscribing the contours of moral communities—the settlers against the Palestinians, the liberal-Left against the community of religious settlers and their supporters, mutual expressions of stunned disbelief, each claiming moral superiority.

But the voice of Moshe was different. His tenor was not one of stunned disbelief at all. When speaking about Palestinian workers who turn on their bosses, Moshe said quite matter-of-factly that they do it for money. "A thousand shekels," he said. He paid them fifty shekels a day and knew that was twice what they could make inside Khan Yunis, if they could find work inside. Moshe's telling refuses the possibility of a political act of local Palestinian resistance and at the same time seems to speak from a place of empathy or identification from within his own experience of economic struggle. "They do it for money," he said, with a gentle smile as we stood between the greenhouses, talking calmly while surrounded by his Palestinian laborers, Palestinian laborers who might kill their bosses for money.

Mizrahi Settlers

Mizrahim as settlers in the occupied territories are noticeably absent from popular and scholarly representations. Ethnicity and class are among the differences that become subsumed within the hegemonic appearance of discourses in conflict, or perhaps consumed by that conflict, which produces two sets of ideologically opposed communities, each claiming the moral high ground. The hegemonic discourse of conflict that came to the fore just prior to the Israeli disengagement from the Gaza Strip participated in the removal of Mizrahim. Like distant cousins who are known and often forgotten, they were twice removed: once from their homes in Gush Katif with the other Jewish settlers, and again from the larger public view as Mizrahim or Arab-Jews. This second removal began much earlier and continues through a number of practices, including the rhetorical move contained in the phrase "not for ideological reasons."

What is at stake in recognizing the presence of Mizrahim as settlers in the occupied territories? I have suggested that their presence in the occupied territories contains the potential to disturb categories that participate in the constitution of the moral, liberal self in contemporary Israel. Mizrahim as settlers seem to disturb comfortable frameworks of the liberal imagination in which

opposing the occupation of land conquered in 1967 and supporting social welfare, including a particular sympathy for the plight of Mizrahim, are included
in the positions that constitute the moral self. Recall that Rachel's father had
the means to pay the extra wages required to hire Thai workers while Moshe
repeated that there was full cooperation among the simple people, that settlers
do not hate Arabs, and that if "we could just get rid of the leaders" on both
sides, the people would work it out. Listening carefully to the words of Moshe,
one hears something uncomfortable, that is, something that does not fit into
the moral arguments between Israeli settlers—those living on both sides of the
Green Line, settlers of greater and lesser socioeconomic and ethnic or racial
privilege. There is something here that seems to have nothing to do with
whether the occupation is right or wrong and nothing to do with the future
character of the Israeli state. That is, his words in this conversation did not
engage with the hegemonic discourse in conflict, the currently available choices
surrounding issues of whether Israel should be a democratic state, one of two
nation-states in the space of Israel/Palestine, a state for all its citizens, a Jewish
state, or what the meaning of a Jewish state might be. Moshe was, however,
talking about security, economic security. In this conversation, he was concerned with making a living, a right that is not guaranteed by the liberal nation-
state. The right to earn and to produce in free-market capitalism is, of course,
a matter of personal responsibility (Comaroff and Comaroff 2001). The very
promise, then, to be a free people in one's own homeland—as inscribed in the
Israeli national anthem—rings hollow when succeeding in fulfilling that private responsibility to provide for one's family in the best way possible may
mean participating as an occupier in hostile territory and becoming the object
of moral outrage and disdain.

Yet, there is an additional discomfort located in this uncanny presence
when descendants of laborers brought to build the Zionist settlement project
now become more blatantly settlers—in forms that defy the political correct-
ness often exhibited among liberal Israelis—than the descendants of the founding socialist Zionist settlers themselves. At first, this might appear to be a form
of colonial mimicry, as Bhabha might have it (Bhabha 1994). Yet it is not so
much an ambivalence that makes room for resistance, but rather a form of
consent by way of conformity[21] that results in an unsettling reflection on Israeli
colonialism in the present.

My purpose here has been to continue shifting the lens through which the
socio-political-religious scene in Israel appears as sets of binary oppositions,
considering what might be learned by engaging more fully with differences
that exceed those categories. Remaining within the discourse of conflict and its
constitutive categories erases complexities like the presence of Mizrahim in the

occupied territories. Recognizing that presence unsettles these categories and poses a particular problem for what I have called the landscape of morality through which moral communities in opposition are constructed on either side of the Green Line. Recognizing the presence of Mizrahim *as settlers* in the post-1967 occupied territories troubles the left-wing, liberal position that opposes the occupation yet is sympathetic to the plight of Mizrahim. The liberal conundrum can be reduced through the rhetorical move that claims these settlers are *not* living there *for ideological reasons* but for economic reasons, an explanation that is more easily accommodated within the liberal rationalism of some secular Israelis. But what happens when recognizing Mizrahim as settlers includes recognition of those who see no moral problem with living in the occupied territories? This, it seems, is far more difficult to contain within existing hegemonic categories and is far more troubling to the moral constitution of left-wing, liberal, secular Israelis whose self-perception depends on an ethics of concern for the economically needy and disdain for those who *choose* to endanger the possibilities of territorial compromise by settling in post-1967 occupied territories. But choice is not attributed to Mizrahim, who are denied agency through the rhetoric of "not for ideological reasons."

Pointing to the absence of Mizrahim as settlers furthers the investigation into nuances and differences found within the population of religiously motivated settlers in Gush Katif that began in the last chapter. Once the aperture is widened, increasing complexities of ethnicity and socioeconomic class that have been subsumed within the hegemonic appearance of discourses in conflict can be brought into focus, raising new questions about how to make sense of the political, moral, and social landscape. I have argued that engaging with the presence of Mizrahim as religiously motivated settlers contributes to unsettling existing categories through which moral communities are discursively constructed in opposition—the moral, liberal Left against the evil settlers from one perspective, and the righteous pious settlers against the materially driven, misguided secular Left from the other. The next chapter continues troubling seemingly settled categories of politics and difference by undoing the couplet that associates fundamentalist religion with violence.

6

The Danger of Redemption

Messianic Visions and the Potential
for Nonviolence

Prior to the Israeli government's implementation of its disengagement plan, which resulted in a withdrawal from the Gaza Strip in the summer of 2005, the religious settlers of Gush Katif had been living their dream, so to speak. They were carrying out their lives in ways they believed expressed the will of the Creator of the Universe, ways of living that were required to bring the coming redemption closer. The tripartite vision at the heart of their belief system—the People of Israel, the Land of Israel, and the Torah of Israel—seemed to be coming to fruition. The People were living on the Land and the communities grew and prospered, clearly signs that the Creator of the Universe was pleased. This overall prosperity and growth was seen by those opposing this project as resulting from government investment in infrastructure and protection by the armed forces. Rather than the fulfillment of a dream, those opposing this settlement project saw the results as endangering the lives and livelihood of Israelis more broadly. But religiously motivated settlers saw their success as a sign of encouragement from God and an indication that they were to continue along this righteous path. Life had been very good, most people reported, at least until 2000, when the second Palestinian uprising against Israeli occupation began affecting the settlers of the Gaza Strip directly and with increasing frequency.[1]

The dream of redeeming the Promised Land through Jewish presence and a commitment to leading a pious life has been directly associated with numerous forms of violence. This includes the violence of settlement in the occupied territories itself, taking possession of scarce and valuable resources like land and water, as well as the concomitant practices of face-to-face violence. The messianic visions of religiously motivated settlers and their attendant discourses resonate profoundly with certain rhetorics of redemption that have also been associated with state power, violence, and exclusions (Shulman 2006; Volger and Markell 2003). The liberal state, promising redemption from violence, "also takes into itself the right to use violence in pursuit of this goal, exemplifying the capacity of redemptive aspirations . . . to motivate and direct the coercive use of force" (Volger and Markell 2003:2). This leads to a concern that the very idea of redemption can be problematic in its justifications of violence when redemptive language is invoked for the purposes of modern political projects.[2] Despite these violent realities, a closer look reveals that among religiously motivated settlers there are also those whose belief in a messianic vision is precisely what allows room for flexibility, patience, and compromise.

In a recent set of essays, George Shulman enters into debate with Talal Asad over the concept of redemption and its potential danger in political contexts (Scott and Hirschkind 2006). Asad argues that "the idea of political redemption is grotesquely out of place in the secular world." It is, he writes, "a danger to politics and a parody of spirituality" (Asad 2006a). Shulman, on the other hand, contends that no matter how problematic the concept and language of redemption may be, it is unavoidably intrinsic to modernity and holds the potential to be politically fruitful and not just dangerous (Shulman 2006). The question arising from this debate is whether there is something inherently perilous in the very concept of redemption. Is it an intrinsically dangerous idea, or is it especially treacherous when transposed onto secular politics? Zionism itself includes a notion of redemption transposed onto a modern, secular political project. However, with the unilateral disengagement plan, dreams of redemption seemed to conflict with the state, resulting in the appearance of an intense struggle between a secular liberal state and religious extremism. That appearance, which resonates so powerfully with widespread representations of a deep divide between some forms of Islam and the so-called West, returns us to the question of what allows such appearances of conflict and struggle on the one hand, and what these appearances might enable, on the other. In the context of Israel/Palestine, this conflict is part of the ways in which settlers on both sides of the Green Line are mutually constituted within a society that continues to struggle with the outcomes of its settler origins. It is a conflict that results, at least partially, from a desire to differentiate, while the groups involved are dependent on each other for their moral constitution.

Contemporary scholarship on "fundamentalism" participates in reinscribing the appearance of a deep divide both between Islam and the West and between liberal, secular Israelis and fundamentalist settlers. In the previous chapter, we saw the discursive removal of Mizrahim as settlers, and particularly as religiously motivated settlers. Mizrahim are removed from the category "fundamentalist," which is often applied to religiously motivated settlers or the religious-political settler project, because they are categorized as "traditional" Jews. There were other religious settlers, or settlers motivated by their religious beliefs, who are also seldom counted in the literature on fundamentalisms, even among those scholars whose work undermines the appearance of a clear division between incommensurable discourses. For example, Roxanne Euben's study of comparative political theory finds continuities between Islamic fundamentalists, postmodernists, political conservatives, and others. Yet, she is very concerned to precisely define the category "fundamentalism" and includes Muslim, Christian, and Jewish forms, as do many other scholars. Euben's definition of *fundamentalism* "refers to contemporary religio-political movements that attempt to return to the scriptural foundations of the community, excavating and reinterpreting these foundations for application to the contemporary social and political world." This definition, she explains, excludes "phenomena such as mysticism," emphasizing "fundamentalism's political nature" (Euben 1999:17–19). This narrow definition, along with the broader impulse to define and categorize, does not leave room for some of the religiously motivated settlers I encountered in Gush Katif, who were both mystical and concerned with applying their beliefs to the contemporary social and political world. According to Euben's definition, the more mystical among settlers should be considered in a separate category. These distinctions are very problematic for the case of religious settlers, as they tend to homogenize a diverse population, removing different beliefs and practices among those settlers.

Removing the more mystical among religious settlers denies the variation found among people living in the occupied territories who believe in the important connection between Jews and the Land of Israel. Rabbi Abraham Isaac Kook is considered the spiritual founder of the religious beliefs and practices found among religious settlers. Some scholars claim that it was Kook's son, Zvi Yehuda Kook, who transformed what is referred to as "the settler movement" into a radical right-wing nationalism, leaving the limited impression of a linear progression that left the father's interpretations behind. For example, Aran writes that the nationalist ideology developed by the Rabbis Kook began with the father but was transformed by the son. That ideology, he contends, turns traditional Orthodox values upside down. "The traditional relation of redemption to repentance, and of the future to the present, is completely reversed, a shift that entails a basic change of values"(Aran 1997:308). For the Orthodox, according to Aran, redemption had always been based on living the moral life according to traditional faith and ethics, studying the Torah, and practicing the mitzvot. The nationalist religious movement, he explains, "sacralized Zionist reality," making the reality of the Jewish state into the reality of redemption. This seems to coincide with Asad's trepidations about the danger of transposing ideas of redemption onto the secular world, which can also be heard among secular, left-wing Israelis who see religious Zionism as a dangerous combination of religion and nationalism. Kook, the son, the rabbi Zvi Yehuda Kook, sacralized political Zionism through his biblical interpretations that emphasized practical acts in the material world, engaging directly with the Holy Land.[3] For the followers of the Rabbis Kook, according to Aran, redemption is not dependent on repentance—the sovereign Jewish state is itself redemption. Thus redemption takes on a character that is more concerned with nationalism and statism than with repentance. The state itself is sacred to the religious settlers Aran describes (Aran 1997:309). These distinctions leave little room for believers who gravitate more toward the father's teachings than the son's, who according to Aran are not really part of the settler movement. These categorizations reinscribe images that associate religious settlers with political violence by denying that other religiously motivated settlers count, both those religious settlers who live in the occupied territories, but not for "ideological reasons," and those religious settlers who are more mystical in their beliefs.

Redemption in This World

If the state itself is understood among religiously motivated settlers as signaling the redemption of the Jewish people, how is it that messianic visions of redemption come into conflict with the state? Such a conflict came to the fore with the 2005 disengagement but is based in deeper struggles within the Israeli polity. A parallel situation arose in 1982 with the Israeli withdrawal from the Sinai Peninsula as part of a peace accord with Egypt, when the settlement Yamit was dismantled and religious settlers came into direct conflict with the state.[4]

We have heard of plots among some radically religious Jews to blow up the mosques on the Temple Mount/Haram-al-Sharif in Jerusalem, of acts of face-to-face violence against Palestinians in the occupied territories, of uprooting olive trees, and of beating or shooting at Palestinians. All this, because of a deep belief that the Sovereign of the Universe promised the biblical Land of Israel to the Jewish people, making it not only their right but also their responsibility to live on that Land, to rebuild the temple in Jerusalem, and to actively bring redemption closer. This deep spiritual connection to the land has been referred to through the terminology of a dream, a vision of redemption that can be used to justify the use of direct physical violence and to justify the expansion of settlements.[5] Of course, secular militaristic rhetorics of security can have much the same effect.

This spiritual connection to the Land that has resulted in numerous forms of violence also inspires intense feelings of wholeness, oneness with the Creator of the Universe. It is an expression of the central belief among messianic settlers that the Land of Israel, the People of Israel, and the Torah of Israel are actively enacted values, all three equally important, and together forming a kind of living body. This is why removal from the Land was often described as amputation, the removal of a limb from a living being. This is a system of beliefs that emerged together with territorial nationalism that has worked for and with the state at various historical moments toward a number of ends, even when it appears to be at odds with the secular national project.[6] While this vision is implicated in interpersonal acts of violence, as well as state violence, it can just as readily lead to nonviolence and even inaction. However, such representations might undermine the appearance of discourse in conflict—the rift among the people. It could interfere with the moral constitution of liberal and left-wing Israelis, who often define themselves in direct opposition to a violent and irrational other in the form of the religiously motivated settler. It also unsettles scholarly depictions of religious fundamentalists.

As we saw in chapter 4, there were religiously motivated settlers with visions of redemption who considered the possibility of remaining on the coveted land by reaching an agreement with the Palestinian Authority, and others who became conscientious objectors, refusing to carry out the order to remove settlers. There were also those who simply called for prayer rather than political action. These nuances tend to be lost in scholarly representations that conflate religiously motivated settlers with the radical right under the category "fundamentalists."[7] In some cases, these nonviolent practices have been represented by those opposing settlement in post-1967 occupied territories as violence of another kind. They were seen as threatening to democracy and the rule of law, acts of incitement that could even lead to civil war.

In fact, the calls that Israeli democracy was facing a precarious moment came from both those in favor and those opposed to disengagement. Right-wing and religiously motivated settlers and their supporters spoke of the end of democracy in then Prime Minister Ariel Sharon's plan to carry out the withdrawal. Sharon had been elected on a platform promising that he would *not* give up territory, while his opponent, Amram Mitznah from the Labor Party, proposed the exact opposite and was defeated. If elections are to be counted as the expression of the will of the people, religious settlers argued, then Sharon's plan was both a betrayal and a mockery of democracy. Among the Left and those in favor of disengagement, the decision to proceed with the disengagement was understood as taken by a democratically elected government. That decision, they argued, must be respected regardless of campaign promises. Otherwise, democracy itself would begin to disintegrate.

Among the Left, this notion of the end of democracy was marked by a curious new problem: the problem of defining a soldier's democratic right to conscientious objection. Right-wing soldiers refusing to carry out military orders justified the act of refusal as "one's democratic right to be loyal to one's faith."[8] But those supporting left-wing conscientious objection argued: "Not all refusals . . . are equivalent . . . refusal by left-wingers to serve in the territories breaks a law to avoid violating international human rights and civilian rights. Refusal to dismantle settlements is also insubordination, but it is aimed at undermining legislation by Israel's . . . democratically elected government."[9]

The arguments over conscientious objection were not easily divided into Left versus Right or religious versus secular. Many liberal and progressive Israelis opposed (and continue to oppose) left-wing refusal, and among settlers and their supporters, there was opposition to right-wing refusal as well. There were arguments between rabbis and disagreements between rabbis and their followers. The uproar over conscientious objection led to a middle ground movement among Israelis opposing the refusal to carry out military orders in both cases. This middle ground argued that political disagreements should be held separate from military duty. And again, the fear of the end of democracy was invoked, as calls were heard for Israelis to come together in opposition to all forms of refusal, to come together and heal the "rift among the people" to protect Israeli democracy and the rule of law.

Conscientious objection can be read as a nonviolent form of resistance. It can, however, also be read as dangerous, as we have seen here, or as a form of resistance that perpetuates existing violence. It also provoked a sense of danger to Israeli democracy because it signaled an arbitrary loyalty to the state.

Dreams of Redemption and Secular Logic

In this chapter, I should like to bring into focus a lesser known way of interpreting and acting on or *not* acting on the vision of redemption among religiously motivated settlers in Israeli-occupied territories by exploring how messianic visions can be understood as requiring flexibility, patience, and compromise among religiously motivated Jewish settlers. I turn now to a story about belief, visions, and the meaning of bringing redemption closer among those who might be described as the more mystical among religiously motivated Jewish settlers in Israeli-occupied territories.[10]

When I traveled to Israel/Palestine in the spring of 2006, almost a year after the disengagement, I made a visit to the home of a Perhia, who had moved from Gush Katif to a community in Samaria/the occupied West Bank, not far from Jerusalem. While I was in Jerusalem, I had been having an e-mail exchange with a colleague about the relationship between my research and that of other scholars who were working on dreams and visions in the Middle East. When I went to visit Perhia, those conversations about mysticism, dreaming, and visions were very clearly on my mind. So, when she began to tell me this story about her son, my interest was piqued. She recalled an evening when God had spoken—communicated directly—to her teenage son, Shomeya. It was a moment both she and Shomeya had been hoping for. Upon receiving the communication from the Ruler of the Universe, Perhia told me, her son rose up—*hitromem.* I imagined this scrawny teenage boy floating above the bare floor of their sparsely furnished living room, the Lord having chosen to communicate with him of all people, a young man who can hardly be described as the most pious. Indeed, he was one who struggled to keep the practices (mitzvot) required of the faithful, struggled quite literally to keep the kippa (yarmulke) from falling off his head. I turned to Perhia repeating the last words of her sentence with a rising intonation: "He rose up?" I inquired. "Yes, yes," she said. "He was uplifted at that very moment. I was sitting at the table here," she recalled, "and he was over there at the desk, and I remember it distinctly." She went on to explain her interpretation of this moment and how she told her surprised son that this could be likened to what is written about Jeremiah the prophet, whom God chose before he was born, perhaps even before he was conceived (Jeremiah 1:4–8). "This is an indication," she said, "that the Lord chooses His messengers for His own reasons and not necessarily based on their success at living according to His rules, on their keeping the mitzvot.[11] Not that it is not important for us to keep the mitzvot," she went on to explain, "but He chooses His messengers for reasons we cannot know." Indeed, the ways in which God works in the universe are beyond human comprehension—recall the tapestry metaphor—although not only do believers try to interpret events to understand the messages the Lord seeks to communicate and to act according to his requirements but their lives are also largely structured by these interpretations.

"What message?" I thought to myself. What had the Lord communicated with her son? A whirlwind of questions flew through my mind. I was not concerned with why her son was chosen but enormously intrigued by the moment of communication. "He was uplifted?" I said again, trying to elicit a more detailed description of this supernatural event. At that point, Perhia turned to me in a matter-of-fact manner and said, "Yes, Joyce, uplifted— spiritually uplifted, like when you're so happy you feel like your feet don't touch the ground. What!? Did you think he actually started floating around the room or something?" I guess I had hoped that at least *she* thought he had. It was a blushing, embarrassing moment when my (secular, skeptical, liberal) lack of understanding became acutely clear. I had failed to understand that it was not that God had sent him a specific message but that he had sensed God's presence and God's approval of him. Shomeya had not been literally levitated but felt spiritually moved and knew God, and sensed Him in his life. The young man felt that he could communicate with God and find direction for his life.

Still, Perhia is among those religiously motivated settlers who do have a vision and strive to live according to it. This is a vision of the coming of the Messiah, a spiritual vision with enormous political implications. Some might say it is in fact a political vision expressed through or couched in religious rhetoric to the extent that it has worked hand in hand with the Zionist project.[12] This "dream" of redemption is perhaps better understood as a set of interpretations of events in daily life, as well as extraordinary or particularly difficult or traumatic events. The passage of time and all that transpires is always understood as leading toward redemption, bringing the coming of the Messiah closer. Yet this shared belief in the coming redemption does not amount to consensus among believers as to required practices.

The protests and actions of the anti-disengagement movement appeared so well orchestrated that those in opposition were at times in awe. Often comments were made about the anti-democratic and irrational foundations that must certainly underlie such a well organized movement. Liberal and secular Israelis often said that religiously motivated settlers must be so easily organized for political actions because "they do whatever their rabbis tell them to do." Despite outward appearances, there has never been complete consensus among the spiritual and political leadership of the settler movement (Lustick 1988). Nor do all believers consistently agree with their leaders. As the disengagement drew nearer, the population of religiously motivated settlers in Gush Katif was thrown into a kind of crisis that led to a great deal of questioning and soul searching, as we saw in chapter 4.

On one occasion, just one month prior to the Israeli withdrawal from the Gaza Strip, a woman who lived in one of the settlements there expressed her deep sense that the coming redemption required a *lack* of action at that juncture. Like Shomeya and his mother, this woman also experienced communication with God that some other religiously motivated settlers chided. ("What? Does she think she has a direct line to G-d?")

"It is a time to turn to G-d," Dahlia explained. "It is time to tell the Lord, Blessed be His Name, what we hope for and to leave the future in His hands." She expressed these ideas with a great deal of anguish both because so many other settlers were, she believed, acting without the direction that would come from prayer and because that direction, those communications, are not always easily achieved. Dahlia's call to prayer came in conjunction with leading rabbis calling for large communal prayer gatherings, while at the same time there were demonstrations and protests. Together with some other women in Gush Katif, she set up a tent in Neve Dekelim, a place for people to seek God's guidance and direction.

"What is it that you hope for?" I asked Dahlia "What is your dream?" Once again, I revealed my lack of understanding. She turned and sat quietly, head in her hands. She said nothing, her silence creating an uneasy interval. Looking back, I wonder that she did not become agitated. She had just finished saying, "we should tell G-d" what we hope for. Did I think I could stand in His place and listen to her hopes? Or to put it differently, did I think that I could translate her vision, her dream of redemption into a secular logic? Such an attempt is based in a belief or desire for translatability or commensurability. It is also based in a desire to know, in which the resulting knowledge is expected to generate a sense of comfort, a desire, I think, that lies behind much of the scholarly research into religious fundamentalism. I wanted to hear an explanation, an in-depth description, a narrative tale of her dream, something to analyze. But she refused. This woman did not need my recognition for her truth. This simple act of silence seemed to signal a radical rupture. It might be interpreted as marking the end of the space of secular, modern logic. Or it could be interpreted as marking my limited ability to understand the meanings this woman was trying to share.

This was not a matter of her specific vision, her dreams and hopes. That was the whole point. It was what I had missed with Shomeya and failed to understand again. Although Dahlia did not articulate a specific vision, one might discern such hopes and dreams from the ways in which the religious communities of settlers were built and how members led their lives. Indeed, many of the people of Gush Katif believed they were building model communities that could stand as an example of pious living, model societies that God expressed approval of by blessing them with many successes, including plentiful crop yields. As we have seen, this is a model society that is so reminiscent of the dreams of the founders of the secular kibbutz and so very like the settlers at the Massachusetts Bay Colony. In the communities of Gush Katif, brothers give loans to brothers without charging interest. No one locks doors, and there is no fear of crime. Strangers (like me) are welcomed and given food and drink and invited into people's homes. Families assist other families through local charitable networks and directly whenever the need arises. But as those communities were about to be evacuated, some of the settlers stopped talking about the vision of the faithful community. Instead, while many were occupied with organized protests, there came a call for an expression of emptiness or openness, a lack, an acceptance of not knowing. This was considered a deeply spiritual moment, a time to be open to the lessons of the Lord.

Anava (Humility)

This call for openness was sometimes described in contrast to "Western ways of life," which are often criticized by religious settlers for lacking certain important values.[13] In this case, it was a certain lack of humility, this sense of knowing and believing that humans can know and can have control.[14] The Judaism of religiously motivated settlers is *not* an inactive faith. It does not propose idly standing by while the Lord does his work. It is rather a system of faith that requires active engagement, taking moral responsibility for working toward good in the world, peeling back the layers to reveal the light. Of course, what is involved in creating a dwelling place for the Lord in this world is open to interpretation.[15]

Still, Perhia, Dahlia, and others echoing voices of religious leaders in their community all warned that it was a mistake to be too certain of our actions.[16] We cannot create the good, they explained; we can only ask to take a part in it, for we are, after all, not the Creator. "The problem is that we are too small, the machine we use (our brain) is just a tiny computer. It just doesn't have the program. We are too limited." Perhia, echoing other interpretations of Hebrew prophecy, went one step further.[17] There were, she believed, times when we must admit that we do not know. Human certainty is tantamount to the sin of pride.[18] There are times to communicate with the Lord and work on being open to hearing His answers, as Shomeya and others have. This requires just *being* and not filling one's time with the kinds of busyness that ultimately amount to the emptiness of what many religiously motivated settlers think of as Western life. Such busyness is often valued among the secular liberal who aspire to belong to a certain articulation of modernity. Being modern Western subjects can include attaching a positive value to taking advantage of one's time (time well spent) toward achieving that which is considered success. This value can also function as a technique of hegemony in which people experience a sense of choice and satisfaction in the ways in which they spend their time, particularly when their busyness is seen as signifying importance or high status. Such busyness can stand in the way of critical consciousness and result in political inaction, often named apathy.[19] "Western reality," I've often heard among religiously motivated settlers, "is problematic. It begins with you thinking you can fix the world." Indeed, Zionism itself is problematic in this way, Perhia told me. "Zionism is Western.[20] It is based on force without G-d. And the Bible teaches us that action, particularly political action, which is not guided by the voice of G-d will ultimately fail."

Following the war in Lebanon in the summer of 2006, another former resident of Gush Katif, not considered mystical in his beliefs, echoed these sentiments. He explained that the war was a misguided effort. It was not fought for the survival of Israel, he said, but for the survival of the prime minister. This man, an ardent Zionist, was adamantly opposed to the 2005 disengagement, which meant he would have to leave his home in Gush Katif. Still, when the overwhelming majority of Israelis favored the invasion of Lebanon, this right-wing, religiously motivated settler was opposed. This kind of opposition can be explained though rational, secular politics.[21] But it can also be explained with reference to the Bible: "This is why King David is the historical example of a good leader. He took care of business during the day, but each night he cried out to the Lord. Asking for guidance he says, 'I am nothing.' This is humility (*anava*). This is what is required. The problem is the way in which the People of Israel (*Am Yisrael*) try to rule itself. Trying to be a kingdom where the human king himself decides." From this insight, some religiously motivated Jewish settlers have criticized leaders and members of their own community. "Their mistake is that they have adopted Western ways to fight against the Western world. We must all start listening, allow ourselves to be open to what G-d will communicate with us. It is hard for us to listen because we can't stand the silence and will fill the silence with words and books and activity; we fill every moment because we cannot stand the silence."

Inaction

At the outset of this chapter, I suggested reconsidering the relationship between dreams of redemption and violence in light of the possibility of such dreams being interpreted as calling for passivity. Whereas Shulman and Asad debate the use of rhetorics of redemption in secular politics, this chapter looks at the political outcomes of religious belief in redemption. This belief is often considered irrational among the secular and liberal, allowing at least one scholar to confidently explain that "in their own eyes, the fundamentalists are reasonable people" (Sivan 1995:35), which, of course, presumes they are not. The belief in redemption and the practices of living that belief are seen not only as irrational but also as frightening and potentially violent. In the case presented here, the belief in redemption resulted not in political violence but rather in a politics of inaction. Inaction, however, like silence, also has consequences. It can be said to accept, condone, or become complicit with a broader status quo. "That's the way the oppressor class thinks," a character in a V. S. Naipaul novel remarks. "They've just got to sit tight and the world will continue to be alright for them" (Naipaul 2004:6). Here the call to stop and listen to the voice of the Ruler of the Universe may even come full circle and meet the busyness of Western life of which it is so critical. That Western (capitalist) busyness also produces a kind of silence, a lack of political action that becomes complicit with an existing social order, with state projects and their attending violences.

Without the danger of messianic visionaries—if dreams of redemption can also be nonviolent and call for inaction—the hegemonic appearance of discourses in conflict is at risk. This in turn carries the potential of undermining the moral constitution of Israelis who identify, at least partially, in opposition to those deemed despicable and dangerous, religiously fanatic others. Each group of Israelis located at seemingly opposite poles of the socio-political-religious spectrum continuing to view the other as threatening and as morally corrupt can prevent a confrontation with the ways in which their beliefs and practices take part in broader processes that may serve interests other than their own. Both constellations of identity can be co-opted for larger state interests. A particular group may find itself to be the darlings of the nation, or favorite son, so to speak, at a particular historical junction, only to fall from favor at a different moment. Such has been the experience of kibbutz members and now the experience of religiously motivated settlers as well. In each case, the group maintained its ideals and ways of life with government support accompanied by a sense of public admiration that led each to feel favored and each to feel betrayed in some sense by what appeared to be an inexplicable change.[22]

The next chapter reconsiders ideas among settlers on hospitality, sovereignty, and citizenship. It continues to widen the lens, opening up the definition of settlers, to reveal ways of imagining the future, beyond the constraints of current hegemonic categories.

7

Unimaginable Futures

Hospitality, Sovereignty, and Thinking Past
Territorial Nationalism

Part I: The Guest

"If you have a guest, you treat him well. You tend to his needs and provide food and shelter." This is one's duty according to the Torah. "But,
you do not give him your house. Not even your porch!"

—Hagar, Neve Dekelim[1]

"The sovereignty of the people and its connection to its past, its land
and its culture is of supreme importance. Here, there is no duality of identity like that among Jews abroad. I am an Israeli without
hyphens. . . . Here the Arab is in the minority and he is an Arab-Israeli,
which is to say he lives in a duality like Jews abroad. He deserves rights
just like those of any Jewish citizen of the United States, and should be
given the same rights as any Israeli Jew."

—Shulamit Aloni, former member of
Israeli Knesset[2]

In these postmodern times of globalization and cosmopolitanism, it
seems nearly anachronistic to focus on the relationship of a people to
a place. Since at least the late 1990s, a great deal of anthropological
thought around issues of identity has been aimed at undoing the
largely taken-for-granted notion that there is an "immutable link
between cultures, peoples, or identities and specific places" (Lavie and
Swedenburg 1996:1).[3] Indeed, as recounted in chapter 3, it has become
an anthropological truism to assert that "all associations of place,

people and culture are social and historical creations to be explained, not given as natural fact" (Gupta and Ferguson 1997:4). And most recently, we have heard the scholarly call to articulate post-territorial forms of identity, in particular, diasporic forms of identity that can subvert nationalist narrations linking people, territory, and sovereignty in a triad that has increasingly come under critical scholarly scrutiny.[4]

This nineteenth-century notion of people, territory, and sovereignty has been eulogized countless times. Yet, here in the troubled space of Israel/Palestine, it is impossible to deny the ongoing significance of people and place to citizenship and sovereignty. It is also impossible to ignore the need people often express to be grounded, to have a home and a sense of stability, and familiarity, including the attending perception of security in known surroundings. The scholarly desire to rationalize, justify, and moralize alternative forms of belonging, emerging from an impetus to increase social justice, necessarily denies certain forms of belonging in which some people are deeply invested. A growing number of socially engaged scholars are involved in struggles to create space for alternative forms of belonging. This call at once opens new possibilities and is blinded to others.

Anthropological theorizing that deconstructs assumptions of a natural relationship between people and territory critically challenges Jewish faith-based calls within Zionism to return to the sacred land. Indeed, Zionism has increasingly come to be considered dangerous in its ethnic-nationalism, which is necessarily exclusivist. In a sentiment encountered in chapter 4, that exclusivist tendency was expressed through a conceptualization of Palestinians as guests or as otherwise superfluous or troublesome to the Zionist national project.[5] I would like to revisit that idea of the guest here and compare it with secular, liberal notions of citizenship, recalling the continuities beneath the appearance of conflict, before continuing to explore what that discourse of conflict conceals.

The idea of the Palestinian or Arab in Israel as guest brings to mind Derrida's (2000) reflections on the notion of hospitality in which genuine hospitality is not a possible scenario. The guest is necessarily a transgressor, and the position of host, which requires mastery of the house, ultimately undermines the possibility of hospitality. Nonetheless, the act of hospitality with its romanticized location in the deserts of the Middle East is widely accepted as a virtue that contains an element of risk, as hosts provide sustenance to strangers who might bring danger. At the same time, hospitality is recognized for its mutual requirements on both host and guest, including the understanding that those roles may be reversed.

Many religiously motivated settlers express a clarity regarding one's duty to a guest or foreigner based on interpretations of sacred texts.[6] One is required to treat a guest or stranger well; however, there are also scriptural expectations placed on the guest. The host provides sustenance, food, and shelter to the stranger unless and until that person or group fails to behave as a guest. As previously suggested, a stranger's status may change to enemy, depending on interpretations of the stranger's behaviors, and the set of expectations may change entirely.[7]

The notion of a hyphenated identity of the Arab-Israeli as expressed in terms of liberal citizenship discourse quoted at the opening of this chapter also contains elements of the notion of the guest. The Arab-Israeli, it is said, is deserving of rights but seems to imply permanent minority status, one who should never expect to become master of the house. His will always be a hyphenated identity, somehow partial if not second-class. Both of these representations, it seems, emerge from a deeper episteme of ownership, mastery, sovereignty; both are premised on the assumption of the land as owned, belonging to, in possession of, and ruled by the Jewish Israeli. "The sovereignty of the people is of supreme importance," wrote Shulamit Aloni, a former member of the Israeli Parliament representing the liberal Citizens Rights Movement and an advocate for separation of religion and state, as well as the protection of basic human rights within Israeli law. It is not uncommon to encounter similar sentiments among liberal Israelis, who may deny a contradiction between ethnic nationalism (Zionism) and democracy or, at the very least, claim that in this regard Israeli citizenship is no different from that of nation-states elsewhere.

The contradictions inherent in struggling to expand democracy while holding on to ethnic/racial nationalism are apparent within this liberal discourse of citizenship. There is no need to rehearse here the well-known limitations necessarily included in such a formulation, the exclusion contained within that inclusion, and the violence intrinsic to the limits of the ethnic/national/religious territorial nation-state.[8]

The liberal and right-wing religious formulations quoted here have very different surface appearances and emerge from incongruous worldviews, yet there is something eerily similar, again evoking the sense of the uncanny. The difference between these two formulations in practical politics lies at the moment of either the recognition or lack of recognition that another people has the right to make the same claim to this piece of territory. Yet in practice, the difference becomes one of quantity, not quality. It is a matter of how much land, not whether the Jewish People (assuming a shared definition of that concept) are/should be masters of the house, sovereign in their homeland, but of how much of that land should or can be governed as a Jewish state. Both conceptualizations share premises with nineteenth-century ideas of nationalism that imagine contiguity between a people, a particular piece of territory, and the sovereignty of that people over the land. And both come into direct conflict with Palestinian ideas of nationalism that rest on the very same set of ideas of ethnic, territorial nationalism. There are other political positions found among Israelis, Palestinians, and other interested parties that call for a binational state, or one state for all its citizens.[9] I would argue that these ideas, emerging from political positions further to the left, are also based on the same categorical system. The epistemic foundation of territorial nationalism, discussed in chapter 1, consists of the sovereignty of a people over a particular territory—people, territory, and sovereignty. The signifier "people," in each of these variations, can stand for Jews, Arabs, both Jews and Arabs, or all citizens. In other words, even in political positions that do not rely on ethnic exclusivism, where the category of citizen is expanded, the underlying system of categories from which these ideas emerge remains constant and limited in its possibilities. Each of these possibilities has been met with trepidations, yet alternatives that move beyond the limits of territorial nationalism seem quite impossible to imagine.

We Are All Guests

Alternative ideas through which a future Israel/Palestine can be imagined that are based on a belief in the active role of the supernatural in worldly affairs have remained on the margins of social science and politics. It seems impossible to represent the supernatural as an actor in Western, rational discourse, and at the same time considering the sovereignty of the Lord rather than of the people undermines a post-Enlightenment faith in the promises of democracy. A woman from the settlement Atzmonah, in Gush Katif, made the following observation about secular faith in democracy:

> It begins with your arrogance, that you think you can change the world. . . . Like the Americans going into Iraq. When they come to repair the world, look at what they've done! They were going to fix things, change the world. What have they done? They do such damage, make such problems. Look at what they did in Serbia. This whole approach that here I come and I'm going to put things in order. It's wrong! You can't do it. Coming in and thinking you can change the world with, what, I don't know, democracy? Who said democracy was the way? What, is democracy sacred?

Some alternative ideas are kept at bay through the categorization of either the ideas or those who propose them as irrational or crazy. At the same time, however, some of these ideas may not be counted since they do not fall into the categories of either secular liberalism or fundamentalist religiosity. One of these marginalized ideas I encountered during this research involves placing a higher value on living on the land than on state sovereignty. This is a belief shared among some so-called fundamentalist settlers that is considered threatening to the rule of law in Israel. A more mystical version of that belief has been voiced by a rabbi of a West Bank settlement town, who participated actively in the anti-disengagement movement. This rabbi has been marginalized within the settler movement even though he was among its founders. Beyond the settler movement, he has generally been considered a rather eccentric member of a small fringe of society and therefore not to be taken too seriously. Insanity marks the boundaries, reinscribing the range of possibilities within a given moral social order.[10] And madness can mark the interface of freedom and danger. The mad can utter the unspeakable while they are kept at bay through separation, condemnation, incarceration, or most basically by their categorization as insane or irrational (Foucault 2006 (1961)).

In chapter 2, the term *crazy* was invoked as a term of endearment by kibbutz members in reference to the pioneering socialist Zionist settlers. But the notion of insanity applied to religious settlers in that chapter was associated with the irrational and the immoral. In this chapter, I introduce another element of "craziness." This one falls outside the neatly delimited boundaries of the hegemonic appearance of discourses in conflict. This craziness is recognized as such among both right-wing religiously motivated settlers and also among left-wing liberals. It is, I would suggest, a threatening insanity, provocative and dangerous to the social order of people, territory, and sovereignty, challenging both democracy and Zionism.

There is a faith-based call to return to the Land among some religious settlers that moves beyond ideas of citizenship that are founded in nineteenth-century notions of nationalism. This is an approach to the idea of sovereignty among some mystics in the Jewish settler movement that does not require one people to be masters of the house and another people in the role of guests. In fact, it calls into question the very notion of sovereign citizenship, so basic to modern democracies.

This vision, like the one calling for inaction and prayer in the previous chapter, emerges from what has been described as a feeling of deep spiritual proximity to the Lord and a place of humility before the Lord. It is an interpretation of the messianic vision that emphasizes the relationship between the Jewish People and the Land of Israel in a very literal sense, which is found among religiously motivated settlers more broadly. Believers find sanctity in the Holy Land, sanctity in the soil itself, which can bring the People of Israel closer to the light of the Lord. This is the belief in oneness, a unity of People, Land, and a life led according to the Torah that left many former residents of Gush Katif feeling torn apart by their removal from the Gaza Strip. This belief has most often been associated with Jewish sovereignty and the Israeli nation-state, but it also allows alternative imaginings that place a higher value on living on the land than on state sovereignty.

In the months preceding the implementation of the disengagement plan, many supporters of the post-1967 settlement project traveled to the settlements in the Gaza Strip to express solidarity and take part in the struggle to remain on the land. Some supporters joined demonstrations or special events. Others rented or purchased housing and moved to the settlements, giving practical expression to their belief that the disengagement would never take place, or, in the very least, that one must do everything in one's power to carry out the will of the Creator of the Universe, who would then reward His followers by preventing the disengagement from going forth. Still others would visit for a weekend (*Shabbat*) to spend time among the residents, lending moral and emotional support. During these months, thousands of devoted believers arrived. Some continued flooding in even after the area was designated a closed military zone and visitors were no longer allowed legal entry.

Among the visitors who came to Gush Katif on several occasions, including the days when the disengagement was being implemented and the settlers were actually being removed, was the rabbi from a town in the West Bank and his family. This rabbi came to the Jewish settlements in Gaza to do more than express symbolic solidarity; he had a plan. Based on his belief in the sanctity of the Land and his faith in the Sovereign of the Universe, the rabbi was among those who thought the Jewish settlers should remain in the Gaza area, even if the disengagement plan would come to fruition. He came to Gush Katif to convince as many settlers as possible to agree to stay, even if the Israeli government withdrew its troops and its protection of settlers. All the while, he tried to negotiate an arrangement with officials in the Palestinian Authority that would allow Jews to continue living in the Gaza Strip.

The rabbi is a recognizable figure and well known among the religious settlers.[11] When he came to Gush Katif to find supporters for his plan, he spent the Sabbath with an old friend with whom he had studied Torah in his youth. That friend, Shlomo, expressed no support for the rabbi's ideas. But characteristically living the ethical ideals he believes are required of him by his faith, he would not turn away a friend or a stranger with whom he disagreed. (Indeed, I was treated with the same hospitality and respect.) "I think he's completely wrong," Shlomo told me. "Still, he is a friend. And I told him not to worry. I would protect him if he came to synagogue with me." Shlomo was concerned that this so-called left-wing rabbi might be met with antagonism among the religiously motivated settlers of Gush Katif because his past actions were seen as cavorting with enemies, particularly Palestinians, including Muslim Palestinian clerics associated with political violence.

According to the rabbi, believing in the sovereignty of a higher power requires putting one's faith in God and letting go of one's faith in human sovereignty. Like Dahlia's suggestions in chapter 6, this rabbi and other religious settlers spoke of the importance of a human political ruler maintaining a degree of humility before the Lord. This rabbi's practical ideas for implementing that humility have caused him to be outcast by members of his own community, criticized from within, and considered crazy by many both in the community of religious settlers and in the broader Israeli community.

"Zionism must undergo a process of feminization," the rabbi told me. "The land is feminine and sovereignty is masculine. We must become closer to the land and let go of our tight grip on the reigns of sovereignty. We must not be afraid to let go." These ideas have found a small receptive audience among religiously motivated settlers and have some appeal beyond the Orthodox community. There is something in the nature of these thoughts that has the potential to traverse the Left-Right and secular-religious dichotomies.

This seems like a rather surprising interpretation to find among religiously motivated settlers who, unlike other Orthodox Jews, have been strong supporters of the Zionist project, including the role of secular Jews in bringing about the return to Zion through the establishment of the state of Israel. There are other streams of Orthodoxy that reject modern political Zionism (Rabkin 2006). Yet, here from within the right-wing religiously motivated settler movement, a group often called the nationalist Orthodox or religious nationalists, are those who explain that their commitment to God takes precedence over their commitment to the government or to the state. However, this shared sentiment did not necessarily result in support of this rabbi's ideas. Instead, it led to further nuances and interpretations. For example, during one of the anti-disengagement protests, Motti, a contractor from one of the agricultural communities in Gush Katif, explained that he and others are strong supporters of democracy. He emphasized the importance attached to acting within the general consensus in a democratic state. However, despite the desire of settlers from Gush Katif to be accepted into this general consensus among Israelis, there were times, he explained, when "the consensus is just wrong." This was case regarding the disengagement plan, he said. It was simply illogical for the Jewish state to remove Jewish citizens from their homes. In these situations, Motti said, there is no choice but to defy the consensus, which might include disregarding government decisions. In the end, Motti and many others who shared his beliefs left Gush Katif without physical resistance, even though they were convinced that the disengagement was illogical, undemocratic, and just plain wrong.

In some cases, the commitment to God above the state was taken as quite threatening and seen as bearing the potential to undermine the rule of law. It is associated with the most radical among religiously motivated settlers, who threaten or employ violence to achieve their goals.[12] It is different from the interpretation of more traditional Orthodox groups who also see their commitment to God as taking priority. Ultra-Orthodox Hasidim may be opposed to the state of Israel because they believe that human beings should not interfere with the return of Zion through Jewish sovereignty but must wait for the Messiah. They may live in Israel but do not necessarily believe that living in Israel is the key to becoming closer to God or to fulfilling God's will and bringing the redemption.

Among the ultra-Orthodox are those who never accepted the Zionist state. They have refused to participate in mandatory conscription in the armed services by invoking their right to practice their beliefs and study Torah.[13] This has been widely criticized (and is undergoing changes) by the secular in Israel, who have harbored anger against those Orthodox who they say benefit from the state through accepting social welfare and are protected by the state while they do not share equally in the responsibilities. The nationalist Orthodox, on the other hand, distinguished by their crocheted kippa (yarmulke) were more favorably received by secular Jewish Israelis precisely because of their support of the state and their participation in the armed forces.[14]

Unlike the thoughts expressed in the previous chapter, where the belief in the inevitable redemption led to a call for inaction, quiet, and prayer, the interpretation of this West Bank rabbi calls for alternative actions. He has tried to organize ways for Jews and Arabs to live on the Land under the ultimate sovereignty of God. His controversial ideas have led him to meet with prominent Muslim leaders, including those designated as terrorists and enemies of the state. One young man told me that a number of years ago, he had assisted in making such a meeting possible. The man, Hanan, shook his head with retrospective disbelief as he recalled hiding a Palestinian, who was wanted by Israeli security forces, in the trunk of his car—all this just to pass a checkpoint marking the borders of occupied territory so that the rabbi could meet with religious counterparts from the other side of the Israeli-Palestinian conflict. Hanan was disappointed that this effort and so many others like it have brought little change to the ongoing conflict. Like the rabbi, Hanan expressed a belief that religion (or more specifically, Judaism) carries within it the moral imperative to make peace. According to the rabbi, faithful followers of Islam and Judaism share an understanding of what it means to submit to the sovereignty of the Lord. For the rabbi, the path to peace through this belief is very clear, yet difficult to express. The rabbi did not use the term *theocracy* in our discussions, but he spoke of submitting to the will of the only true Sovereign. Indeed, he spoke little, and with a certain impatience, between walking away as often to answer his cell phone as to meditate and pray.

While he expressed a complete commitment to the idea of seeking and reaching agreements based on shared faith, the rabbi also spoke about important differences between Muslim and Jewish believers. He explained that he first met faithful Palestinian Muslims in Israeli jails, having been incarcerated himself for illegally settling land in the occupied territories. He spoke about his many meetings over the years with those in the Palestinian community, often considered Muslim extremists. "They are not like you and me," he said. "Do not misunderstand. I do believe we must talk to them, but I do not think they are angels. . . . They practice violence and brutality and do not sanctify human life as we do." Nevertheless, he said, the Muslim clerics with whom he has met share his deep belief in God as the only true Sovereign. And this, he contends, can be the basis for living together in the Holy Land, albeit each according to his own practices. He expressed a hope that Jewish settlers can take the role of what he calls an "outstretched hand" toward the Palestinians. This seems like a very strange idea, since so many incidents of clenched fists or other violent behavior have been reported between settlers and Palestinians. Still, the rabbi maintains his determination and is convinced that this is the right and righteous path.

The rabbi's vision can be described as a kind of fluid citizenship. When speaking about Jewish families who might have stayed in the Gaza area with the agreement of the Palestinian Authority, the rabbi told me this would not have to entail giving up citizenship in Israel, nor would it mean necessarily living under Palestinian jurisdiction. Instead, it would mean rethinking our current ideas of territorial contiguity, borders, and fences. This rabbi, like many other radical, religious settlers, abhors fences and boundaries.

Beyond Borders

On one occasion, I met the rabbi when he was spending a few days visiting near the Dead Sea, and he decided we should conduct our conversation on the shores of the sea. I drove down along the shore, looking for an entrance to a beach, with the rabbi in the back seat and his wife seated beside me.[15] Leading a simple life that privileges spirituality over material wealth, the rabbi and his wife have few material possessions. They do not own a car and often travel by hitching rides. I once invited his wife to a conference in Jerusalem and was convinced she would never make it on time. But she put her faith in the Lord and went out to the road as she always does, was picked up and dropped off at intersections by passing cars, and arrived early for the conference in Jerusalem.

As I drove along, all the entrances to the Dead Sea seemed to be marked by fences and parking lots that required paying a fee to enter. Finally, we found a place to park and got out of the car. I began walking toward the sign desig-nating the beach area, but the rabbi and his wife walked in the opposite direc-tion. The couple walked toward a fence with a sign warning against entering this dangerous area that was closed by the military. The sign said the area might have undetonated land mines. Paying no heed, the rabbi, his long white beard blowing in the breeze, found a hole in the fence and proceeded through, while I grudgingly followed. "Isn't this a bad idea?" I grumbled. "It could be dan-gerous." He just frowned and went forth. His wife smiled, an enormous, glow-ing grin. This reminded her of the old days when they had participated in establishing the first settlement in the newly occupied West Bank. She seemed to be having fun recalling those exciting days when defying the rule of men was an enactment of deep faith in a Jew's connectedness with the Holy Land. Our current trespass seemed far less meaningful but consistent with the practice of the belief that the holy bond to the Land should never be impeded by fences; there should be no mortal constructs interfering with this connection. When a security guard approached and asked us to remove ourselves, the couple calmly but assertively argued, displaying an ease apparently cultivated over time and with experience in similar situations. We stayed at our own risk, as the guard put it, while he explained that we were placing ourselves in danger. I'm not sure whether I sensed danger or just felt silly, but the experience also reminded me of demonstrations by the radical Left when protestors entered closed military zones to voice opposition to the Israeli occupation of post-1967 territories. On those occasions, participants also seemed to take pleasure in the excitement of crossing borders and breaking rules. Protestors faced possible arrest to meet with Palestinians on those occasions, just as the rabbi had. It was for these seemingly comparable experiences that the rabbi was sometimes called a "left-wing settler," which within current hegemonic categories is, of course, a con-tradiction in terms. The rabbi's passion for the Land and the Lord took him beyond those categories, making his actions and words fall instead within the category of the eccentric or crazy.

The Unimaginable

Among settlers opposed to fences on the Land are those often considered the most radical, including the hilltop youth, who continue to set up new outposts in the occupied territories. They are considered among the craziest and most violent of settlers from outside the settler movement, or alternatively diagnosed as delinquents. Some of these youth came to Gush Katif in the final days preceding disengagement. It was said that they were the ones who acted violently, holed up in a synagogue in Kfar Darom and throwing cans of paint and nails at the police who had come to remove settlers. Shira, the woman who first showed me Gush Katif, described those young people as out of control and in need of an educational framework and setting. The rabbi and his wife did not condone this violent behavior, but among their ten children, some were arrested during the disengagement struggles, and empathy was expressed for their behavior. That empathy, it was explained, emerges from a shared love of the sacred Land and an understanding of the impatience and ideological purity of youth.

The rabbi's feelings about the Land have been expressed through poetry describing an intimacy with the sacred soil, which waits in silence. His poetry gives emotional representation to the idea that we—signifying both the Jewish people and humanity more broadly—are not the owners of this land (ha-aretz), this country, this soil, this earth. The rabbi quotes the bible: "for the land is Mine; you are but strangers resident with Me" (Lev. 25:23–24). We are not the owners (the word *owner* in Hebrew is also the word for husband) but partners (*b'nei zug*, meaning a couple including a married couple). It is a call for humility, for an understanding that we are nothing more than guardians, or stewards of this land, and we are strictly accountable to the true owner the true sovereign, *the* Sovereign of the Universe. This poem plays with the words *adama* and *dmama*—soil and silence.

> And all the speakers (spokesmen) go forth on their way—
> On the land
> And all that is spoken goes unto the silence
> Accumulating upon the earth (soil)
> Like the ten articles of creation
> They return to Him
> With love until the end

The land bears all and is silent. And we, who seem yet to have learned that we are not the owners of that land, continue speaking out. What is called for here is trust in a power greater than ourselves and humility before that power, the creator and true ruler. As the rabbi once said to me, "There is, after all only one true sovereign." Then smiling with a knowing twinkle in his eye, "The Sovereign of the universe." And indeed, he argued that in keeping with that faith in the Sovereign, we must come to understand that one group of people cannot designate the other as guests. According to the rabbi and others who share this conviction, such a concept is a mistaken interpretation. It fails to realize that we are all guests on this earth and all guests in the Land of Israel. The Lord can allow us to stay or remove us from that land. And finally, according to this point of view, Arab and Jew have been placed together in the Holy Land by God. This is an indication that these peoples should carry out their lives together, according to God's expectations. That is, if the Jewish people are to be a "light unto the nations," it will be through the ways in which they live on the land together with the people God has placed them with. This vision seems fraught with contradictions. At once defending the right of Jews to live anywhere in the biblical Land of Israel and at the same time working for peaceful coexistence with Palestinians seems ironic, contradictory, or even cynical. But is it any more problematic than other visions for possible futures?

The idea that a two-state solution for the conflict in Israel-Palestine is no longer possible has been raised by a number of scholars and activists. It has been argued that post-1967 settlement activity has made such a solution geographically untenable since the landscape is now defined by scores of Jewish settlements separating Palestinians from each other and making territorial contiguity dependent on large population transfers.[16] Following the withdrawal from the Gaza Strip, the second Lebanon War, the rise of Hamas in Gaza, and the subsequent violence between Israel and Gaza, another problem has resurfaced. If the Israeli populace was once convinced that land for peace was the best possible option for the future of the state of Israel, this may no longer be the case. The Oslo Peace Process of the 1990s enjoyed widespread support among Israelis and carried a hopefulness that was ultimately undermined by the realities on the ground.[17] But the majority of Israelis only knew that their prime minister was offering the Palestinians a state and large tracts of land while anti-Israeli terrorism continued. At the same time, Palestinians knew that deals were on the table while settlements were expanding all around them, and dispossession continued as leaders shook hands on the White House lawn.

The disengagement, carried out in the summer of 2005, was presented by the Israeli government as a positive step toward peace. It was represented as a unilateral, generous act of giving territory to the Palestinians, a difficult move that proved Israeli willingness to compromise and make sacrifices. The fact that it was not a negotiated withdrawal seemed less significant than setting a precedent for the return of territory. "Land for peace" had been the slogan that many Israelis had adopted since the mid-1990s. But following the withdrawal in the summer of 2005 and the consequent election of Hamas in the Palestinian Authority, many Israelis lost faith in this possibility. Missiles continued to fly over the border between Gaza and Israel, rekindling a deeply ingrained Israeli fear that Palestinians will never be satisfied until the end of the Israeli state. A year later, the second war in Lebanon gave more credence to the growing belief among Israelis that land for peace may be more dangerous than they once believed. That war was largely presented to Israelis as a result of Israeli withdrawal from southern Lebanon, which was seen as allowing the conditions for Hezbollah to amass arms to attack Israel. Then, in the winter of 2008, a war took place in Gaza between Israel and Hamas, leading many Israelis to conclude that territorial compromise was extremely dangerous.

In light of current political, geographic, and demographic constellations, the idea of establishing a democratic state of Palestine alongside a democratic state of Israel seems very difficult to imagine. And reaching widespread agreement on a one-state solution, either binational or one state for all its citizens, seems an even more distant imaginary, as hatred and mistrust grow and multiply. The ideas put forth by the rabbi who asks that people let go of the belief in human sovereignty seem equally as unimaginable.

To press the imagination beyond the current binary oppositions of hegemonic discourses in conflict might require stopping, listening, and taking note, once again, that something is deeply amiss in the Holy Land. Voices from within the religious settler movement say "stop what you are doing" and "stop thinking that you know what to do." Voices from within the academy might warn against continuing to act from within hegemonic categories or against the impulse to continue categorizing. Instead of reproducing those categories or critically re-analyzing and recategorizing, perhaps it is time to consider what makes those categories possible and what those categories support.[18] Perhaps it is time to take note, too, of ideas and actions that seem to defy categorization and resist the urge to redefine, confine, and marginalize. Perhaps it would be wise to notice the unlikely places where seemingly bizarre alliances emerge.

Consider, for example, the ways in which those categorized as the far Left converge with those categorized as the far Right and support a cause that many Palestinians support. There are religiously motivated settlers and those in favor of a larger state of Israel who have voiced opposition to the construction of the separation barrier. Among the settlers of Judea and Samaria/the occupied West Bank, there have been calls to protest not only the construction of the separation barrier/wall/fence, which they say destroys the beautiful landscape and breaks Jewish hearts that feel a connection to those landscapes, but also the military checkpoints that are supposed to protect Israel from dangerous Palestinians. Some settlers feel their freedom impeded by these checkpoints and fear that the wall and checkpoints leading to occupied territory where they live will create an image of two separate states in the minds of Israelis.[19] That, of course, is exactly what many liberal Israelis (including the Peace Now movement) would like to see happen. It seems quite impossible to consider alliances between right-wing, radical settlers and Palestinians in the occupied territories. Yet these groups do share common interests despite their antagonistic relationship.

Another convergence that is equally difficult to imagine within current hegemonic political categories might find some relationship between those so-called radical settlers and the international anti-globalization movement. There are settlers who are armed and dangerous and have been known to beat or shoot at Palestinians. And there are settlers who call for an end to the fences and boundaries of territorial nationalism. They and others in the settler move-ment denounce what they see as empty Western, secular values, including ma-terialist values and excessive consumption. They are environmentalists and live simply off the land. Some religiously motivated settler youth have criticized materialist comforts even among their parents' generation. Such convergences stretch the imagination beyond what currently makes sense to quite unimagin-able futures, unsettling categories, and disturbing commonly held perceptions.

The next chapter takes a reflexive look at the work of disturbing categories undertaken in this book.

8

On Disturbing Categories

The powerful centrifugal force created through the interactions of hegemonic discourses in conflict pulls particular ways of being to the center of attention and conflict while casting alternatives to the margins. It conceals the continuity between settlers in a settler-colonial social formation and hides the anxiety that lies beneath the appearance of conflict. The anxiety stemming from the fear that Jewish presence and sovereignty in the space of Israel/Palestine stands to lose its legitimacy, or lose itself—its center of identity—is an important driving force behind the conflict between settlers on both sides of the Green Line.

Poststructural theorizing recommends deconstructing and digging beneath categories, identities, and the commonly accepted terms of political debate. The motivation behind this impetus is a quest for greater social justice and increased human freedom. Postcolonial scholars, and notably feminists, have suggested paying closer attention to the margins. However, even such scholars have struggled with recognizing certain marginalized groups, particularly certain variations of religiosity.[1] In addition, the academy or, more specifically, the predominantly secular academy remains wary of those "repugnant others," in Susan Harding's words, especially when they are seen as linked to power.[2] This means, for example, that Christian Fundamentalists in the United States and right-wing, religiously motivated settlers in Israel/Palestine often remain essentialized others; those others with whom the secular liberal would not or could not seek alliances as they fall beyond the limits of liberal tolerance.[3] They hold the place of the evil others who, as Povinelli (2001) says, remain a requirement so that the liberal subject is not undone. In this chapter, I shift the lens again to illuminate some otherwise shadowy places, to continue considering constellations of identity that do not fit easily into existing categories within the Jewish Israeli sociopolitical spectrum. My purpose here is not only to continue to challenge the tendency to essentialize those often categorized as fundamentalists (those others we love to hate) and open up the category of settler in the space of Israel/Palestine but also to reflect on the complexity or potential danger of such challenges. Chipping away at confining frameworks and tearing apart the powerful ways in which we order the social world is important work. It helps us see past the well-fortified bunkers of "us" and "them." It also creates a certain discomfort as we recognize similarities, seeing ourselves mirrored in our sworn enemies, a discomfort that might push us to question our own beliefs and practices. Yet, as we break out of well-known categories, looking beyond and beneath, we can never know just what we will find. There are no guarantees that the complexities of identity, beliefs, and practices that fall beyond hegemonic categories will be any more appealing than what we've left behind.

I would like to invite the reader to join me at an event that took place in the settlements of Gush Katif two months prior to Israeli withdrawal from the area. That event, a Women's Sabbath (*Shabbat Nashim*), brought together Israeli Jewish women, including religiously motivated settlers and women expressing opposition to settlement in the occupied territories. This event provides an opportunity to reflect on what can be found beyond and beneath the Left and Right, secular and religious, those in favor and those opposed to the settlement project.

Categories

It is comforting to have categories through which to organize the world. This allows a sense of order and serves a very human, psychological need. Yet, anthropologists have long known that the categorization of humanity is always problematic and that identity itself is better conceptualized as a process rather than as sets of static categories. We know that identities and alignments between people shift and vary. In addition, when we position people along a political continuum, the locations of Left, Right, and center are not only inadequate, and always relational, but also form hegemonic discursive categories that hide power relations. The comfort and assurance found in well-known

categories can be easily disturbed, like a turn of the wheel at the end of a kaleidoscope. Before turning that wheel, let me lay out, once again, the more familiar categories on the Israeli Jewish sociopolitical scene.

The Left of Israeli Zionist politics emerged from the socialist or labor
Zionist movement.[4] It tends to be associated with a liberal or secular humanism
and with what is known as the peace camp in Israel. It generally includes those
Israelis who are opposed to the occupation of territories gained in the 1967
war. This Left, however, is not necessarily exclusively secular but includes
shades and variations of secularity and religiosity, including some Orthodox
Jews,[5] particularly those often called "modern Orthodox," which is another
category including variations but generally viewed as distinctive from the
ultra-Orthodox or Haredi Jews.[6] The Right, on the other hand, is historically
associated with a more hawkish position and a belief in the right of the Jewish
people to establish a state on what is known as "the whole of Israel" (*Eretz Israel
ha-Shlema*). This position has historically been opposed to relinquishing territory and has often been aligned with more religious Jews who share a belief in
the right of Jews to settle on the ancient biblical Land of Israel.[7] Of course, the
Right is also not exclusively the domain of the religious but includes versions
and shades of religiosity and secularity. Racial, ethnic, and class dimensions
further complicate these categories.[8] There are, of course, many nuances
within each category, and as this chapter progresses, I would like to further
consider some of the less familiar constellations of identity that are among
those most difficult to articulate. I begin by illustrating the powerful context of
a hegemonic discourse of conflict that makes those less familiar constellations
so difficult to express.

Insanity

They're crazy, insane, not normal, disgusting people, not like us.
                                   —Common liberal views of religious settlers

Such ideas reverberate with other times and places:

"I met many white South Africans who were . . . horrified and disgusted
(by the system of Apartheid) . . . (this) rendered their life in South Africa
tolerable. It gave them the certainty that they were different."
                                   —Vincent Crapanzano (1985:23)

Some of the liberal views about religious settlers were expressed by Israeli
men who carried out army reserve duty guarding settlements in the occupied

territories. Some of the most disturbing stories came from Hebron, where soldiers told of settler children throwing stones at an elderly Palestinian woman
laden with packages. Why don't these children who are being raised in a deeply
religious manner offer to help the old woman with her packages? A soldier said
he asked the children what they were doing; why were they throwing stones?
What had the woman done to deserve this? The children explained that they
were throwing stones in retribution for the Arab massacre of Jews in Hebron.
That was in 1929, and this incident was 2005. The soldier was confused. A
stone memorial placed in a wall of the Muslim quarter in the Old City of Jerusalem marks the site where a Jewish man was killed in the 1990s, presumably
by local Palestinians. The placard reads: "On this spot Elhanan Aharon Atteli
was murdered by the evil ones. . ... By the spilling of his blood, we shall live on"
(approximate translation; see figure 8.1). This is followed by: "Remember what
Amalek did to you on your way" (Deut. 25:17). The Amalekites are depicted in
the Bible as a tribe of nomadic people who attacked the Israelites during the
exodus from Egypt (Exod.17:8–17). They appear in other places in the text, and
the interpretations of what is required by the injunction to "remember Amalek" are varied. In this case, the term has come to stand for any and all those
who are considered "enemies" of the Jewish people.

Time, in this case, is not that troublesome Western, linear, progressive
time that some critical scholars have argued leaves no room for representing
subaltern others.[9] This time is cyclical and spiraling, and place is spiraling, too.
The past is the present, and Amalek is the Palestinian woman in Hebron. In
some cases, it seems wise and compassionate to try to amend that linear time,
to hear the voices of others and push the boundaries of possible representations. Here, that same move is far less comfortable. It is the discomfort of
coming face to face with that "repugnant" other. But such discomfort is not
reason enough to reject attempts to understand—quite the opposite, in fact.

Pathology

"I once thought it was possible to understand the left-wing from a rational
perspective, but now I'm convinced that it is some kind of pathology."

—Religious Settler

"It's time to dismantle the settlements because living there in isolation is a
recipe for social deviation. Like juvenile delinquents who only spend time
among their own—they are cut off from the norms of society."

—Israeli Sociologist

FIGURE 8.1 Remember Amalek. Author photo.

The notion of a pathology of the Left is an interesting twist, when *pathological* and *deviant* are precisely the adjectives that some among the Left use to describe the religious Right.[10] The pathology of the Left is a result of diasporic (*galut*) mentality, a man from the settlements in the Gaza Strip once told me. It is the way of thinking of a people still in exile, "as though we had not yet come out of Egypt," Judah said. This exile mentality makes Jews concerned with what gentiles (*goyim*) think. They are more interested in pleasing the gentiles than they are with basic Jewish values. "It is very difficult," Judah went on to say, "to understand how the left-wing just doesn't seem to learn. You would have thought that after the Oslo disaster, they would understand that it is impossible to make peace agreements."[11] A friend of Judah's agreed: "The Arabs want to destroy Israel. We're like a bone in their throat, in the middle of the Arab world. They want us out. There will never be peace because the Arabs don't really want it. They say they do for the media and to influence world opinion. But you can't trust them."

The "left-wing" being referenced includes a wide range of points of view. But at that moment, just prior to the Israeli withdrawal from the Gaza Strip and his own removal from his community and home in Gush Katif, the "left-wing" was the signifier for the opposition within. It was not the Palestinian Amalek but those Israeli Jews who did not take to the streets to oppose the disengagement plan calling for withdrawal from Gaza. For Judah, the opposition from within was characterized by Jewish Israelis who had become too concerned with Western, materialist values, with pleasing American leaders, and with finding ways to lead an easier life. This worship of false idols, he thought, would ultimately pose a threat to the very survival of the Jews as a people.[12] That cosmopolitan "easy life" of McWorld, propelled by the market forces of globalization that many believe (or once believed) are a "major force advancing peaceful coexistence in the Middle East" (Ram 1999),[13] might be just what forced the Israeli government to disengage from the Gaza Strip. But should the Israeli withdrawal from post-1967 occupied territories necessarily be read as part of the path to "peaceful coexistence"?

Unusual Opposition

Although unilateral withdrawal from the Gaza Strip was most vocally and theatrically opposed by the far Right and religiously motivated settlers, there was other opposition as well. There is as much to be learned from these lesser known positions as there is from those more often encountered. To ignore these positions would participate in the continuous reinscription of hegemonic categories of politics and identity that set the limits of debate and ways of being in the present that also limit ways of imagining a future. The first constellation of identity/politics emerged from what is usually called the left side of the political spectrum, which has been strongly aligned with the politics of ending the occupation and of partitioning the land in order to establish a Palestinian state alongside Israel.

Anti-occupation/Anti-withdrawal

A number of people opposed to the withdrawal took a position that might be described as the far or radical Left, yet this opposition was also controversial within the radical Left. The actual number of people who might have held this position is difficult to determine. In part, this point of view emerged as a critique from within the more mainstream left wing. In part, it emerged from alternative readings of Jewish religious texts. For individuals who consider themselves situated on the left side of politics—whether religious, secular, or containing elements of both—this was an extremely difficult position to articulate. For those opposing Israeli expansion, opposition to the withdrawal could easily be read as supporting the ongoing military occupation of post-1967 territories. Indeed, it was almost exclusively read this way and nearly always so intended. Opposition to withdrawal, then, would mean supporting those "crazy" and "disgusting" settlers, which was not what this opposition intended. There were people who did not support the beliefs and actions of those settlers but did not refer to them in these disparaging terms, instead expressing an ethics of tolerance that extended to those with very different political positions and theological interpretations. This position was so problematic because it could be interpreted as supporting the same settlers who shoot at Palestinians, uproot olive trees, and throw stones at elderly Palestinian women. Certainly, these kinds of acts were strongly opposed by those opposing occupation and opposing withdrawal, many of whom were political activists in coalition with Palestinians against the violence of occupation. In addition, this position risked voicing support for those settlers in the occupied territories who do not partake in any of those immediate, face-to-face forms of violence but seek a higher quality of life in places where government incentives have reduced the cost of living,[14] as well as those settlers who are deeply motivated by their religious beliefs to populate the ancient Land of Israel with Jews, would never engage in individual acts of violence, yet serve proudly in the Israeli Defense Forces. And what about those Israelis who are usually not referred to as settlers?[15] Then again, what about Israelis who make their homes inside the Green Line, may voice opposition to the military occupation in post-1967 territories, but continue to serve in the Israeli Defense Forces (IDF), that is, Israelis who are not conscientious objectors? What about those secular and liberal settlers who are looking for a higher quality of life and feel no particular sentiment toward the ancient land and holy places? What about those liberal settlers who want to trade land for peace or make unilateral withdrawals from post-1967 occupied territories without too much engagement or fuss, just as long as they can get on with their lives? How can a position that opposes *both* military occupation in post-1967 territories *and* unilateral withdrawal from those territories be heard amid all that clamor?

That most difficult position to articulate within current categories was often in favor of an Israeli state inside the Green Line—a complete withdrawal to pre-1967 boundaries. But that same voice found a breach of moral responsibility in carrying out the withdrawal in the absence of negotiations with a Palestinian partner. It was argued that Israel's disengagement would not liberate Palestinians but create the conditions of a large prison.[16] Among the Israelis expressing this opinion were those who did not want to be the wardens of that prison and saw such a situation as detrimental to Israelis and Palestinians alike. In addition, some were convinced that leaving the Gaza Strip in the way it was being proposed would set up the conditions for another Israeli invasion. Next time, it was predicted, would be far more violent. The Green Line surrounding the Gaza Strip would become what James Ron calls a "frontier," authorizing increasingly extreme forms of state violence (Ron 2003).[17] Some people who expressed both anti-occupation and anti-withdrawal positions also criticized the force of Israeli militarism that was being imposed on the residents of Gush Katif. Perhaps the people of Gush Katif should not be there, but they should also not be forced out. They should not be treated as though they were unable to make these decisions on their own. The state could withdraw the military and offer assistance in moving the Israeli citizens living there. But why should the state force their removal? The difficulty expressing an anti-occupation/anti-withdrawal position was evident when it was dismissed as unrealistic. The dismissing voices often spoke as if to a child who could not possibly understand the complexities of the real world. That no-nonsense voice had once been the Left in Israeli politics.

On one occasion, a proponent of an anti-occupation/anti-unilateral withdrawal position recounted for me his experience as an invited speaker at a secular, liberal kibbutz.[18] A member of the kibbutz who had been participating in a dialogue group with religiously motivated settlers organized a panel in December 2003 to discuss the impending disengagement from the Gaza Strip and parts of the West Bank. The kibbutz member, Tzodeket, had invited three speakers to present differing opinions on the disengagement plan; two were opposed to disengagement, and one was in favor. The two who were opposed were described as the radical Right, represented by a religiously motivated settler who lived in Gush Katif, and the radical Left, represented by a political activist for peaceful coexistence with the Palestinians, advocating an Israeli state within the pre-1967 borders.

Amos, representing the anti-occupation/anti-unilateral withdrawal position, was pleased to have the opportunity to explain to Israelis situated on the political Left why they should oppose the Sharon government's disengagement plan. He came prepared with facts and figures describing the conditions of unemployment, poverty, and overcrowding suffered by Palestinians in the Gaza Strip, as well as the details of the proposed plan that would, he predicted, worsen the conditions of Palestinians but would not pave the road to peace. This, he argued, was because Israeli forces would retain control of the seacoast and border crossings. It would be like placing the Palestinians of Gaza in a very large military prison in desperate conditions. Ultimately, this would undermine the leadership of the Palestinian Authority, who would not have the resources to take over. Amos recounted that he received very little support from the kibbutz audience. He was not treated with hostility, like the religiously motivated settler opposed to disengagement. Instead, he was spoken to in a patronizing voice by the secretary general of the kibbutz movement, who was in favor of the disengagement plan. This man represented the more conventional "Left" at this moment in Israeli politics. He said that Amos's position was unrealistic; it was a position that revealed a lack of understanding of the way politics worked in the real world. In the real world, we must make compromises, and the secretary representing the so-called left-wing[19] of Israeli politics thought it was best to withdraw from Palestinian territories occupied in 1967 under any conditions.

Settler-Left

The left-wing anti-occupation/anti-disengagement position is as marginalized as the position of the settler seeking to live with and among Palestinians that was introduced in the previous chapter. The anti-disengagement position that might be described as the "settler-left" does not fit comfortably into any of the existing categories either. How can a person live in the post-1967 occupied territories, support religiously motivated settlement, oppose the construction of the separation barrier/fence/wall, and insist that these positions come from a place on the far Left? This critical voice from within the religiously motivated settler movement refuses to accept the removal of Jews from any part of the biblical Land of Israel and encourages expansion. But at the same time, those voicing this position do not insist on national territorial sovereignty, as we currently know it. The settler-left, introduced in the previous chapter by the West Bank rabbi, represents a position that was delegitimized even by some from the marginalized anti-occupation/anti-withdrawal position. It was called an irresponsible position that could not claim a humanistic concern for Palestinians, nor claim the possibility of being a good neighbor unless and until its proponents physically removed themselves from their homes across the Green Line. That would be a sign of truly caring about Palestinian suffering. That would be proof of a true willingness to live together. The settler-left is also pushed to the margins from within the very settlements its proponents pray for. It is a position that represents the voice of the traitor; one who does not understand that Jewish sovereignty cannot be separated from living on the Land.

In the shadows beneath the headlines, proponents of the anti-occupation/ anti-unilateral withdrawal, and settler-left positions spoke out wherever someone else might listen. These are people who found or created spaces to encounter others who do not accept their points of view, often believing firmly in the importance of dialogue. They were also often activists taking part in political actions that expressed at least some of their beliefs—some associated with the far Left, others with the far Right, and others with acts aimed at protecting human rights. The deep faith in the importance of meeting and speaking to others who disagree can be read as the practice of democratic values or, alternatively, as an expression of a drive to unity among the Jewish people in the face of impending disaster. One of the places where such a meeting took place was a weekend gathering for women in Gush Katif, a women's Sabbath or *Shabbat Nashim.*

I was invited to attend this weekend gathering. Here I present some of the conversations that took place in the following notes, interspersed with my own reflections in italics. This encounter and the discussions between the women represent a break from the antagonism between Left and Right, secular and religious, and those in favor against those opposed to disengagement. There are a number of organizations that arose is Israel following the 1995 assassination of Yitzhak Rabin to heal the rift among Israelis and encourage dialogue between left-wing secular and right-wing religious Jews. This meeting, however, was different. It was not a formal gathering arranged by a particular organization, there were no fees to be paid, nor was there a group facilitator or a program. This was a group of women, some of whom had met each other on other occasions, each bringing a few others along to talk and to listen. It was also different because some of the women participating expressed ways of being and believing that do not fit comfortably into existing hegemonic categories of religion or politics. The secular and left-wing women were not so secular—like Rina, for example, who came from Tel Aviv. Rina was not an Orthodox or traditionally observant Jew, nor was she completely secular or anti-religious like many left-wing, secular Israelis, but she did feel a deep spirituality and enjoyed the Sabbath prayers and songs. And the right-wing religious were not so right-wing. Tikva and Ruth, both religiously motivated settlers, expressed opinions that exceeded typical right-wing religious points of view, particularly regarding Palestinians, as will become clearer in what follows. This meeting was also different because it was held in Gush Katif. Most left-wing, secular Israelis would not come to Gush Katif, and those who did would rarely be willing to spend a night. In fact, there were two women from Tel Aviv who came down on Friday afternoon but left before sundown. Many were afraid to stay in the communities of Gaza after dark, and many others simply would not want to give their free time to an event like this. Most Israelis, particularly those with left-wing positions, wanted nothing to do with the settlers of Gush Katif.

Saturday is the only day off for most Israelis, and the secular use their Saturdays for leisure activities. They travel in the country, visit friends, go out to restaurants, or hike in the countryside. Observant Jews, on the other hand, cannot travel, work, write, cook, or spend money between sundown on Friday until three stars appear in the sky on Saturday night, marking the end of the Sabbath. The Sabbath, for observant Jews, is a time for prayer but also a time when families and friends get together. This unusual gathering was a moment that moved beyond powerful categories of difference that defined the Israeli sociopolitical scene. Yet as my reflections will clarify, this event illustrates how disturbing well-known categories is not a panacea. It may reveal alternatives that are equally as problematic, or worse, than what we started with.

Shabbat Nashim/Women's Sabbath

May 20–21, 2005, Shirat Ha-Yam, Gush Katif

The women's Sabbath was hosted by Ruth, who lived in a trailer in a relatively new and humble community (or a settlement outpost) on the Mediterranean Sea called Shirat Ha-Yam, Song of the Sea (see figure 8.2 and 2.1). It will be recalled that the Song of the Sea (Exod. 15:1–18) is a lyric poem celebrating God's defeat of Egypt at the Red Sea. It seems beyond coincidence that the spiritual poetess living in a trailer at the Song of the Sea would invite secular and religious women from different places in the country to come together to study, converse, pray, and celebrate the Sabbath.

Saturday evening, after having shared in a process through discussion, prayer, song, sharing food, and just being together, Tikva decided that it was time to talk about the issue that had been there all along, the burning issue we had not yet approached. Tikva began to talk about the disengagement itself, the struggle, prompting others to engage in discussion.

Tikva had made her way to Gush Katif from her home in the West Bank. She and Ruth are friends, and she had offered to help lead the discussions during the weekend. She began by telling us that two of her sons had been arrested during the recent protests that past Monday when demonstrators blocked major intersections and had ended up in jail. Her sons asked her what she thought about what they had done, and she told us that she gave them two answers. First, she said she doubted that "these kinds of activities would further the cause. They may even be counterproductive. Second," she said, "I understand the need to shout out loud and express the pain and resistance to the disengagement plan." Rina, who came to Gush Katif from a town near the center of the country, not far from Tel Aviv, was very upset at hearing that Tikva's children had participated in these demonstrations. In Tel Aviv, Rina facilitates groups of women that include Palestinian citizens of the state. Some of the demonstrations had become violent and dangerous, setting fires on the

FIGURE 8.2 Inside the fence at Shirat Ha-Yam. Author photo.

roads and at intersections, and "this is not the way," Rina said. Sitting on the back porch, facing the sea, Rina lowered her head in disapproval. Her words came slowly at first, measured, as though she was trying to explain to herself first, disapprove, yet still listen. *Did she disapprove of the methods of protest? Or was it disapproval of the settlements or the settlers?*

The discussion turned to an assessment of the current situation and how to proceed. Dahlia, who lived in Gush Katif, spoke at length, sharing her convictions that this was not a time for action. "It is a time to turn to G-d. It is time to tell the Lord, Blessed be His Name, what we hope for and to leave the future in His hands."

"What do you hope for, what future do you seek?" I asked Dahlia. She spoke about a vision in which all the People of Israel would live with the revelation of the Lord. Ruth offered to pick up from where Dahlia had left off, trying again to explain to the more secular among us what it is that she and Dahlia dream of and pray for. "What is called for," Ruth said, "is a coming together of the Jewish people in Israel, a return to a certain wholeness that is missing when we each retreat to our corners—the Left or Right, the secular or religious—and each to our own ideology." She explained, as she had on other occasions, that each group has been holding on to one aspect of its ideology.

This is what Dahlia called worshipping idols. Putting all your faith in one thing, one answer, is a kind of idolatry. *So the secular and left have often said of religiously motivated settlers. Coveting the land, placing the value of the land above all else, that is a form of idolatry.*

Ruth was more broadly critical of the different sectors among the People of Israel. "It means," she explained, "that the secular Left has put all its faith in humanism. As part of that they have been concerned for the rights of Palestinians. But," she continued, "their humanism is not complete because it does not extend to Jewish settlers." One could feel the bristle as these words brushed against the secular, liberal sensibilities of some of the women in the group. *Humanism. Humanitarian concern. Compassion. Surely, the Palestinians were in far greater need. Surely the poor and unemployed, the single mothers struggling to get by in Israel/Palestine were in far greater need. In fact, it was nearly impossible to feel compassion toward "settlers" who cried out for sympathy at their impending loss as they faced removal from their homes. Anger was abundant. "They deserve it!" I often heard people remark. "They should have known from the beginning that this was the wrong thing to do." Beyond this tiny group of women who chose to come together and hear each other, who would even want to try to find compassion for these "insane," "disgusting" people? Is such compassion the morally responsible act called for? Could the practice of a pedagogy of compassion be usefully applied here?*

Ruth went on, slowly with measured and careful words. Her soft, small voice required quiet and concentration. "The Left," Ruth said, "has ignored the importance of the land itself because, being so concerned with human rights, they forget the importance of living on the Land. This is something they once knew in the earlier days of Zionism. The religious Right on the other hand has also placed all its faith in one thing," she said. "They have been totally committed to the one mitzvah that suited their needs," she said, "the mitzvah of settling the Land of Israel. And because of this narrow view, they have ignored the rest of the picture, thinking the Lord will take care of the Palestinians, for example." Each side, according to Ruth, must heal and repair itself. Each side must make the adjustments and changes to include what is missing.

Ruth's words are both compelling and disturbing. She calls for a morality of self-critique that resonates powerfully with a skeptical, liberal subjectivity. But there is also a strong dissonance between the words and the place. Here we are once more, settlers talking among ourselves, reconstituting ourselves in light of each other, speaking for and about Palestinians without a Palestinian interlocutor. And there she is on the other side of the fence! Literally, on the other side of the security fence surrounding this beachfront outpost, Palestinian women and their children walked by. There on the beaches of the Gaza strip, we sat out on the back porch of a crumbling beach house, one of a row of small square concrete structures lining the coast, a house once used by vacationing Egyptian military officers when the Gaza Strip had been under Egyptian sovereignty. In that place, facing west, looking out onto the sea, the present absence of Palestinians and Palestine screams in your ears and scratches at your eyes.[20]

Kabbalat Shabbat

On Friday night, we spoke about the meaning of the Sabbath, sang Sabbath songs and prayers as the sun set over the Mediterranean Sea. Some of the women were so moved, they spontaneously began to dance, as others stood, eyes closed, and palms raised, calling on the Sabbath to arrive. In the midst of the singing and prayer, the sound of the muezzin could be heard behind us. They, too, were calling to prayer. I exchanged glances and smiles with Tikva and said, "Listen, they are praying, too." A questioning face turned toward me. *I was interrupting thoughts and concentration, interrupting the process of prayer. The face turned toward me did not register my words. We didn't stop, we didn't listen, and we didn't talk about the voice of the muezzin calling Muslim Palestinians to pray. The woman leading the singing sang a little louder, trying hard not to let the other melody interfere with her own. She must have been aware of the sound to sing over it with force, even though, in that eerie, uncanny way, the voice remained.* Later that evening, I said to the group, "We called the Sabbath and heard an answer." They laughed, softly, nervously, but said nothing.

Later, when I was ready to walk back to the trailer where I would spend the night, Esther suggested walking along the beach behind the houses rather than on the road in front. "Why?" I asked her. "Why should I walk along the beach? I am more familiar with the road." "Yes," she said, "but it is unpleasant to walk along the road. There is no concrete barrier, only a fence. The Arabs drive by on the other side of the fence, and it's unpleasant and frightening," she said.

"There are no concrete barriers," *I thought to myself, means the Palestinians living in the area known as the Muassi are not hidden from view, as are those in Khan Yunis. But what does "unpleasant" mean? Is it more pleasant to live surrounded by concrete barriers?* (See figure 8.3.) *Or is it just more pleasant to live in a small community in the United States where all that remains is a monument to the last Indian? I have heard Israelis say they are "jealous of Americans for whom the problem of the native is a thing of the past."* Esther, who described walking next to the fence as uncomfortable, did not live in this community. She had not developed that sense of comfort and security that many of the Jewish residents in the Gaza Strip claimed they had. It was rare to hear the local residents speak of fear, but on occasion a grandmother might confide her fear for the safety of her

FIGURE 8.3 Living surrounded by concrete barriers. A house behind a wall at the edge of Kfar Darom. Author photo.

grandchildren.[21] Or residents would express their understanding for other Israelis who were too afraid to visit.

The next day, a group of women from Neve Dekelim walked through the Muassi to join this gathering, accompanied by a young man, the son of one of the women. *Did he come as an escort, or just to visit some of his friends as his mother claimed? The people who lived in Gush Katif described the people living in the area called the Muassi as a kind of "primitive people" who one need not fear. "They do not make trouble." On the other hand, the people of Gush Katif also pointed out that the area along the beach populated by Palestinians had grown. Palestinians from Khan Yunis had been moving to the Muassi; they were "taking more land." This is why it was important to set up the trailers on the beach. Those trailers at the Song of the Sea did not constitute a new settlement, it was explained. They were part of the original, approved plan for Neve Dekelim. Khan Yunis is a city and a refugee camp in the southern part of the Gaza Strip. The refugee camp was established following the 1948 war and populated mainly by refugees from the southern regions of what is now Israel. The struggles over land and resources continue in both places.*

On Friday night, Tikva said that in Judea and Samaria there is still the possibility of taking a hilltop and setting up a house, as indeed some of her children have. "Inside Israel, such possibilities no longer exist," she remarked sadly. Tikva spoke with a longing reminiscence of those days, when she joined her husband and a handful of others taking hilltops and establishing what would become the first settlements in the newly occupied West Bank. Dahlia pointed out that here, in the Negev, there is a new wave of people setting up individual small farms. "They grow grapes for wine or raise goats for cheese. It is difficult," she said, "because it is hard to receive the amount of land that people want. But," she went on, "otherwise the Bedouin would just take over and that wouldn't do anyone any good." *Yes, those farms in the Negev can also be thought of as part of the larger strategy, a longer historical process—the most possible land with the fewest possible Arabs.*[22] *Those farms are part of a current government strategy to contain the Bedouin of the Negev. Tikva's children take hilltops and imitate earlier ways of life. What does it mean to return to the land, to care about the environment, to live simply and oppose the forces of Western materialism? What does it mean in the context of Israel/Palestine and the Zionist settler movement? What does it mean in the United States when survivalists return to nature or left-wing liberals promote recycling? Is there room for coalitions here?*

Ruth spoke about her vision, about those identified with the right wing learning to respect the human dignity and the rights of Palestinians from those identified as the left wing. She spoke about the left wing learning to appreciate the value of living on the Land of Israel from the right wing. But Rina stopped her and pointed out what she thought was a serious problem. She said that in the current reality Ruth's vision was impossible. "You say you want to show concern and behave differently toward the Palestinians. Yet, in the meantime, you live here like this with the fence between you and the soldiers guarding you. In this situation, you have not changed and cannot change the way in which you relate to the Palestinians. The very fact of your living here, and living here in this way, precludes such changes." But Ruth protested, and Rina compromised, saying that she realized she could not suggest removing the fence. "At this point, that would not be realistic. . . ." *Had she internalized the patronizing voice of the liberal left Amos encountered? Was this one more way of saying "we have no choice"?* "In any case," Rina continued, "as long you continue living here and living like this, you have not changed your relationship with Palestinians, you have not become more humanistic in your approach."

The Jerusalem Summit advertises a "neo-Zionist answer to post-Zionist appeasement." It is called a Humanitarian Regional Solution to the Israeli-Palestinian Conflict (www.jerusalemsummit.org). This is a political document that demonstrates precisely how the Right can learn from the Left. The so-called humanitarian solution suggests that "to successfully resolve the Palestinian problem, the Political Paradigm must be replaced by a Humanitarian Paradigm," which involves, among other steps, the "de-legitimization of a Palestinian narrative," along with generous relocation grants given to Palestinians living in Israeli-administered territories. In other words, a form of transferring Palestinians out of Palestine through financial incentives that might encourage them to move to other countries. Was this the humanitarianism that Ruth had in mind?

If this is what counted for humanitarian concern among religious settlers who moved beyond the powerful categories of difference, did it really represent something better than the well-known attitudes of settlers toward Palestinians? Was this a move toward increasing social justice and freedom? Or is this position somehow worse? Couched in humanitarian rhetoric, it seems like nothing more than a more palatable version of violent, forceful means of removing Palestinians. In any case, it seemed to raise a whole new set of troubling questions. Would the removal of Palestinians from the region through financial incentives be a form of humanitarianism or a form of nonviolent ethnic cleansing? Who has the right to answer such a question? What would the people of the Muassi think? How would the refugees in Khan Yunis respond? How far away is an idea like this from the possibility of a post-territorial future proposed by postmodern scholars?[23] Is this the place where the Left and Right meet?

Earlier in the day, there had been an outpouring of tears. One very young woman, Tuvit, suddenly began crying. She had been listening quietly to the discussion and then suddenly, out of what seemed to be frustration, she cried out, tears streaming down her face. Tuvit, in her late teens, did not live in Gush Katif. She had come from Jerusalem to express solidarity with the people of Gush Katif. Tuvit's words burst forth with emotion: "The people of Gush Katif are very good people. They live here on G-d's Land for all the right reasons. They are committed to fulfilling His will, and they live their lives according to the commandments, so why are they being removed? The people of Sheinkin (a bourgeois section of Tel Aviv) should be removed, if anyone!" This was very problematic for Rina, not because Tuvit thought the people of Gush Katif were more righteous than the people of Tel Aviv, Rina said, but because of the collective attitude Tuvit expressed. Rina was looking for individual concerns, and Tuvit's tears were for the nationalist religious collective. "That is problematic," Rina said, as she tried to shift the conversation to a more personal level. When she runs discussion groups, the focus is always returned to the individual. This is a place from which to begin talking to each other, according to Rina's methods and philosophy.

Rina thought of herself as a deeply spiritual person. It was in this way that she found connections with religious settlers. But her rather New Age style of spirituality called for a journey of personal fulfillment. On the one hand, this point of view moves away from what we often imagine as the left-wing, secular liberal in Israel. Moving *away from a core principle of rationality creates the potential for a kind of false compassion, which can result in a collapse of the fragile alliance between Left and Right, secular and religious. Seeking personal fulfillment does not amount to support-ing settlers and their program, even if one finds some spiritual connections. Personal spiritual development actually leaves politics aside altogether. Is this an improvement over other left-wing positions? What happens when we abandon politics? This sounds very much like the religious settler calls to stop and listen to the voice of God, a call that ultimately results in inaction that can work to maintain the status quo.*

Ruth was critical of Tuvit's opinion, too, but from a completely different perspective. Ruth said, "You cannot look to the other group and try to deter-mine what is wrong with them. This is useless. It is a way of justifying yourself and a way of preventing a closer inspection of your own way of life," she said, as Esther comforted Tuvit and wiped away her tears. Ruth said that each group has to look to itself for the answers. "Don't say 'we're perfect' and look for flaws in the other. Try to determine what is missing in your ways." *Ruth is wise, I thought to myself; be critical of the groups to which you belong, find what is missing in your ways. But this is so much harder than blaming the "pathological" Left/Right. Then again, it is harder still to recognize the ways in which we are similar to the "pathological" Left/Right against whom we would like to identify.*

Disturbing Categories

There were a number of deep believers in Gush Katif who recalled their earlier removal from Yamit in 1982. The Yeshiva in Neve Dekelim was an amazing architectural structure. Built in the shape of the six-pointed star symbolizing Judaism, it was an enormous, ostentatious protrusion on the landscape, which, in addition to educating young men, held a central symbolic position. It housed a glass mural depicting the fall of Yamit, an Israeli community removed from the Sinai Peninsula as part of a peace agreement between Israel and Egypt.[24] Some of the deep believers living in Neve Dekelim and elsewhere in the com-munities of Gush Katif had been the young radicals who took their families down to Sinai to oppose the Israeli withdrawal. The loudest voices opposing disengagement from the Gaza Strip said, "Never again," evoking Holocaust imagery and recalling the removal in 1982. There were quieter voices, too, look-ing for housing inside the Green Line, looking for ways to raise families in the best possible conditions. Among these, one could find Jews of different ethnic and class backgrounds, people with various levels of belief and disbelief, and a range of opinions on how to proceed. There were some families getting along well financially; others depended on contributions from their neighbors. There were other quiet voices, too, who said stop demonstrating and start listening to the voice of God.

This chapter began by illuminating some of the more unusual opposition to Israeli unilateral withdrawal from post-1967 occupied territories, troubling commonsense categories that are not always the most helpful ways of understanding conflict or the ways in which power works. The first constellation of identity/politics, emerging from the radical Left of Israeli politics, is perhaps easier for the predominantly secular academy to recognize. Indeed, we hear the radical secular Left in published scholarship, in a language with which we are familiar. Here I have suggested that we must continue to push the limits of our own thinking by trying to listen to other marginalized voices as well, like the "settler-left." I am not suggesting a greater sympathy for that position, nor is this intended as admonishment for lack of upholding the moral imperatives of universal humanism. It is quite simply to say that there is something to be learned by seeing and listening to those "others" we have grown accustomed to hating or, at the very least, disregarding. But there is a cautionary note here: Looking into the hidden spaces and facing those others reveals commonalities and differences both between and within various subject positions, but it does not necessarily provide answers, nor will it necessarily reveal something better than what we had when we remained stuck inside our hardened shells. Here, for example, we encountered the right-wing, religious settler who is perhaps not so very right-wing and expressed humanitarian concern for the plight of Palestinians. But those humanitarian concerns raise a whole new set of issues. Do these concerns represent a break, or are they a continuation of settler desires to remove Palestinians, this time with a carrot rather than a stick? Is this humanitarianism or ethnic cleansing made more palatable? Why are the settlers carrying out this conversation about Palestinians without a Palestinian interlocutor, when she is right there on the other side of the fence?

We also encountered a left-wing secular perspective, which was not quite so secular. Spirituality provided a sense of shared meaning among the women. Yet that commonality also carried the potential to be read as a false compassion for settlers and their project, which might lead to a collapse of the alliance in an even bigger explosion. This happened in other places where religious and secular Israeli Jews met to heal the rift among the people and support Israeli democracy, which seemed threatened after the assassination of Yitzchak Rabin and in the wake of the disengagement. Religious settlers believed they had new allies among the secular and Left, people who had come to understand their position and their plight. Yet, when the moment arrived, the left-wing and secular Israelis who met cordially with religious settlers, ultimately opposed the settler project and supported disengagement. This resulted in an anger even deeper than before.

Right-wing settlers who want to live with Palestinians and left-wing liberals who opposed the disengagement seem to have moved even further beyond the comfortable categories through which Israelis constitute their identities in opposition to each other. These positions require actions that directly engage with Palestinians and might lay the foundations for a very different way of living together. These, too, almost certainly, will contain problems, contradictions, and constraints.

Spinning the wheel at the end of the kaleidoscope also requires that we continuously consider what inconsistencies, contradictions, and irreducible alterities mean for future forms of social organization, ways of living together or apart.

The final chapter moves beyond the case of these antagonizing settlers to consider how this case may speak to other instances of the problematic interface of liberalism with religious ways of life.

9

Beyond Antagonizing Settlers

On Demonized Muslims and Vilified Jews

"'Thou shalt love thy neighbor as thyself.' Why should we do it? What good will it do us? But above all, how shall we achieve it? . . . Even more incomprehensible . . . is 'Love thine enemies.' . . . What is the point of a precept enunciated with so much solemnity if its fulfillment cannot be recommended as reasonable? . . . I think I can now hear a dignified voice admonishing me: 'it is precisely because your neighbor . . . is your enemy that you should love him as yourself.'"

—Sigmund Freud, *Civilization and Its Discontents*

This book has been concerned with the hegemonic categories through which the Israeli socio-religious-political scene is ordered. I have considered the mutual othering that takes place, the hierarchy of difference, and pointed to what is enabled through the appearance of a discourse of conflict and what is missed as a result of its centrality. I have suggested that the appearance of deep difference can enable the continuation of settler colonial practices while at the same time allowing people to maintain liberal values with a clear conscience, since someone other than the secular liberal subject can be blamed for the outcomes of those practices; someone else is doing worse than what we've done and left behind, we—living on Native American tribal land after centuries of genocide—who are opposed to such things. The division makes it possible to be in two places—one physical, one intellectual—at once, maintaining a split self without experiencing a split consciousness, because the unspeakable abhorrent other within the self has been projected outward onto the socially defined and visible Other. I have suggested that studying the categories through which we order humanity and through which politics takes place is crucial because the ways in which we order, divide, and categorize our sociopolitical world are not innocent. These categories do not simply arise, giving names to already existing essences in the world. There are no essences out in the world waiting to be named (Foucault 1972). Instead, groups, subgroups, and divisions between people are constructed through discursive practices. These divisions have very real outcomes, including the constitution of categories of identity, religion, and politics, delimiting the contours of action and debate in the present, as well as the boundaries within which we might imagine possible futures. The narratives that emerge through these divisions become familiar to us; they take the form of common knowledge upon which we base our judgments and take action in the world. The case of antagonizing settlers in Israel resonates powerfully with broader appearances of deep divisions between liberalism and religiosity, in particular with representations of a stark division between Islam and the West. This chapter considers the implications of this study beyond the Israeli context. It asks what kinds of questions and challenges this case poses for scholarly interventions into contemporary issues of religious/secular conflict and how those studies inform this case. Finally, it considers what kinds of approaches might be most useful in considering how we can live together with the experience of radical alterity.

Neighbors and Enemies, Politics and Religion, Muslims and Jews

The comparative literature on religious fundamentalism includes the case of religiously motivated Jewish settlers, among other religious groups.[1] But the scholarly work aimed at unsettling powerful binary distinctions between the secular liberal and particular forms of religiosity have focused primarily on the case of Muslims and the West, and ignored similar discursive distinctions between other secular and religious groups, such as the Israeli case considered in this book. The problematic interface of political liberalism with certain forms of religiosity has been of growing concern to scholars across disciplines. With emerging global power struggles, and in particular following the defining moment of September 11, a wave of scholarly analyses have addressed Islam and the West. Among these are scholars who see some form of "clash" of cultures or civilizations and others who reject the idea of such a clash. There are some who go to great pains to explain Muslim "others," while another group of scholars is determined to focus on responses to those Muslim others. Some argue that if there is an "us against them" situation, it results from our own actions in the West. And others still call for a more nuanced understanding of historical relationships and commonalities that make it quite impossible to understand current conflicts as a clash between certain kinds of religious ways of life and formations of the secular.

For those analysts in the last two categories (we created them, and we have a lot in common with them), studying the limits of liberal tolerance and the recognition of certain forms of religiosity has taken on a greater urgency with the case of Islam. A number of scholars have pointed to the contradictory ethics contained in liberal and secular humanism, which on the one hand abhors violence on the basis of difference and at the same time engages in violent practices to protect its way of life (Asad 2003, 2007; Brown 2006b; Butler 2008; Mahmood 2006; Povinelli 2001). Indeed, within current global political constellations, numerous scholars have come to the defense of Muslims as the religious group currently most targeted as enemies of the so-called West. But this raises questions about the broader applicability of theorizing that defends a particular religious group through a critique of modern liberalism and secularism. Can this kind of theorizing be applied beyond the case of today's targeted, vilified other? Would it clarify cases of discrimination against, containment of, or attempts at removing religious groups in other places or at other historical moments? Surely the question of the Jew comes to mind. Recall Hannah Arendt's concerns when reflecting on Jews in pre–World War II Europe that those who "heard the strange compliment that they were exceptions, exceptional Jews, knew quite well that it was this very ambiguity—that they were Jews and yet presumably not *like* Jews—which opened the doors of society to them" (1968 (1951):56). It was an ambiguous acceptance based in a double difference—difference from the gentiles who could accept Jewish others who had become in some ways similar to the gentiles and different from other Jews. Thus, as with many circumstances concerning contemporary Muslim individuals and communities, some religious others could be accepted through exception. They were accepted once changed in specific ways, making "them" more like a particular version of a modern, post-Enlightenment "us." Certainly, I would not be the first scholar to point to a commonality between Muslim and Jew or, even more specifically, to point to the conflation that results in a representation of Arab against Jew. Most recently, for example, Anidjar (2003) has suggested a relationship between Arab and Jew as different facets of "the enemy" of a Christian Europe.[2] Others have pointed to a need to investigate the ways in which Orientalism (Said 1978) has affected Jews as well as Arabs, in particular Arab Jews, or those Jews who lived in Arab countries (Raz-Krakotzkin

2005). However, my concern here is not with the broad category of Jews in modernity, nor with anti-Semitism or Orientalism as such, but more specifically with the form of Jewish religiosity often categorized as radical, extremist, fundamentalist, or violent.

This chapter explores both the usefulness and unease of applying such theorizing to the contemporary conflict between liberalism and religious extremism addressed in the book, a conflict that arguably exists within a particular project of modernity, which is usually represented as part of Western power—the modern political Zionist project in Palestine.[3] Moving away from what appears as a global showdown between Christianity and Islam, or the so-called West and certain forms of Islam, this book has focused on the case of religiously motivated Jewish settlers in the space of Israel/Palestine and the liberal and secular public, both in Israel and beyond, that is vehemently opposed to the post-1967 settlement project.[4]

Despite the political unease this case brings, in particular to left-wing and progressive activists and scholars, it is important to understand it as a case that is comparable to that of Islam and the West. It, too, is a case of powerful representations that conceal as much as they reveal. Like the appearance of a clash between Muslims and the West, the antagonism between Israeli settlers inscribes differences that forget the connections and continuities beneath the appearance of a deep divide. The Israeli case requires a comparable application of theory, or it stands to undermine the theoretical integrity of those scholarly interventions that question the limits of liberal tolerance for currently demonized Muslim others.[5] Those whose politics place them in opposition to Zionism—or in opposition to religiously motivated (or nonreligious nationalist) Zionist expansion in the occupied territories—may argue that this case is *not* comparable or perhaps that it in fact undermines the theorizing under consideration in this chapter. It is my contention that the case *is* comparable, and that means understanding interpretations of and interventions into the lives of religious settlers, which are similar to interpretations and interventions concerning Muslims, as equally problematic and contradictory to the ideals of tolerance and freedom, including freedom of religious expression. It, too, is a case that lays bare some of the contradictions that inhere between the theory and practice of liberal humanism. It is an uncomfortable case because it troubles politics in the guise of theory. Scholars today who express concern over the demonization of Muslims tend to align themselves in opposition to the Israeli occupation and are concerned with the rights of Palestinians, which means they are opposed to the beliefs and practices of religiously motivated Jewish settlers. Thus, expanding notions of freedom to included recognition of these religious others means making room for people whose beliefs and practices are deemed morally repugnant. It is, therefore, precisely the kind of problem that requires thinking beyond comfortable categories of politics.

The hegemonic discourse of conflict in Israel presents a parallel case to the apparent division between what is often depicted as the liberalism of the West in conflict with Muslim fundamentalism. The idea of a clash of values, beliefs, and practices results in vilification or marginalization of one group by the other. One group establishes its identity in contrast to the other, and in many ways each is construed as the constitutive outside of the other, marking group boundaries of identity, politics, and ethics. The differences between groups, however, are not equivalent. Religiously motivated settlers are the marked group within the broader Israeli context. They are the others to the unmarked hegemonic secular. Throughout my research, I have often found that liberal, secular, and left-wing Israeli Zionists are particularly determined to demonstrate that religiously motivated settlers and the settler project in post-1967 territories represent a break both from Judaism and from the socialist Zionism of the founders of the state. These two moves—not really Zionism, and not really Judaism—echo broader responses and analyses at the interface of liberalism and religiosity with regard to certain beliefs and practices among Muslims. We often hear denunciations of the acts of those referred to as Islamists, Jihadists, or radical Muslims, with the twin claims that this is not really Islam and that it is also starkly opposite to the tenets of Western political ideology, democracy, and liberal humanism.

Demonized Muslims, Vilified Jews

The case of these Jews, I argue, presents an uncomfortable position. It is a case that has yet to be approached in the same way as what seem to be similar cases of certain Muslim populations. This leads me to ask what is at stake in comparing liberalism's problematic interface with certain forms of religiosity to these *other* religious others? At bottom, according to Asad, it is our *recognition* of other people's very humanity that is at stake (Asad 2003). For Arendt, this meant recognition of religious and political differences, as she noted the danger of reducing the person to a "human being in general" (Arendt 2003 (1951):43). This, of course, has very serious outcomes for civil and human rights, both within multicultural or plural democracies and in the international community. More to the point, however, it seems that there is a move among scholars to carve out a moral position that both draws on liberal sensibilities and pushes at the limits of liberal tolerance.[6] I argue that the similarities between the case of so-called radical Muslims and the case of so-called radical

Jewish settlers require both a reconsideration of this scholarship and a reconsideration of the case of Jewish settlers.

I have chosen to engage with the work of three scholars, each of whom addresses reactions to Muslims or interventions in their lives (rather than trying to explain Muslim ways of life) in the United States and Europe, and each of whom is critical of the treatment of and reactions to Muslim groups that are traced to inconsistencies in liberal thought and practice. I begin with Saba Mahmood, who recently argued against U.S. involvement in trying to alter the theology and practices of Muslims in the Middle East. Next, I consider a recent article by Judith Butler that addresses Muslims in the Netherlands, the problems of citizenship, and the right to religious freedom. Finally, I turn to Talal Asad, who speaks to issues of violence, arguing that suicide bombing practiced by radical Muslims is really not all that different from state violence perpetrated by the United States and Israel. Each of these arguments contains critiques of secular liberalism, or liberal humanism and democracy, and the contradictory ethics and inconsistencies contained within liberal thought and practice. My purpose here is to begin to explore the possibilities of applying the analyses of these scholars to the case of conflict between left-wing, secular, and liberal Israeli Jews in opposition to religiously motivated settlers in Israeli-occupied territories. The questions raised through this uncomfortable comparison, I hope, will contribute to broader conversations on the challenges and complexities of living together with differences that may be threatening if not altogether incommensurable.[7] I begin with Saba Mahmood's critique of U.S. interventions in the lives of Muslims in the Middle East.

Secularism and Subjectivity

In a recent article "Secularism, Hermeneutics, and Empire: The Politics of Islamic Reformation," Mahmood (2006) interrogates the way in which "secularism" works today. It is not so much a matter of separating religion from the public sphere, she argues, but has to do with attempts to intervene in the lives of certain religious people. According to Mahmood, a problematic conception of secularism underlies the idea that Islam needs to be reformed and has resulted in attempts to alter the theology and practice of Islam to produce "the kind of religious subject who is compatible with the rationality and exercise of liberal political rule" (Mahmood 2006:344). Her case study details the ways in which the U.S. State Department and the Rand Corporation have been engaged in a "theological campaign aimed at shaping the sensibilities of ordinary Muslims whom the State Department deems to be too dangerously inclined toward fundamentalist interpretations of Islam" (2006:329). It aims at transforming Islam from within by aligning with those Muslims deemed moderate, tolerant, and prone to democratic values, while trying to transform those Muslims labeled "traditionalists" (332). Mahmood's objections to State Department practices of intervention come at two levels, that of practical outcomes and that of intellectual consistency. First, she argues these interventions are mistaken because they do not actually target those Muslims who tend toward violence (333). Thus, we should refrain from intervening in the lives of Muslims because, in any case, we get it wrong.

The second level of objection follows from a critique of the contradictions within a particular liberal conception of secularism that is rooted in religious tolerance. The separation of church and state (in its U.S. formulation) is meant to provide a political solution that maintains the right to practice religion freely. However, according to Mahmood, the tension between establishing and maintaining a boundary between religion and state while at the same time defending the right to practice religion freely is a problematic inconsistency within liberal doctrine. Thus, she argues, promoting liberal political rule actually contradicts liberal moral standards of tolerance for religious differences because the political doctrine of secularism does not really work by separating religion from the public sphere. Instead, it works to determine the kind of subjectivity that a secular culture authorizes by defining the exception. Mahmood draws on Talal Asad's argument that even though secularism presupposes the mutual independence of political power and religious life, the state actually has the power to make decisions that affect religious practices and doctrines, while the reverse is not true. The state retains the exclusive authority to define the exception. Asad writes that secularists miss how certain discourses become part of the powerful practices that cultivate sensibilities essential to a kind of contradictory, or impossible, individual. This is one who is morally sovereign but at the same time is obedient to the laws of a secular republic (Asad 2006b). Secularism, Mahmood argues, determines what counts as truly spiritual and how faith should be practiced.[8] It is not really about tolerating difference and diversity, but rather it is about remaking religious subjectivities who will be compliant with liberal political rule (Mahmood 2006:328). What Mahmood categorizes as secularism might be more accurately described as a kind of hegemonic Protestantism.[9] However, my goal here is not a critique of the accuracy of specific terms, but rather to consider the possibility of applying Mahmood's theorizing to the Israeli case.

What would happen if we applied a similar line of thought to religiously motivated settlers in Israeli-occupied territories? On the one hand, Mahmood's argument for what she calls the "force of secularism" to produce the kinds of subjects who are more compatible with liberal rule and state projects seems to apply to this case. When the Israeli government decided to implement a unilateral withdrawal from the Gaza Strip, including the forcible removal of about 9,000 Israelis from their homes in the settlements there, many of the settlers who were removed had a sense that this was precisely a matter of the state trying to send them a message, to rein them in and weaken their project by moving them and breaking up their communities and by making sure they understood they must respect state decisions, even when those decisions contradicted their religious beliefs. If Mahmood's argument can be applied, the implication might be that we (the state of Israel and, by extension, U.S. foreign policy) should *not* interfere with the lives of these settlers. We should not intervene in ways that undermine their belief system, first because we have a tendency to get it wrong when we do. Certainly, this would be clearly aligned with what many settlers and their supporters have argued. Interfering with settler beliefs and removing them from their homes was the wrong thing to do, they argue, often offering the rise of Hamas in the Gaza Strip and the ensuing violence in southern Israel and the Gaza Strip as evidence of this mistaken action. And second, according to Mahmood, such intervention contradicts the values of liberal humanism and democracy, as such interventions attempt to create certain kinds of subjects who are compatible with liberal rule. On the other hand, one might argue that it is theoretically problematic to apply these conclusions to the Israeli case, either because the issues of religion and state take a different form in Israel or because this is not a case of foreign intervention; instead, it takes places within a particular polity.[10] (And after all, aren't all states involved in producing their subjects either through force or other disciplining processes?) In that sense, the Israeli case may be closer to the case of Muslims in Europe and issues of citizenship rights and religious freedom.

Citizenship, Sexual Orientation, and Religious Freedom

Judith Butler recently wrote an article interrogating a hierarchy of difference through the case of Muslim migrants to the Netherlands (Butler 2008). For Butler, what is at stake in cases of citizenship for Muslims in Europe is a matter of competing freedoms that are differentially valued within a modernist linear temporality. Citing the procedures that Muslims must undergo to become Dutch citizens, Butler is concerned that to maintain a certain kind of society with particular freedoms for some citizens, the rights of Muslim immigrants would be denied. In the case of the Netherlands, according to Butler, Muslims applying for citizenship were asked (among other things) to respond to an image of two (homosexual) men kissing. They are asked if they find this kind of behavior offensive to their religious sensibilities. The implication is that this might be a way of discouraging or controlling immigration. Butler is concerned that the freedom of sexual preference and expression not be used to deny freedom of religion and citizenship rights. Most broadly, this is a maxim underlying an American sense of what freedom should mean. It is the idea that the freedoms of all citizens should be protected to the extent that one's freedom does not interfere with someone else's. However, Butler says hegemonic conceptions of progress interfere with such freedoms by distinguishing between what or who is modern, and who has not yet arrived in modernity. Her work is addressed to progressive politics, which she says can rely on a concept of freedom that is understood to emerge through time, and often secularism is associated with this progression toward freedom through time. The result for the case she is considering is that acceptance of homosexuality comes to be positively associated with embracing modernity, and the freedom of gay people can be a marker exemplifying a culturally advanced position. Through a critique of this concept of secular time, Butler calls for a multifaceted modernity that allows for multiple freedoms; a modernity in which sexual freedoms would not depend on the foreclosure of rights of religious expression (2008:6).[11] If Butler's concerns can be applied to the case of religiously motivated settlers, what would its implications be?

The maxim that requires the most possible freedom for individuals and groups as long as those liberties do not interfere with the liberties of others is clearly applied in Israel when the secular feel their rights limited by religious impositions like closing places of business or public transportation on the Sabbath. But following Butler's critique, we might argue that secular freedoms should likewise not interfere with religious freedoms. So, what happens in Israel when secular freedoms interfere with the religious? What happens when working or playing music interferes with the right to observe the Sabbath? And far more profoundly, what happens when secular decisions about trading land for peace interfere with what some religious Jews construe as not only their right but also their obligation to hasten the coming of the Messiah by living according to their interpretation of sacred texts? Clearly, the expectation of not interfering with the lives of others, or accepting those others without attempting to contain or change their way of life, is not reciprocal.

Butler's argument for free religious expression and the rights of citizenship for Muslims in Europe is more concerned about protecting the rights of minorities or subaltern groups, those relatively lacking in power who have been discriminated against or subject to coercion. Again, one might argue that inside Israel, religiously motivated settlers are a relatively small minority. They are not accepted by the more mainstream in Israel and have been derided as problematic members of a democratic society because their religious beliefs are seen as unreasonable, irrational, and dangerous. In short, in terms of Butler's argument about secular time, these religiously motivated settlers fall outside the progressive modern. At the same time, however, to the extent that it has coincided with state interests, the settler project in Israeli-occupied territories has been supported by state funding for decades, despite the instances of withdrawal and dismantling of communities (Zertal and Eldar 2007). This seems to indicate that religious ways of life are not in and of themselves considered problematic but can be co-opted or interfered with, depending on state interests at any given moment. Indeed, the beliefs of secular citizens can and have been similarly co-opted. This brings us back to Mahmood's discussion of subjectivity and the ways that states or suprastates are involved in disciplining processes to create certain kinds of subjects.

Based on Butler's arguments about competing freedoms and the importance of carefully assessing political situations and protecting rights, to what extent should we feel compelled to protect the rights of religiously motivated settlers to practice their beliefs about living on the Land of Israel? That right clearly interferes with the freedoms of others. Many secular and left-wing Israelis who are opposed to Israeli occupation of post-1967 territories are especially concerned when it comes to having to participate in the military defense of those settlers and to the state spending for building and protecting settlements. All this, of course, is a debate that takes place on the backs of the Palestinians, so to speak, as it is their rights to land, sovereignty, and freedom, including the right to freedom of religious beliefs and practices, that is at stake.

Comparable Violence

Finally, I turn to Talal Asad and his most recent book, *On Suicide Bombing* (2007). Asad focuses on the kind of critique that requires reflection on the collective self either prior to or instead of criticism of those categorized as dangerously different. Unlike those scholars who support the "clash of civilizations" thesis, Asad opposes the idea of absolute differences (between "us" and our "enemies"). And instead of looking at, for example, Islamic fundamentalists (or Islamists) as the dangerous others to be explained, he suggests looking at the ways "we"—in the United States, the liberal West, or secular humanists—are like "them." That is, we should reflect deeply on the ways in which our collective behavior is and has been both inseparable from and comparable to the behavior of those enemy others (like radical Islamists, including suicide bombers). For example, considering modern uses of violence, Asad writes of suicide bombing that "the creation of terror and perpetration of atrocities are aspects of militant action in the unequal world we inhabit" (2007:3). It is a mistake to view that world as made up of distinct and self-contained civilizations that have remained unchanged through time. At least in part, the logical conclusion of this line of thought is that if we find the violent practices of others (like suicide bombers) abhorrent and morally reprehensible, we would do well to remember that our histories are intertwined and that we are at least partially responsible for the unequal world in which live and therefore at least partially responsible for creating the conditions in which such violence has arisen. In addition, there are many ways in which we have carried out violent acts on far larger scales, causing much more damage, including deaths of civilians, which we call collateral damage. We express remorse, marking ourselves as different while continuing to engage in these violent practices. For Asad, then, before condemning Islamic fundamentalists, terrorists, and suicide bombers, we should recognize the ways in which we participate in practices that we abhor when carried out by others, and we should recognize the need for change within our own ways of life. The question here is, can we extend Asad's arguments? Before condemning Muslims involved in suicide bombings *and* before condemning religiously motivated Jewish settlers, should we recognize our own practices that bear distinct similarities to those we condemn? Should we also always recognize the broader context in which these practices arise and consider our participation in creating these situations?

Religiously motivated settlers in Israeli-occupied territories are often condemned by their opposition for the violence of their settlement project. This includes both the structural violence of territorial expansion and the face-to-face violence between settlers and Palestinians. Applying Asad's analytical framework to religiously motivated settlers means that those who oppose these settlers should look for the ways in which they (we) have been complicit in creating the conditions in which the violence of settlement takes place, as well as their (our) own complicity in similar forms of violence. At first glance, this means noting the support post-1967 settlements have received since their inception by Israeli administrations led by both the left-wing and the right-wing. Beyond this, continuity can be found in recognizing post-1967 settlement as an extension of the Zionist project itself, which is at base a settler project in Palestine.[12] Some would argue that considering the context of this project means looking back to the anti-Semitism in Europe in the nineteenth century, against which the modern political project of Zionism emerged. Others contend that the modern discourse of anti-Semitism in nineteenth-century Europe and political discourses of nation-states and Zionism are related in more than the usual causal fashion traditional histories would suggest (Halevi 1987:155–157).[13] That is, rather than thinking of Zionism only as a reaction to anti-Semitism, it has been argued that these ideologies share a common set of conditions that allowed them to emerge. The racist theories of the nineteenth century that classified the Jews as a race (genealogically tied together as a people rather than a group who could chose affiliation with a religious institution) and the conditions that created the need and the right of citizens to rule themselves underlie the combination of nationalism and democracy in which self-rule is a right granted to a people, in this case, the Jewish people. These are the same conditions in which this people (the Jews as a nation) is constructed against another people (the Palestinians as a nation) vying for sovereignty of the same territory. Following Asad, then, we can find historical connections and commonalities at many levels. But what are the implications of this kind of analysis for the case of religiously motivated settlers and their opposition in the present? If we find historical connections and continuities between the Left and Right, secular and religious practices of Zionism, and we find one set of practices morally problematic, does that result in undermining the moral legitimacy of the entire Zionist project? It is largely this fear—that the moral legitimacy of the entire project will be undermined—that propels the vilification of religiously motivated settlers. While this might provide an explanation for the intense virulence expressed toward religiously motivated, right-wing settlers by members of the secular and liberal Zionist Left, the problem of living together with significant differences remains.

The Work of Vilification

The antagonism between the groups of variously situated Israeli Jews in my study reinscribes existing categories that constitute the parameters of discourse and practice in ways that parallel the broader appearance of a clash of cultures between the West and Islam that Mahmood, Butler, Asad, and numerous other scholars have written against. There is a certain work accomplished through the appearance of a discourse of conflict, again very much like the work accomplished through the appearance of a clash of cultures between Islam and the West. For the case of Israel, that work is (at least) twofold. First, through establishing the hegemonic categories of identity and political positions, the discourse of conflict sets the limits of debate and marginalizes different ways of being Israeli and alternative possibilities for enacting the present or imagining a future. Second, the discourse of conflict conceals continuities and commonalities among Israelis who participate in the settler project in Palestine.

For example, preceding the disengagement, unilateral withdrawal from the Gaza Strip was most vocally opposed in Israel by the far Right and religiously motivated settlers. But as we have seen, there was other opposition as well. A number of people took an anti-occupation/anti-disengagement position, which was an extremely difficult position to articulate within the space of Israel/Palestine because of the powerful understandings of identity and politics established though the discourse of conflict. For those opposing Israeli expansion, opposition to the withdrawal could easily be read as supporting the ongoing military occupation of post-1967 territories. Opposition to withdrawal, then, would mean supporting religiously motivated settlers, which was not what members of this opposition intended. Instead, those voicing this opposition found a breach of moral responsibility in carrying out the withdrawal in the absence of negotiations with a Palestinian partner. It was argued that Israel's disengagement would not liberate Palestinians but create the conditions of a large prison. Among the Israelis expressing this opinion were those who did not want to be the wardens of that prison and saw such a situation as detrimental to Israelis and Palestinians alike. In addition, some argued that leaving the Gaza Strip in the way it was being proposed would set up the conditions for another Israeli invasion, a prediction that has since proved true. Some people who expressed both anti-occupation and anti-withdrawal positions also problematized the force of Israeli militarism that was being imposed on the residents of the Gaza settlements. Some argued that forcibly removing people from their homes is wrong, whether those people are Palestinians or Israeli settlers. This constellation of identity/politics emerging primarily but not exclusively from the radical Left of Israeli politics is perhaps relatively easy for the predominantly secular academy to recognize. However, there were other marginalized positions that emerged from within the religiously motivated settler community.

In the communities of Gush Katif, as we have seen, during the months preceding disengagement, there were a great number of people reflecting deeply on the impending crisis. Among the religiously motivated settlers in Gush Katif were those who saw the impending disengagement as one very important sign among the many signs from God that require interpretation. Among the interpretations offered was the idea that "we"—in this case, the settlers themselves, or sometimes the people of Israel (Am Yisrael)—should reflect on their (our) lives and wonder why God would allow this to happen. Some settlers suggested reevaluating their own practices and offered a range of possible interpretations. While some suggested that perhaps they had not been leading pious enough lives, others thought they had not reached out sufficiently to the secular community. Some questioned the motives for living in

Gush Katif. Was it was really a matter of devotion to serving the Lord, or had people come for the beautiful seaside landscape? Others were concerned that they had put too much emphasis on settling the Land of Israel and not enough on fulfilling other commandments. And still others thought the disengagement was a sign from God that called for humility and prayer rather than continued protest or political actions, because expressing certainty for human actions is tantamount to the sin of pride.[14] But perhaps most surprising were those who thought God was sending a message about how they and all of the People of Israel should be living together with Palestinians on this sacred land. This included some who considered the possibility of remaining on the coveted land by reaching an agreement with the Palestinian Authority, and those who sought commonality between their beliefs in the Sovereignty of God and the beliefs of pious Muslim Palestinians. These are among the ways of being and believing that are pushed to the margins through a hegemonic discourse of conflict between Left and Right, secular and religious, and those opposed versus those in favor of Israeli settlement in post-1967 occupied territories. The parallel between this case and that of Muslims and the West suggests seeking ways of being and believing that move beyond the appearance of deep divisions. It suggests that we pay more attention to the variations and nuances among religious Muslims—even those considered most radical[15]—and within the secular, liberal West.

The appearance of this conflict between Israelis establishes and reinforces the categories of identity and political positions that set the limits of debate and of ways of being in the present and imagining a future. The same is certainly true for broader conflicts between the liberal West and its constitutive outside—other ways of being and believing that do not fit easily into taken-for-granted categories that are silenced through the vilification of a particular group.

In Israel, the appearance of incommensurable discourses in conflict conceals continuities and commonalities among Israelis who take part in the settler project in Palestine. The discourse of conflict enables settler practices to continue throughout Israel and the occupied territories while maintaining a sense of moral legitimacy for the Zionist project as a whole through denouncing and delegitimizing religious settlers. The appearance of incommensurable discourses in conflict between the West and the rest similarly participates in constructing a moral high ground for Western interventions and violence. I have argued that the intense antagonism between these variously situated groups of Zionist Israelis is located less in their deep differences than in a *desire* to differentiate, which is particularly pronounced among the secular and Left. To paraphrase Mahmood, the conflict between the secular Left and religious Right in Israel and the vilification of religiously motivated settlers work to authorize certain kinds of subjectivities (as good citizens or true Zionists) through marking the exceptions (as radical, irrational extremists). Is the supposed clash between the liberal West and radical Islam also located in a desire to differentiate? Certainly Asad's arguments that Western violence is often far more damaging than that perpetrated by the Muslim extremists we abhor would support such a claim.

The appearance of conflict among Israelis further conceals the historical relationship between racism, anti-Semitism, and nationalism, reinscribing the categories of Arab and Jew as binary opposites. The discourse of a clash of cultures forgets the work of Orientalism and the history of European imperialism. Numerous scholars (and activists) have engaged in deconstructing the powerful categories that emerge through these discourses in order to undermine limitations on the possibility of new coalitions and alliances against various forms of oppression.

While I am suggesting that it is analytically productive to interrogate these hegemonic categories of conflict to understand the work accomplished through them, I must also maintain that it is crucial to recognize the beliefs, practices, and ways of life through which people identify themselves. To discard as meaningless that which gives meaning to so many lives seems impractical if not impossible, but more importantly, it is a form of violence that contradicts its very rationale. Maintaining this tension requires a consideration both of the politics of powerful binary divisions and the political implications of undermining those divisions.[16] This means analyzing the work of these categories of difference, but also respecting the meanings they have in people's lives. It returns to Arendt's refusal to reduce people to "human beings in general" and poses challenges to the prospects of living together with the experience of radical differences. In the case of vilified Jews, this means recognizing commonalities and continuities between "us" and "them" and the complexities that are concealed through the appearance of binary oppositions, yet also recognizing the kinds of differences that are meaningful to the populations under consideration—meaningful differences like, for example, the belief among religiously motivated settlers that the Jewish People have not only the right but also the responsibility to live on the Land of Israel as promised and commanded by God, a belief that directly conflicts with secular and liberal understandings of Zionism, which often coincide with Palestinian ideas about their rights to sovereignty. This means recognizing those often considered morally repugnant, vilified Jews and contemplating what it might mean to allow a place for their beliefs and practices in the contentious space of Israel/Palestine.[17]

Somehow, the imperative to recognize in the fullest sense of the word—that is, to accept as different without interference, or to re-cognize, allowing the self to think again and be changed[18]—certain religious others seems far more palatable when those others can be counted among the subaltern, or demonized others who are relatively lacking in the powers associated with the (secular) projects of contemporary liberalism. This leads to a certain discomfort that seems to be located in politics but might not be altogether disconnected from a theoretical uneasiness. On the one hand, if it is a theoretical mistake to extend the analysis of the problematic relationship between liberalism and certain forms of religiosity—as in the cases cited here—to the division between religiously motivated Israeli settlers and their liberal opposition, the reasoning behind the very analyses may come into question. If, on the other hand, this theorizing can be applied, we are left to ponder the implications of a moral imperative to recognize not only currently demonized Muslims but also the implications of recognizing the humanity, as it were, of currently vilified Jewish settlers.

Asad's work suggests that "we" begin by reflecting on ourselves, considering our historical relationship to the projects we denounce and the ways in which we have behaved similarly, but without offering any simple solution or clear path of action. Such reflection, I would like to point out, is not specific to scholarly thought. Indeed, such reflection was echoed among religiously motivated settlers of the Gaza Strip. Asad wrote *On Suicide Bombing* as he reflected on the events of September 11 from the standpoint of a resident of New York City. A crisis had occurred, causing him to consider what had happened and the reactions to what had happened and to think about what might be learned by reflecting on the collective self rather than on trying to explain the suicide attackers as completely separate and totally different cultural others. In the settlements of Gush Katif, during the months preceding disengagement, there were similar reflections on the impending crisis. Religiously motivated settlers in Gush Katif saw the impending disengagement as one among many signs from God that required interpretation, including a call for reflection on the lives of settlers and a consideration of why God would allow the disengagement to happen. We should look for what is lacking in ourselves rather than looking for enemies to blame, not because we must love our enemies as ourselves, but because that enemy is perhaps ourselves. We participate in reinscribing conflict and binary distinctions as we constitute our moral selves in opposition to others, setting the limits of ways of being and believing and living together. We fall back on well-known narratives that have become common knowledge to simplify our fast-paced and complicated lives, making judgments and taking actions based on these problematic ways of ordering the social world. Destabilizing binary distinctions and defamiliarizing categories of identity, religion, and politics do not provide a cure for injustices or a solution to violence in the world. Like the reinscription of categories of humanity, digging beneath those discourses is also a work in progress, as new categories and constraints replace the old, requiring renewed efforts to see past powerful representations and open up room for alternative ways of being, believing, and acting. For religious Jews (including settlers), this may take the form of *Tikkun Olam*, to heal and repair the world, an ongoing process requiring interpretation and reinterpretation to gather divine light and create a dwelling place for God in this world and prepare for redemption. For the skeptical liberals seeking increased social justice, freedom, and peace, it may be as Gramsci would have it, an ongoing process that requires "pessimism of the intellect and optimism of the will."

Notes

CHAPTER I

1. Such sentiments were expressed by Leah Rabin following the assassination of her husband. See Juergensmeyer (2000b:47).
2. I have chosen the word *story* rather than *history* to signal complexities and variations in national narratives. *History* has come to stand for that "intellectual, secular telling of the past" (Nora 1989:9), which is also included in the story I have in mind.
3. While the use of the term *fundamentalism* has been widely debated and often deemed inappropriate when applied to Jewish religious groups, the term has become commonplace both in academic writing and in everyday use inside Israel. For example, see Gideon Aran's work in Marty and Appleby's fundamentalisms project (Aran 1991). I use it here following the common usage to refer to ideologically or religiously motivated Jewish settlers in the Israeli-occupied West Bank and Gaza Strip, as well as their supporters.
4. Nagata (2001) suggests an anthropological approach to fundamentalism that would seek common elements in diverse categories, including extreme forms of nationalism, socio-religious movements, especially Islamist, and "other forms of extremist ideological expression." This is very similar to Lustick's (1988) use of the term, which includes the non-religious right wing in Israel.
5. "Land of Israel" is capitalized to distinguish it as a concept different from the modern state of Israel. The idea of the biblical Land of Israel has been variously interpreted; its meanings and geographical borders are subject to dispute.

6. Inside Israel, these contexts might be described as mainstream Israeli culture, bearing in mind the problematics of such a term. Of the popular television comedies that aired on Israel's Channel Two, prior to the disengagement, one satire that sometimes made fun of religious peopled and settlers, *Fixed Game*, appeared on Friday nights at 10:00 P.M., during the Sabbath, when religious Jews would not turn on their televisions. A number of religious settlers refrain from watching television more generally.

7. An editorial in the *New York Times* on November 5, 2008, read: "Israel is becoming a nation at war with itself. The conflict is not just with militant Palestinians. Militant Jewish settlers in the West Bank regularly clash with Israeli police . . . security officials have warned of possible assassination attempts on peace-seeking Israeli leaders."

8. The positioning of right-wing settlers as dangerous or impeding peace has been central to left-wing depictions since settlement in the occupied territories began. But the mainstream political initiative to remove some settlers may be read as a kind of betrayal, since this population previously enjoyed a privileged status of having been mobilized as an extension of Zionist discourse and practices. The changing representations of settlement activity blur distinctions between Left and Right.

9. The People of Israel, or *Am Israel*, refers to the Jewish people rather than the citizens of Israel. It therefore includes all Jews.

10. This position is explained in greater detail (in Hebrew) from the point of view of religiously motivated settlers on the Torah and the Land Institute Web site www.toraland.org.il. Prior to the disengagement, the institute had been located in the Gaza settlement of Kfar Darom and was part of the visitor's center. Similar viewpoints can also be found in English on Arutz Sheva at www.israelnationalnews.com. Arutz Sheva means Channel Seven and was once a pirate radio station that was outlawed in Israel. It continues to broadcast in a number of languages on the Internet.

11. Yesh Gvul was established in 1982 after the Lebanon War, in 1988 Women in Black was established in opposition to the occupation and all violence, Gush Shalom was established in 1993, and others have been established since then. Peace Now, the largest left-wing peace movement in Israel, was founded in 1978 and about a decade later adopted the position that a Palestinian State should be established in the territory occupied by Israel in the 1967 war.

12. While Tamara Neuman (2004:53) writes that in the context of settlement (post-1967), maternalism "serves to create sympathies that extend beyond the people who directly participate in religious Right activities," in this case, there was no such extension of sympathies.

13. These ideas can be traced to the teachings of Rabbi A. I. Kook. See, for example, Bokser (1978).

14. While popular reaction tended toward expressions of shock, this was not the first instance of political violence between Jews. An earlier incident of such political violence occurred in 1983, when Emil Grunzweig was killed during a Peace Now demonstration by a right-wing activist, Yona Avrushmi, who threw a grenade into the crowd. And even before the establishment of the state, a Zionist activist who turned anti-Zionist, Yaacov De Haan, was reportedly killed for his anti-Zionist activity (Rabkin 2006).

15. I am referring here only to the Zionist Left. There are also non-Zionists and anti-Zionists who may or may not be part of the Left. It includes what Shafir and Peled call the Labor Settlement Movement (2002).

16. The notion of "religious" in the Israeli context does not mean affiliation as it might in other locations. Instead, it usually refers to observance and tends to be associated with more Orthodox forms of observance that include keeping the Sabbath and the dietary laws of *kashrut* (keeping Kosher). Jewishness in Israel is, of course, the unmarked category parallel to whiteness in the United States, for example.

17. The term *modern Orthodox* has been employed by Fischer to reveal the specifically modern character of those Jewish nationalists often called fundamentalists (Goodman and Fischer 2004). However, the modern Orthodox also include non-Zionist Jews and left-wing liberal Jewish Zionists.

18. On how the secular and religious have been mutually dependent in the Zionist project, see Raz-Krakotzkin (1994).

19. There are Orthodox Jews inside Israel and around the world who reject the modern political state of Israel because the state was created through worldly politics. It is their belief that Jewish rule in Israel can/should only occur with the coming of the Messiah and that worldly interference is blasphemy. In addition to Rabkin (2006), see Boyarin and Boyarin (1993).

20. Examples of this work include Deeb (2006), Hirschkind and Mahmood (2002), and Mahmood (2005).

21. Foucault, for the most part, did not direct his attention to politics except in later works.

22. On the front page of the daily English-language newspaper, the *Jerusalem Post*, on November 10, 1995, staff writers reported that Amir's mother had disowned him.

23. Ammiel Alcalay writes of the long historical process of transformation in Jewish history: "the gradual exchange of the legal, communal and cultural basis of Jewish existence for the racial the ethnic and the national . . . [which] assumed a final physical form in the Levant" (1993:221). This is the formation that underlies these discourses by providing the surfaces on which they emerge as incommensurable, a formation that is deeply related to that which it rallied against, anti-Semitism in Europe. The modern discourse of anti-Semitism in nineteenth-century Europe and political discourses of nation-states and Zionism are related in more than the usual causal fashion traditional histories would suggest (Halevi 1987:155–157). That is, rather than think of Zionism only as a reaction to anti-Semitism, we find that these ideologies share a common set of conditions that allowed them to emerge. The racist theories of the nineteenth century that classified Jews as a race (genealogically tied together as a people rather than a group who could chose affiliation with a religious institution) and the conditions that created the need and the "right" of citizens to rule themselves underlie the combination of nationalism and democracy in which self-rule is a right granted to a people, in this case, the Jewish people—and against which this people is constructed against another people vying for the sovereignty of the same territory. This issue is taken up again in Chapter 9.

24. Ella Shohat, perhaps the first to deconstruct this binary, provided a sustained analysis through her work on Jews from Arab countries, *Mizrahim* (1988, 2003). Ammiel Alcalay later contributed to this effort through his work on literature and culture that describes a time preceding the dichotomous split between Jew and Arab in the Levant (1993). Smadar Lavie employed her own positioning as a Mizrahi Jew in Israel and as an occupier opposed to occupation to further undermine this distinction (1990, 1992). Yehouda Shenhav has been strategically employing the term "Arab Jew," which undermines the distinction between Arab and Jew on which Jewish nationalism (modern political Zionism) depends (2003a). Gil Anidjar writes a history of the relationship of Arab and Jew as enemy to a Christian European (2003). Amnon Raz-Krakotzkin advocates writing a Mizrahi history that challenges Zionism and offers the potential for a binational perspective combining Jew and Arab to redefine Palestine (Raz-Krakotzkin 2005).

25. For a useful literature review (in Hebrew), see Goodman and Fischer (2004).

26. Examples include the work of Aran (1991, 1997), Lustick (1988), and Sivan (1995). For a more complete analysis of representations of settlers, see Dalsheim and Harel (2009).

27. The popular study of Israeli settlers by Zertal and Eldar (2007) documents how right-wing and religious settlers have been winning in this struggle between the Left and the Right and how their settlement project has dramatically changed Israeli society, once again reinscribing the discourse of conflict. This participates in a fetishism of the Green Line, a point I take up later.

28. Gershon Shafir was probably the first Israeli sociologist to use this analytical framework, building on and refining the work of Maxime Rodinson (1973). For a systematic typology of colonies and Shafir's argument of how Zionism fits into that typology as a "pure settlement" colony see Shafir (1989a:8–10). More recently, see Shafir and Peled (2002). Sociologist Baruch Kimmerling (1995) used the term *immigrant-settler* rather than *settler-colonial* to describe Israeli society. Comparative studies of settler-colonial societies are still few, but an article by Johnston and Lawson (2000) in a study guide for students of colonial studies might be counted as establishing this as a subcategory for postcolonial theory. On Israel and South Africa in comparative perspective, see Greenstein (1995). A broader comparative volume is Stasiulis and Yuval-Davis (1995). I have found it most useful to compare the Israeli settler imagination with that of Australia (Dalsheim 2004).

29. This argument is laid out in historical detail in Masalha (2000). Zertal and Eldar also show how Israeli governments led by both the Labor and Likud parties—by the Left and the Right—have participated in developing the settlement in Israeli-occupied territories (Zertal and Eldar 2007). In addition to Eldar, an Israeli journalist, other journalists continue to comment on the participation of left-wing Zionism and the kibbutz movement in settling territories gained in the 1967 war. Most recently, with talk about the possibility of territorial compromise with Syria, the issue of left-wing Jewish settlement in the Golan Heights has been discussed (Gorenberg 2008).

30. On the colonization perspective and its place in the history of Israeli sociology, see Ram (1995a). Probably the first analysis of Israel as a settler-colonial society was the work of Maxime Rodinson (1973).
31. See Yiftachel on the idea of frontier and internal frontier (1998, 2006).
32. For a concise historical overview of Gush Emunim in English, see Lustick (1988).
33. Some argue that Gaza was never the home of ancient Israelites. See chapter 3.
34. For more information, visit the YESHA English-language Web site at www. yesha-israel.com/index/home/.
35. See Aran (1997) and Fisher (2004) for differing conceptualizations.

CHAPTER 2

1. A great deal has been written on the relationship between memory, history, and identity. For useful theoretical discussions on this relationship, see Brow (1990), Gillis (1994), and Lowenthal (1985). This chapter deals with representations of the past on school trips. On the uses of collective memory and history in schools, see Wertsch (2001).
2. See Amos Ron (2001), in addition to my own data.
3. For a recent anthropological analysis, see Simon Harrison's argument that aspirations to distinctiveness are key to understanding the dynamics of ethnic opposition (2002).
4. Lewis Coser, in his introduction to Halbwachs's work on collective memory, shares a personal note on this point. He recounts the experience of having immigrated to the United States and making friends or contacts but always feeling there was something lacking. He came to the realization that not sharing enough collective memories blocked the possibility of a fuller communication with his newly acquired friends (Halbwachs and Coser 1992:21).
5. In Israel, it is common to use first names, expressing a kind of informality that is part of the culture of establishing a new way of being Jewish, different from life in the Diaspora. In many schools, for example, teachers and administrators are called by their first names.
6. Tali Hatual and her four daughters were killed by Palestinian gunmen on the road from Gush Katif to the Kissufim crossing on May 2, 2004.
7. See Chapter 1, pages 24, 25 and 37.
8. I stress that there *seemed* to be less ambivalence among religiously motivated settlers in Gush Katif. But this apparent certainly is explored further in chapter 4 where I suggest that religiously motivated settlers may be no more certain of their actions than the secular Left.
9. Retrieved from the Gush Katif Web site (www.katif.net) on December 13, 2004, at 11:19 A.M. The communities of Gush Katif are no longer there, but the website remains.
10. For updated figures, see the Peace Now website at www.peacenow.org.
11. In a conversation, a reserve soldier expressed his exasperation with the enormous state expenditure on protecting settlers. He spoke of his 2004 reserve duty at

Morag in Gush Katif, where 200 soldiers, tanks, jeeps, and other equipment were in place to protect thirty families.

12. See Ilan Pappe (1997) on the new historians and Silberstein (1999) on the post-Zionist debates in Israeli scholarship. See the work of historian Benny Morris (1987, 1994) on the treatment of Palestinians in the prestate era and around the 1948 war. See also the recent interview with Benny Morris (Shavit 2004).

13. See Michael Walzer (1997) on the limits of liberal toleration.

14. Michael Herzfeld (1997) suggests the use of this concept for anthropologists to contribute to the study of nationalism. Indeed, in the case at hand, nationalism, an intense sense of caring for and belonging to the nation, is a common denominator among these Israelis. For Herzfeld, embarrassment or a reluctant recognition of the collective self is central to this concept. In the case at hand, cultural intimacy may be the source of critique, but as this chapter will show, far more than embarrassment over quaint, local traditions is at stake.

15. Thinking through formations of the secular, Talal Asad writes about the important place of intentions in secular ideas about agency. The responsibility of individuals, he explains, refers to actions that are distinguished from passions—that is, rational actions. This is why crimes of passion are not considered to be the consequence of an agent's own intentions in modern, Western secular legal systems. Intentions, then, come to play a very important role both in making moral judgments on individual actions and in legal judgments (Asad 2003:74, 75). More recently, Asad compares intentions and outcomes in acts of violence, noting that when civilians are killed as a result of state military actions, remorse is expressed, denying intent and providing moral justification (with sadness) for these deaths. At the same time, when civilians are purposely killed as a result of a non-state actor's attacks, like a suicide bombing, the violence is condemned, based on the intentional death of civilians (Asad 2007).

16. See Glen Bowman's reflections on the separation barrier or wall (2004).

17. Walter Benjamin (1968 (1940)), of course, warned us about belief in this idea of progress in his Theses on the Philosophy of History.

18. The tour guide is speaking figuratively, of course, as though this place was the sacred source of the secular kibbutz movement.

19. See Michael Feige (2001) on the struggle between social movements over defining space.

20. Known as *homa u'migdal*, literally a wall and tower, these settlements took advantage of the British Mandatory rule that would destroy unauthorized buildings with the exception of those that had a roof. These outposts were built under cover of darkness to avoid detection by the British.

21. Religious Zionists argue that the Land of Israel belongs to the Jews and that it is their homeland, sometimes referring to the Jews as the true indigenous people. They argue that a portion of biblical Israel east of the Jordan River has been given away, and they resist what they call foreign rule over any part of the Land of Israel.

CHAPTER 3

1. Post-disengagement heart attacks and other physical ailments have been attributed to this severing. Many experienced the time following disengagement as a period of mourning.

2. See, for example, Boyarin (1994), Brow (1990), Lowenthal (1985), Ram (1995b), Trouillot (1995), and Zerubavel (1995). On the Israeli case of producing a usable past for the nation, see Ram (1995b), and on constructing traditions for the Israeli nation, see Zerubavel (1995). On the struggle to tell an alternative narrative of the history past, see Dalsheim (2007).

3. Some of the people living in Gush Katif claimed that they had not moved there for ideological reasons. They came for practical reasons because there was an opportunity to acquire land and begin building a community. However, over time and with the changing political situations, some of these people became strong supporters of the settlement movement. They became "ideological" as result of living in the settlements.

4. For anthropological interventions in the contest over the past between Israelis and Palestinians, see Abu El-Haj (1998), Slyomovics (1998), and Swedenburg (1995).

5. That memory is continuously evoked in public rituals like Holocaust Memorial Day, which is linked directly to Israeli Independence Day (Ben-Amos and Bet-El 1999; Zertal 2005).

6. On this kind of collective memory, see Seremetakis (1994).

7. On the historians' debates in Israeli, see Pappe (1995) and Ram (1996, 1998). Post-Zionism, the definition of which is itself debated, is generally a counter-hegemonic political and ideological position that emerged in Israel in the 1990s. It exposed a central tension or contradiction between Jewish domination over the state of Israel and the ideal of an Israeli democracy. For more detail on post-Zionism and the debates between Zionism and post-Zionism and what some call the second wave of post-Zionism, see Nimni (2003), Ram (2008), and Silberstein (1999).

8. For a critical analysis of the newer texts and their limits, see Raz-Krakotzkin (2001).

9. *Tekumah* refers to a documentary series of Israel's history that aired on Israeli television in the 1990s, coinciding with the new history textbooks. It tells a revised historical tale that angered many on the Right. The twenty-two-part series aired for the first time during Israel's fiftieth anniversary. *Tekumah* means "rebirth," and the documentary chronicles the first half-century of the Jewish state's existence. The series was an attempt to shatter myths of the Zionist past, provide a more critical perspective on Israel's early leadership, and include the perspectives of Mizrahi Jews and Palestinian Arabs.

10. On landscapes and politics of separation in the West Bank, see Tom Selwyn (2001) and Eyal Weizman (2002).

11. See the article by Gideon Levy that appeared in *HaAretz* on January 9, 2005, "From Khan Yunis, You Can't See the Settlers," for the view from the other side (Levy 2005).

12. As in the writings of C. R. Condor from 1878 cited in Gasteyer and Flora (2000).

13. On the erasure of Bedouin presence in Israel, see El-Sana (2005).

14. The Negev Coalition for Coexistence, also known as DUKIUM, is one such example. See their website at http://dukium.org/ for more information. There are other organizations, as well as less formal instances of cooperation.

15. See Don Handelman's discussion of present absence in Israel and the role of the dead in nationalism (2004:chapter 8).

16. Eyal Weizman has described in great detail how Israeli infrastructure works to avoid and encapsulate Palestinians in the West Bank. In addition to the bypass roads that connect Israeli settlements to the rest of Israel by avoiding Palestinian villages, he writes about the sewer systems that flow beneath and the airspace above that encapsulate Palestinians not only horizontally in geographic space but also vertically (Weizman 2002).

17. See my 2004 article on the "uncanny presence" of Arabs and Palestinians in settler imaginaries.

18. For more on these processes see Zerubavel (1996) and Bardenstein (1999) on trees and forestation, and Whitelam (1996) and Abu El-Haj (2001) on archeology.

19. Oren Yiftachel has written extensively about the historical and ongoing struggles over land that are integral to the ethnic hierarchy of rule in Israel (1999, 2000, 2002, 2006). See the Ta'ayush Web site for some of the most recent cases of removing Palestinians through legal quandaries of official residency in the Jerusalem area and in other areas: www.taayush.org/. See the Web sites of Israeli and Palestinian civil and human rights organizations, B'Tselem at www.btselem.org/English/index.asp and PCHR at www.pchrgaza.org/.

20. Excerpt from Kook's writings on the Land of Israel reprinted in Hertzberg (1959). For more translated writing, see Bokser (1978).

21. See also their reference to De Shalit (1995) on p. 129 comparing Israeli, Canadian, U.S., and Australian immigrant perceptions of the landscape and lifescape.

22. A flyer handed out to visitors at the museum in Kfar Darom that explains the history of the town includes the following: "Kfar Darom is located in the region of G'rar, where our forefathers, Avraham, Yitzhak, and Ya'akov lived and is included in the area allotted to Shevet Yehuda." See a posting on Katifnet of an article that appeared in the *Jerusalem Post* attesting to the Jewish historical connection to Gaza (Mazar 2005). However, today Grar (Nahal Grar) is found outside the Gaza Strip in the Eshkol Region. This is one of a number of disputed points regarding whether the Gaza region should be considered part of the Land of Israel.

23. Indeed, it has been argued that the Zionist movement arising in eighteenth-century Europe required parts of the belief system of Orthodox Judaism to provide the ideological ties to that particular piece of land. Theodore Herzl, often called the father of modern Zionism and an assimilated, secular Jew, contemplated establishing a homeland for the Jewish people in Uganda (Tessler 1994:55–57). That idea was short-lived and quickly replaced with the biblical yearning for return to the holy and Promised Land of Zion. A land without a people, so the myth goes, for a people without land, *terra nullius*, manifest destiny, and so on. The land was sometimes imagined as empty, sparsely populated, or a place that could benefit

from Jewish settlement and the modern improvements the Jews could bring. It was thought of as the land of promise and the Promised Land for people coming to terms with the failure of assimilation to protect their collective continuity and survival as a people. This is not to deny international political forces and historical decisions allocating the land. It is to recall that the Jewish people themselves seeking refuge and a means of continuity considered a number of alternatives. For a concise overview of Jewish history prior to and including the emergence of modern political Zionism, see Tessler (1994:7–68).

24. Shenhav writes that this fetishism of the Green Line purifies the occupation in post-1967 territories and allows the artificial separation between the good guys and the bad guys; it hides the fact that the Israeli colonial occupation is found everywhere, not only over the Green Line.

25. That was what Gideon Levy wrote in a blurb for *Lords of the Lands* by Idith Zertal and Akiva Eldar, a widely acclaimed book that makes the same argument.

26. There is a long list of scholars who have written against hegemonic Zionist narratives and called into question the events of 1948 and the treatment of Palestinians and of Mizrahi Jews. Within Israel, such scholars are sometimes referred to as "the new historians" (Kimmerling 1995; Pappe 1997). For an early commentary on the place of Israeli revisionist history in a broader critical scholarship, see Moughrabi (1989). Most recently, scholars have turned a critical eye on the treatment of Arabs in Israel in the 1950s and 1960s. According to Di-Capua, in a review of some of this scholarship, this work stands to undermine a deep-seated "left-Zionist myth" of pre-1967 as a sort of Golden Age in Israel (Di-Capua 2007).

CHAPTER 4

1. See Goldstone (2007) on how this belief can be understood as a form of secular disciplining of religious ways of life. Chantal Mouffe argues that the idea that politics should be envisaged in terms of "interests" or "reason" and "morality" misses the important role that passions, values, and beliefs play in various forms of collective identification and political action (Mouffe 2006).

2. The taken-for-granted belief in the autonomous subject on which many modern projects rest has been taken up by a number of scholars. That belief comes into conflict with this apparent certainty. On some of the processes through which this autonomous subject has been constituted, see Keane (2007).

3. Michael Walzer (1997) argues in favor of limited tolerance to preserve a democratic social order. His work has been criticized by a number of scholars, including Povinelli (2001) and, even more extensively, Brown (2006a). See note 8 for more detail.

4. There are numerous struggles between secular and religious communities in Israel, perhaps most famously in Jerusalem, where Orthodox Haredi neighborhoods are closed by barriers to prevent traffic from interfering with the Sabbath and where Orthodox Jews have thrown stones at the secular who drive by. Many

secular Jews have left Jerusalem for Tel Aviv or other more secular places, and the struggle between these communities is reflected in local elections.

5. This process might well be viewed as a kind of Foucaultian governmentality (1991 (1978)), which results in actions that support state projects.

6. By now, the critiques of Habermas and the possibility of free and equal debate in the public sphere are well rehearsed. Many have pointed to the ways in which the public sphere systematically excludes certain kinds of people. See the collection of articles in Calhoun (1992). Note also Talal Asad's assertion that the public sphere is necessarily, not contingently, articulated by power (Asad 2003:184). Contra Habermas, see Charles Hirschkind (2001) on religious reasoning in public.

7. The processes described here are analogous to those described by Lustick with the evacuation of settlements in Sinai. See Lustick (1988:61–62).

8. Michael Walzer makes the case that there must be limits of liberal tolerance to maintain the freedoms of liberal democracy. His critics, including Povinelli (2001) and Asad (2007), call attention to this limit and what they see as its problematic implementation. Similarly, Wendy Brown (2006a) makes an argument against what she sees as the problematic work of tolerance, which is employed as means of regulating aversion. The problem of contradictory ethics will be explored further in chapter 9.

9. For a powerful (and controversial) argument on the ways in which modern narratives are contained by linear conceptions of temporality see Hayden White (1987). Max Weinreich offers an explanation of a particular Jewish way of being that understands all of Jewish history as one indivisible whole, exact periodization is not attempted, and events in the ancient past can be understood through the lens of the present, just as the present can be understood as motivated by the ancient past. Just as Jacob is Israel, identified with the people of Israel, Esau is Edom, and Haman descended from him. Edom is also Christian Europe, and its opposition, and Jews and Muslims are prefigured in Isaac and Ishmael. What is taken by modern linear thought to be problematic or anachronistic is a different sense of temporality, which Weinreich calls panchronism (Weinreich 1980:208).

10. Lara Deeb (2006) documents the variations found among faithful Shi'i in Lebanon, construed as a single homogeneous community of Hezbollah, who actually choose between interpretations of different religious leaders.

11. At first glance, this suggests an issue of gender differences. Yet to make such a claim would require both additional fieldwork and analysis. Based on my experiences in the field, it seems to me that these expressions found among women reflect a broader phenomenon. The range of interpretations found in Gush Katif can be compared with the range of interpretations reported by Lustick for the withdrawal from Sinai (1988:61–62).

12. Emmanuel Sivan (1995) is considered a leading expert on fundamentalists and includes members of Gush Emunim in this category. He suggests that such groups require clarity and cannot sustain ambiguity or confusion (p. 29). Contra Sivan, the data provided in this chapter demonstrate how such ambiguity is endured.

13. Clearly these are discourses and practices associated with nationalism and/or conquest more broadly.

14. See Zertal and Eldar (2007) for a sustained historical analysis.

15. Not *the* Torah (the Five Books of Moses), but to engage in rethinking the nature of Israel and the basic set of ideas or ethics or laws by which daily lives are lived in Israel. An interesting parallel in secular politics is the movement to write an Israeli constitution. Israel has a set of basic laws, but no constitution. Writing one would involve bringing the citizens of Israel to some agreement about the nature of the state.

16. A mitzvah is a commandment or precept of Jewish law. It is a good deed that is performed out of religious duty, but is sometimes also used to refer to good deeds more generally. Here its meaning should be understood as a commandment, one of the 613 commandments required of the People of Israel in the Torah. There are positive and negative mitzvot (plural), things one ought to do and things one should refrain from doing. For the pious Jews in this study fulfilling the mitzvot not only brings individuals closer to God, it also brings the nation closer to holiness and is thereby necessary for redemption.

17. Lustick (1988) described this as the slogan of Gush Emunim and wrote of the primacy of the land. The explanation of equivalency here is differently nuanced.

18. Lustick writes about a similar range of responses within Gush Emunim following the evacuation of Yamit. "In symposia sponsored by Gush Emunim to discuss the meaning and implications of the Yamit disaster, some argued that the failure was due to over confidence displayed by many religious leaders that . . . God would intervene. . . . Others argued that it was the spiritual imperfection of the Yamit settlers. . . . Others interpreted it as the inscrutable will of God" (1988:62).

19. A central argument of *Lords of the Land* by Idith Zertal and Akiva Eldar (2007).

20. There is a long list of scholars who have written against hegemonic Zionist narratives, calling into question the events of 1948 and the treatment of Palestinians and of Mizrahi Jews. Within Israel, such scholars are sometimes referred to as "the new historians" (Kimmerling 1995; Pappe 1997). For an early commentary on the place of Israeli revisionist history in a broader critical scholarship, see Moughrabi (1989). Most recently, scholars have turned a critical eye on the treatment of Arabs in Israel in the 1950s and 1960s. According to Di-Capua, in a review of some of this scholarship, this work stands to undermine a deep-seated "left-Zionist myth" of pre-1967 as a sort of Golden Age in Israel (Di-Capua 2007).

CHAPTER 5

1. Pnina Motzafi-Haller (2001) has written about the absence of scholarship on Mizrahi women in particular since the 1970s. She reviews earlier literature that tended toward Orientalist representations of these women in Israel but notes that what followed has been a noticeable *lack* of scholarly attention.

2. The Hebrew word *mizrah* means East. The term *Mizrahi* and its plural *Mizrahim* refers to Jews of Middle Eastern origin, from the Arab world, who live in Israel. While it is common usage to refer to "*Mizrahi* Jews," I find this a bit redundant

and have chosen the Hebrew plural form *Mizrahim* instead. They are only Mizrahi/Eastern because that term describes their Jewishness and the category is specifically meaningful in the Israeli context where they are sometimes called "edot ha- Mizrah", which means ethnically Eastern Jews.

3. Shohat's title was a reference to Edward Said's famous essay called "Zionism from the Point of View of Its Victims" that was published in 1979. The outcomes of the Zionist project and the Israeli state, which had generally been considered a positive project and a success in the eyes of much of the West was now being criticized for the effects it had on the local Palestinian population. Shohat added to this critique of Zionism and Israel by claiming that the creation of the state was not even necessarily positive for Jews, as she documented the negative effects on Middle Eastern Jewry.

4. Lavie took herself as an example of this problematic positioning in her work on the Bedouin of the Sinai Peninsula by describing herself as both occupied—as an Arab-Jew in Israel subject to Israeli racism—and occupier—as an Israeli in Sinai, or the occupied territories more broadly—who was opposed to occupation. Her later work continued investigating this ambiguous positionality of Mizrahim in Israel.

5. I stress the word *acute* rather than *unique* as this ambiguous positionality is not limited to post-1967 occupied territories. Instead, the military occupation in territories acquired during the June 1967 war is best understood as a continuation of the settler project in Palestine. This is an issue I have dealt with in depth elsewhere. See Dalsheim (2005).

6. For example, historian Raz-Krakotzkin advocates a revision of history that would not simply write the Mizrahim into history or include them in the master narrative. Like other critical and postcolonial historians, he calls for a rewriting of history that moves beyond the boundaries of colonial discourse, recognizing the ambivalent location of Jews in the Orient that "combines the perspective of the colonizer with that of the colonized" (Raz-Krakotzkin 2005).

7. For example, Palestinians are figuratively removed from conversations when Israelis argue among themselves about the future, the peace process, and solutions to the conflict with the Palestinians. Their perspectives had been largely missing from formal national historical narratives, including those taught in Israeli schools, although this has been a focus of debate among Israeli historians (Dalsheim 2007; Pappe 1995; Ram 1998; Rogan and Shlaim 2001).

8. Hegemonic Israeli history has privileged the story of Ashkenazi Jews, silencing the stories of Mizrahim (Shenhav 2001). Referring to Mizrahim as "Sephardi" Jews also contributed to obscuring their Arabness and thus their relationship to the region and to other Arab groups in the region. The existence of these Arab-Jews (Shenhav 2003a) destabilizes dichotomous distinctions between Arabs and Jews on which Israeli identity is largely premised.

9. The precise numbers are difficult to determine. New neighborhoods or illegal outposts were not always counted or reported, and the number of people claiming residency varied as the disengagement drew nearer. The number of settlements does not include Alei Sinai, Dugit and Nissanit, which were located in the Northern Gaza Strip but were not part of Gush Katif.

10. Jews of Middle Eastern descent living in development towns in the Negev reported visiting their families in Gush Katif and described a certain hierarchy among the communities there. Some were known for the high number of Mizrahi residents and considered less desirable within Gush Katif.

11. This is not to suggest that all Jews of Middle Eastern and North African descent share these beliefs. Indeed, they do not.

12. This often includes analyses that associate Mizrahim with right-wing or racist (anti-Arab) political parties that have appealed to voters' economic distress. See Shafir and Peled (2002:87–94).

13. Aziza Khazoom, Pnina Motzafi-Haller, Yehuda Shenhav, Ella Shohat, and Yossi Yonah are perhaps the most prominent among current Israeli scholars (and scholars of Israel), and numerous others continue to analyze the forms and outcomes of Israeli racism. See, for example, the special issue of *Social Identities* (2004, 10/2) that was dedicated to forms of Israeli racism against Palestinians and Jews of Mizrahi descent. While Shenhav has taken up the complex reality of Mizrahi identities in history (2003a, 2003b), none of these scholars, to my knowledge, has dealt with the complex identity of Mizrahim as settlers in the occupied territories.

14. The majority of these violent acts have been reported in the West Bank settlements, which are much larger than those in Gaza and include a number of settlements that are considered particularly extreme.

15. See chapter four, note 15, for the meaning of mitzvah.

16. See Yiftachel (2006) on real estate and Israeli ethnocracy for an in-depth analysis of the adverse effects of state policy and planning on Mizrahim.

17. It should be noted that there are also kibbutz communities established by religious Jews who showed far more empathy toward the communities of Gush Katif, as their members also identify as religious Zionists, like many in the settlements of the occupied territories.

18. For updated information on post-1967 settlements, see the Peace Now Settlement Watch on their website at www.peacenow.org.il/site/en/peace.asp?pi=51, and the settlement monitor, which is a regular part of the *Journal of Palestine Studies*.

19. This act of grace was based on scripture as the Torah prohibits usury (Levit. 25:37). There are a number of Jewish organizations that provide interest-free loans based on this and rabbinical teachings.

20. See "Our Trauma Is Greater Than Yours," in *HaAretz* newspaper online (Ilan 2006).

21. Gramsci's notion of educating consent (1971:242) lies behind this idea of conformity.

CHAPTER 6

1. This is a reference to what is known as the Second or Al-Aqsa Intifada. The settlers in the Gaza Strip often represented the time preceding this as one of calm and peaceful coexistence with Palestinians.

2. I think of *political* parenthetically because imposing distinctions between political and religious projects presumes a particular version of a secular modern.

3. There are religiously motivated settlers who identify in distinction to Orthodox Haredi Jews, those who generally have not participated in such worldly affairs as serving in the army and who place a great emphasis on religious study. However, the lines between these two communities are not so clear. Orthodox Haredi Jews sometimes support the settlers, and there are families that include members of both of these communities. There is an additional category of Orthodox, sometimes called "*Chardalim,*" indicating a mixture of Haredi and Leumi (nationalist). It has been reported that this group has been increasing in numbers since the disengagement.

4. For a description of events at Yamit in English, see Lustick (1988).

5. An article appearing on *Arutz 7* recounts the decision of a number of rabbis condoning the use of violence against non-Jews when such violence would protect the Jewish people, even if that meant "hitting or even killing Palestinians who are not involved in terrorism" because "arch-terrorists consciously sit among their own civilians in order to protect themselves" (*Arutz 7* IsraelNationalNews.com, September 7, 2004). Such incidences have been increasingly reported in the last year.

6. The relationship between religious Judaism and political Zionism has been the subject of a great deal of scholarship, but perhaps the best source for understanding the place of territory in Judaism is W. D. Davies (1991 (1982)). Modern political Zionism required a particular literal interpretation of some of beliefs rooted in Judaism for the claim to this particular piece of territory. Davies demonstrates that this modern form of Jewish nationalism was preceded by a longer tradition of concentration on The Land, which he writes has at no time since the first century been wholly without a Jewish presence. When it suited state purposes, both left- and right-wing Israeli governments have supported the expansion of settlement in post-1967 occupied territories (Masalha 2000). The 2004 disengagement from the Gaza Strip and parts of the West Bank created an enormous uproar as right-wing and religious Zionists opposed the withdrawal, which was presented by state officials as a move toward peace through ending the occupation. In contradistinction to the appearance of the state of Israel taking courageous steps toward peace through the unilateral withdrawal, see Gordon (2004), Beinin and Stein (2006), and Yiftachel (2005).

7. The conflation of religiously motivated Jewish settlers who believe their acts will hasten the coming redemption with the political far Right into a category of fundamentalists (Lustick 1988) is echoed in the work of Nagata (2001), who calls for an anthropology of fundamentalism. Such conflations fail to recognize the strength and depth of meaning of faith among believers. It is, I would argue, a form of erasure emanating from a liberal secular anxiety around belief in the supernatural. On anthropological atheism and the disciplinary taboo against belief, see Ewing (1994).

8. Rabbi Melamed, quoted on *Arutz 7* (www.israelnationalnews.com), February 27, 2004.

9. Dahlia Scheindlin, quoted in *HaAretz*, February 4, 2004.

10. Among those Jews who have or continue making their homes in post-1967 Israeli-occupied territories are those who live there for explicitly ideological reasons. Although the distinctions are never completely clear or static, there are people who have chosen to live in the territories for economic reasons, others based on religious beliefs, and still others for political reasons. The mystical may be aligned with any of these, depending on their interpretation of God's messages at a given historical moment. It should be recalled that the Rav Abraham Isaac Kook, a chief rabbi in Mandatory Palestine, whose thoughts were reinterpreted by his son Tzvi Yehuda, becoming the spiritual foundation of the religious settler movement, articulated his approach in terms of Jewish mysticism (Aran 1997; Lustick 1988). In other words, this mysticism, which has since been greatly diminished by later religiously motivated Jewish settlers, can be traced back to the spiritual foundations of the messianic settlement project.

11. These thoughts resonate deeply with the teachings of the mystical religious leader, the elder Rav Kook. According to Aran, the mystical aspects of the father's (Avraham Kook) faith were greatly diminished as concrete messianic aspects took on greater importance under the interpretations of the son (Tzvi Yehuda Kook). Thus the emphasis on the practical, physical components of settling the land within the vision of redemption took primacy in the settler movement of Gush Emunim (Aran 1997). Among those who continue to believe in the sanctity of the Land and the wholeness achieved by a Jewish presence on the Land of Israel, there are discrepancies and disputes. Not all of these settlers would describe themselves as part of Gush Emunim. Some, indeed, have publicly denounced the movement.

12. In his book that provides an English presentation of religious Zionist thought, Yosef Tirosh (1975) contends that the secular founder of modern Zionism, Theodor Herzl, himself recognized that only in Eretz Israel (the Land of Israel) could the Jewish people come into its own and find peace. That is, even though Herzl famously considered other geographical options, eventually he conceded the interdependence of the Land of Israel with the Jewish People. Others, of course, have interpreted this as a cunning political move that uses religious Judaism toward the goal of establishing a modern Jewish state in Palestine.

13. A common criticism of secular Israeli "Western ways" by messianic settlers is the concern the secular state has with how it will be viewed by the rest of the world—modern diplomacy, in other words. There is a messianic insistence that the major concern should be with how Israel is viewed in the eyes of the Lord, not the gentile world (see Lustick 1988, chapter 4).

14. See the opening quote in chapter 4.

15. There are deep disagreements among Orthodox Jews regarding the extent to which human intervention is allowed or whether it is required for bringing the coming redemption. Traditional Orthodox views include the anti-(political) Zionist interpretation that human beings must not intervene with the Will of God, which alone can bring the redemption. This contradicts religious Zionism as presented here. See Sivan (1995:40–41).

16. This is an interesting twist when compared with scholarly depictions of the fundamentalist ways of life as seeking certainty, which is seen in contrast to the other ways of life. Nagata (2001) writes that fundamentalism should be understood as special forms of identity politics, meaning, and labeling, characterized by a quest for certainty, exclusiveness, and unambiguous boundaries. My research reveals that uncertainty is as much a part of life among religiously motivated settlers considered fundamentalists, although it is practiced quite differently in ways that may be difficult for liberal skeptics to recognize.

17. For a useful, concise overview of redemption in Hebrew prophecy, including redemption from pride, see Shulman (2006:161–170).

18. See the writings of the Rabbi Abraham Isaac Kook, whose thought has been adopted by many religious settlers. On the problem of pride, see the English translation of Kook's writing by Ben Zion Bokser (1978:153–157).

19. For a fuller analysis of busyness as a technique of hegemony, see Dalsheim (2007).

20. Here the speaker is making a distinction between political Zionism and return to the land. Living on the land can be seen as distinct from sovereignty, as will become clear in the next chapter.

21. A secular, rational explanation would be that these settlers opposed the program for continued withdrawal from the occupied territories proposed by Prime Minister Ehud Olmert, thus they were in political opposition to his ruling party. Following the second Lebanon war, there was a great deal of dismay among the Israeli populace against a war that was not wisely managed. The postwar demonstrations against the government were interpreted by some Messianic settlers as the "truth coming to light," as Israelis understood that this war and the kidnapping of Israeli soldiers resulted from the mistake of leaving the occupied territories, or of abandoning *Eretz Israel*.

22. Shafir and Peled (2002) account for the changing dynamics as shifts in the balance of (contradictory) objectives between the creation and maintenance of a Jewish state and commitment to being what they call a "Western-style democracy." The liberalization of the Israeli economy has been a major factor in these changing dynamics. According to Yiftachel (2006), the changes in Israeli state policy from expansion to contraction (disengagement) are both parts of the same process of maintaining the system he calls "ethnocracy."

CHAPTER 7

1. See chapter 4, page 88.

2. This is an excerpt from an opinion piece that appeared in the Israeli daily newspaper *HaAretz* around Israeli Independence Day in 2006. It is a response to the anger provoked by the author A. B. Yehoshua, who made a speech to delegates of the American Jewish Committee in which he emphasized differences rather than a connection between Israeli Jews and those living outside Israel (Aloni 2006).

3. See Slyomovics (1998) for a useful analysis of some of the ways in which identities in Israel/Palestine are constituted through complex and contradictory relationships

to place, and see Boyarin (1994) on the politics of memory in the space of Israel/Palestine.

4. See Rabinowitz's (2000)—who draws on Appadurai (2002) and Scott (1999)—reflections on the failure of national sovereignty as a postcolonial solution. On the importance of articulating a specifically diasporic, nonterritorial Jewish identity, see Boyarin and Boyarin (1993).

5. See also my article on the desire among secular, Ashkenazi, liberal, Jewish Israelis to somehow magically imagine away the Palestinians (Dalsheim 2004).

6. Perhaps the best known example of how one is expected to treat strangers or travelers is the story of Abraham (Gen. 18:1–15) welcoming three strangers into his tent and providing them with food, water, and shelter. Or the story of Lot (Gen. 19:8), who offered his own daughters to an angry mob rather than betray the guests who had come under his shelter.

7. See the short interview with the Rabbi of Tsfat, Shmuel Eliyahu, in Neslen (2006) for an example of these viewpoints from an Orthodox rabbi outside the community of settlers in post-1967 Israeli occupied territories. It should also be noted that there are biblical injunctions to treat enemies fairly as well.

8. There is by now a very large literature on the postcolonial problems of secular democracy and multiculturalism, and the discussion of these issues has moved beyond the academy as issues of difference and living together have come to the fore for citizens in numerous places. For a brief introduction to the debates on multiculturalism, see Goldberg (2004). For an excellent early analysis of the Israeli case of Arab citizens of the state, see Lustick (1980). For a historical overview and updated analysis on the dynamics of citizenship in Israel, see Shafir and Peled (2002).

9. Azmi Bishara, a Palestinian citizen of Israel and former member of the Israeli Knesset (parliament), is among those who have called for one secular, democratic state, but also calls for a Palestinian state. Edward Said wrote about a single democratic state as the only viable solution in the space of Israel/Palestine where the geographic and demographic reality has made separation of the two peoples impossible. (His article is reprinted at www.mediamonitors.net/edward9.html.)

10. A great deal of philosophical attention has been given to Descartes' separation between reason and madness. For Derrida, this exclusion of madness from reason constitutes the very possibility of identity (and reason). It is an originary structure of difference—difference that always exists at the center of identity for Derrida ((1967)1990). However, for Foucault, the separation of madness from reason was a historical moment and one that he uses to explain the powerful ways in which such categorizations of humanity or unities and disunities work to constrain and contain (1972, (1961) 2006). See Grossberg (1996:94–95) for a brief, clear discussion of the debate between Derrida and Foucault.

11. I have neither named him nor given him a pseudonym. Some readers will recognize him, but I have chosen to keep him anonymous like all the other people in this study, both to maintain the anonymity of others and to suggest that while he is most well known, he is not alone in his ideas.

12. This includes the settlers in Hebron, those known as the hilltop youth, and followers of Meir Kahane. See Juergensmeyer (2000b).

13. This option was instituted as part of a larger decision to maintain the status quo in the transition to statehood by Israel's first prime minister, David Ben Gurion.

14. Indeed, for a period of time, when post-1967 settlements were receiving a great deal of support through government funding of infrastructure, it seemed that Orthodox Zionists were the darlings of the nation. From the mid-1970s through the 1990s, the settlement project in the West Bank and Gaza Strip never stopped expanding, even as peace agreements were signed with the Palestinians that promised otherwise.

15. He would not sit next to a woman other than his wife and would not meet me alone without his wife being present.

16. For current and updated maps, see the Palestinian Academic Society for the Study of International Affairs website (www.passia.org) and the Peace Now settlement watch website (www.peacenow.org.il/site/en/peace.asp?pi=51). See also Eyal Weizman (2002) on the multidimensional intractability of the conflict in Israel/Palestine. Despite the reality on the ground, some scholars continue to call for a two-state solution, even if that will only be a temporary move, as in Yiftachel's suggestion of "gradual binationalism" (2006). For the opinions of scholars and activists promoting a one-state solution, see the Association for One Democratic State in Palestine/Israel, which includes the article "The Only Alternative," by Edward Said (www.one-democratic-state.org).

17. For an analysis of the failed Oslo process, see Beinin (2006).

18. See chapter 1.

19. See Fendel (2007), who writes of fears among West Bank settlers that the wall and checkpoints will be used to seal off their communities to ease their removal. The call by the Yesha Council not to participate with regulations that require permits or stickers on settlers' cars was reported as a form of resistance against other possible evacuations of settlers.

CHAPTER 8

1. On the marginalization of religious women within the women's peace movement in Israel/Palestine, see Emmet (1996). Saba Mahmood (2001, 2005) was probably the first to pose serious challenges to feminists who have tended to think of religion, and particularly those forms considered fundamentalist, as another means of oppression against women. The most relevant and recent example of that tendency would be Tamara Neuman describing the religiously motivated settlers of Hebron. Neuman writes that "one would be hard put to see women's activities as liberating for the participants themselves" (2004:54).

2. See Harding (1991). On the link between Christian fundamentalists in the United States, settling Jews in Israel and the occupied territories, and the erasure of the problem of Palestine and the Palestinians, see McAlister (2003).

3. On toleration and its limits, see Walzer (1997). For a detailed description of the radical Right in Israeli politics, see Sprinzak (1989). For some scholars, the term *fundamentalists* includes those on the radical Right, whether they are religiously observant or not. For example, see Lustick (1988).

4. I am referring here only to the Zionist Left. There are also non-Zionists and anti-Zionists who may or may not be part of the Left. It includes what Shafir and Peled (2002) call the Labor Settlement Movement.

5. The notion of "religious" in the Israeli context does not mean affiliation as it might in other locations. Instead, it usually refers to observance and tends to be associated with more Orthodox forms of observance that include keeping the Sabbath and the dietary laws of *kashrut* (keeping Kosher). Being Jewish in Israel is the unmarked category parallel to whiteness, for example, in the United States.

6. The term *modern Orthodox* for Shlomo Fischer (2004), includes "radical, extremist or totalistic political religion" in Israel, that group which other scholars have called fundamentalists. Fischer aims to reveal the specifically modern character of these Jewish nationalists.

7. On how the secular and religious have been mutually dependent in the Zionist project, see Raz-Krakotzkin (1994).

8. See chapter 5.

9. Dipesh Chakrabarty (2000) demonstrates the impossibility of representing certain subaltern voices within Western historiography because of the reliance on a particular linear narrative. Judith Butler (2008), as we shall see in chapter 9, argues that linear, progressive understandings of modernity create particular divisions that preclude potential alliances between groups, thus interfering with some people's freedoms for the benefit of others.

10. See Weisburd (1989) on settler violence as social deviance.

11. Oslo refers to the negotiation process between Israel and the Palestinians that began in Oslo in 1993 and collapsed with the Camp David summit of July 2000. For a most recent detailed analysis, see Beinin (2006). See also Robert Malley and Hussein Agha (2001).

12. It is ironic that Judah, who built his family a rather large house far less expensively than many other Israelis and who travels with his wife to Europe for vacations, felt certain that the Western values held by others was the cause of his own demise.

13. For a similar kind of optimism, see Shafir and Peled (2002).

14. One such settler explained that they are often construed in local parlance as "settler-lite"—as in a low-calorie beverage—and are distinguished from those considered "ideologically motivated."

15. The scholarship analyzing the Zionist project as a form of settler colonialism remains rather small, and the term *settler* is rarely used in reference to Israeli Jews living inside the Green Line. The terminology has been used historically to reframe the immigration of Jews to Palestine, the subsequent establishment of the state, and the ongoing struggles over land and labor. See Shafir (1989a) for a comprehensive analysis of the early years of Zionist immigration and the origins of the Israeli Palestinian conflict. See Abdo and Yuval-Davis (1995) for a succinct

discussion of the Zionist settler project in comparison with other settler societies. In most recent critical scholarship, "colonialism" has been used exclusively to describe the military occupation of post-1967 territories, including the West Bank and the Gaza Strip. Within the Green Line, struggles over territory and citizenship rights tend to be presented through the discourses of multiculturalism, civil rights, and human rights. We might expand our understanding of the processes of decolonization by adding these to the more well-known anticolonial nationalist struggles. I am indebted to a conversation with Gershon Shafir for this insightful comment.

16. This perspective is also expressed by Beinin and Stein (2006:13).

17. These predictions have been coming true, as revealed in the numerous attacks and counterattacks around the area of the Gaza Strip and southern Israel, as well as Israeli closures of the Gaza Strip.

18. This was a kibbutz founded by the Shomer Ha-Tzair, considered the more left-leaning or communist wing of the kibbutz movement. Kibbutz communities today are less homogeneous in the political positions of their members and residents than they were in the early years. Today there is one united kibbutz movement, an umbrella organization composed of the earlier TAKAM and the Shomer Ha-Tzair together.

19. Uri Ram writes that what is known as the left-wing in Israel today might be better understood as the Right because they tend to be liberal, secular, and particularly driven by materialist desires. Ram refers to this segment of the population as the Right even though in popular discourse they are known as the Left because of their liberal ideology. See Ram (1999). In addition, on the terms left and right and how that division conceals and silences the oppression of Mizrahi Jews, Chetrit (1997) has written that according to the new Mizrahi analysis, "There is no Left among the Ashkenazim and the use of the Left/Right is a manipulation." Raz-Krakotzkin (2000) has argued that for the so-called Left, believing in peace and compromise with the Palestinians is more a matter of self-image than an actual political stand.

20. I have written elsewhere on what I called the "uncanny absence" of the Palestinian or Arab other in the settler nationalist imagination of liberal, left-wing Jewish Israelis. This refers to a particular kind of silence that might well be described by the legal terminology used to expropriate Palestinian land that was owned during the British Mandate, "present absentee." Arab landowners who were not present on their land between December 29, 1947, and May 19, 1948, who most likely fled the violence of the war, lost their ownership to the new Israeli state (Dalsheim 2004). On "present absence," see also Wood (1994) and Atran (1989).

21. Compare to the women of Rachelim in the West Bank who, according to El-Or and Aran, were not embarrassed to verbalize their fears for the safety of their children and the safety of the settlers in general (1995:70).

22. Patrick Wolfe (1999) argues that settler colonialism must be understood as a structure rather than an event, its development charted over time, and events and policies understood within its specific context. This is the longer process to which I refer here. According to Wolfe, certain characteristics will be common to all such

societies, including the "logic of elimination," since the central conflict is over land and the natives are superfluous to settler society. Following the work of geographer Oren Yiftachel (1999), it is my contention that these struggles are ongoing. The Israeli/Palestinian national conflict is not yet past the frontier stage of settler colonialism, as final borders have not yet been drawn, and land seizures continue in the form of Jewish settlements in Israeli-occupied territories and with the current construction of the separation wall. Within the current state boundaries— the internal frontier—structural racism in the form of "ethnocracy" involves a number of struggles over land between dominant Ashkenazi Jews and other ethnic and racial groups, including Palestinian citizens.

23. Postmodern scholars write of diasporic identity, suggesting it presents a possible solution to the conflicts and violence of territorial nationalism. Daniel and Jonathan Boyarin (1993) suggest the value of Jewish diasporic identity as opposed to the Zionist territorialism. Rabinowitz (2000) exceeds this with a suggestion that sovereignty in one's own nation-state is not necessary for either Jewish or Palestinian identity and that each may benefit from models of diasporic identity.

24. The scenario of the Israeli withdrawal from the Sinai and the removal of settlers from Yamit was replayed in very similar ways in Gush Katif. For a description in English on the removal of settlers from Yamit, see Lustick (1988).

CHAPTER 9

1. See the five volumes produced by the Fundamentalisms Project from the University of Chicago Press, edited by Martin Marty and Scott Appleby, as well as comparative work by Silberstein (1993), Juergensmeyer (2000a), and Antoun (2008).

2. Reflecting on Derrida, Anidjar writes: "The enemy—as a concrete, discursive, vanishing field, 'the shadow of an ageless ghost,' as Derrida puts it—is structured by the Arab and the Jew, that is to say, by the relation of Europe to both Arab and Jew . . . they—the Jew and the Arab on the one hand, religion and politics on the other—are distinct but indissociable" (2003: preface).

3. This is to distinguish modern, political Zionism from traditional Jewish beliefs, which might also be considered a form of Zionism. It is also to call attention to the polysemic quality of political Zionism itself, which is so often conflated.

4. This is to distinguish between those people who voice opposition to settlement in the territories gained by Israel in the 1967 war, often referred to more simply as "the occupied territories," and those who oppose the state of Israel in its entirety as a foreign imposition in the Middle East.

5. This is not to say that only progressive or left-wing scholars would find this comparison problematic, but this chapter addresses the work of scholars who I believe fall into this category.

6. In addition to the three pieces considered here, Povinelli (2001) and Asad (2007) engage with Michael Walzer's (1997) On Toleration, criticizing the limitations of tolerance that Walzer outlines as both reasonable and necessary to protect a

particular way of life. Brown (2006a, 2006b) provides a sustained critique of how tolerance is employed or deployed in liberal democracies like the United States. However, none of these authors calls for the end of liberal democracy. Instead, for Brown in particular, there is a call to "open liberal regimes to reflect on their false conceits" and to open them to the "possibility of being transformed by their encounter with what liberalism has conventionally taken to be its constitutive outside, its hostile other" (2006a:174).

7. The three pieces I engage with here are all aimed at addressing this issue. See also Povinelli's discussion of radical differences and "incommensurable worlds" (2001).

8. This includes an emphasis on a kind of reasoning that questions religious authority (Mahmood 2006: 334). See chapter 4 for a similar situation between Jews in Israel.

9. Gregory Starrett argues that what Mahmood is describing is in fact a powerful, widespread, and very explicitly Protestant ideology (personal communication). This coincides with the argument put forth by Webb Keane. In his recent book, Keane quotes a friend who remarks, "We are all Protestants now," which Keane uses as shorthand to describe the spread of Protestantism and the kinds of subjectivities it engenders that are integral to a particular, powerful vision of modernity (2007: 201).

10. It might be argued that the case of Israel is different because its internal contradiction does not arise from the problem of religion and state in the same way, but rather from its attempt to be at once a Jewish state and a democratic state. This has meant that from its earliest days, there have been numerous compromises made to avoid alienating religious Jews. This included special provisions allowing Orthodox Jews to claim exemption from military duty, which is mandatory for all citizens. It has also meant allowing religious control over certain legal matters like marriage and divorce.

11. In fact, Butler suggests common interests between religious Muslims and homosexuals in the Netherlands in opposition to both forms of discrimination. While I doubt actual coalitions are possible, I would point out that moving beyond well-known categories of politics and difference allows us to see certain common interests even among groups in opposition. For example, in the space of Israel/Palestine, religiously motivated settlers and Palestinians are in direct conflict over territory, but both groups have opposed the construction of the separation barrier, albeit for very different reasons. It is hard to imagine a coalition between religiously motivated Jewish settlers and Palestinians (and their left-wing supporters). However, both have demonstrated against the separation barrier or wall that is being constructed on contested land.

12. Gershon Shafir was probably the first Israeli sociologist to use the designation settler-colonial as an analytical framework for Israeli society, building on and refining Maxime Rodinson's work (Rodinson 1973). For a systematic typology of colonial formations and Shafir's argument of how Zionism fits into that typology as a "pure settlement" colony, see Shafir (1989a:8–10). More recently, see Shafir

and Peled (2002). Sociologist Baruch Kimmerling used the term *immigrant-settler* rather than *settler-colonial* to describe Israeli society.

13. Ammiel Alcalay writes of the long historical process of transformation in Jewish history: "the gradual exchange of the legal, communal and cultural basis of Jewish existence for the racial the ethnic and the national . . . [which] assumed a final physical form in the Levant" (1993:221).

14. See the writings of the Rabbi Abraham Isaac Kook, whose thought has been adopted by religious settlers. On the problem of pride, see the English translation of Kook's writing by Ben Zion Bokser (1978:153–157).

15. For examples of studies that move beyond the demonization of radical Muslims, see Brown (2006b), Deeb (2006), Euben (1999), and Mahmood (2005).

16. Asad asks, "What politics are promoted by the notion that the world is *not* divided into modern and non-modern, into West and non-West? What practical options are opened up or closed by the notion that the world has *no* significant binary features, that it is, on the contrary, divided into overlapping, fragmented cultures, hybrid selves, continuously dissolving and emerging social states?" (Asad 2003).

17. As the potential for a two-state solution that might have made the claims of religiously motivated settlers practically irrelevant seems to be fading from the horizon, the need to think seriously about how to live together—to love thy neighbor/enemy as thyself—becomes increasingly urgent.

18. I borrow this sense of the term *recognition* as including re-cognition from Johannes Fabian (1999).

Bibliography

Abdo, Nahla, and Nira Yuval-Davis. 1995. Palestine, Israel and the Zionist Settler Project. In *Unsettling Settler Societies*. D. Stasiulis and N. Yuval-Davis, eds. London: Sage.

Abu El-Haj, Nadia. 1998. Translating Truths: Nationalism, the Practice of Archaeology, and the Remaking of the Past and Present in Contemporary Jerusalem. *American Ethnologist* 25(2):166–88.

Abu El-Haj, Nadia. 2001. *Facts on the Ground: Archeological Practice and Territorial Self-Fashioning in Israeli Society*. Chicago and London: University of Chicago Press.

Alcalay, Ammiel. 1993. *After Jews and Arabs: Remaking Levantine Culture*. Minneapolis: University of Minnesota Press.

Aloni, Shulamit. 2006. An Israeli without Hyphens. *HaAretz*, Opinion Page. May 16 http://www.haaretz.com/print-edition/opinion/an-israeli-without-hyphens-1.187829

Alonso, Ana Maria. 1994. The Politics of Space, Time and Substance: State Formation, Nationalism and Ethnicity. *Annual Review of Anthropology* 23:378–405.

Anderson, Benedict. 1983. *Imagined Communities: Reflections on the Origin and Spread of Nationalism*. London: Verso.

Anidjar, Gil. 2003. *The Jew, The Arab: A History of the Enemy*. Stanford, CA: Stanford University Press.

Antoun, Richard. 2008. *Understanding Fundamentalism: Christian, Islamic, and Jewish Movements*. New York: Rowman & Littlefield.

Appadurai, Arjun. 2002. Disjuncture and Difference in the Global Economy. In *The Anthropology of Globalization*. J. X. Inda and R. Rosaldo, eds. Blackwell Readers in Anthropology. Oxford: Blackwell.

Aran, Gideon. 1991. Jewish Zionist Fundamentalism: The Bloc of the Faithful in Israel (Gush Emunim). In *Fundamentalisms Observed*. M. E. Marty and R. S. Appleby, eds. 265–344. Chicago: University of Chicago Press.

Aran, Gideon. 1997. The Father, the Son, and the Holy Land: The Spiritual Authorities of Jewish-Zionism Fundamentalism in Israel. In *Spokesmen for the Despised*. R. S. Appleby, ed. 294–327. Chicago: University of Chicago Press.

Arendt, Hannah. 1973 (1951). *The Origins of Totalitarianism*. New York: Harcourt.

Arendt, Hannah. 2003 (1951). The Perplexities of the Rights of Man, from *The Origins of Totalitarianism*. In *The Portable Hannah Arendt*. P. Baehr, ed. 31–45. New York: Penguin.

Asad, Talal. 2003. *Formations of the Secular: Christianity, Islam, Modernity*. Stanford, CA: Stanford University Press.

Asad, Talal. 2006a. Responses. In *Powers of the Secular Modern: Talal Asad and His Interlocutors*. D. Scott and C. Hirschkind, eds. 206–43. Cultural Memory in the Present. Stanford, CA: Stanford University Press.

Asad, Talal. 2006b. Trying to Understand French Secularism. In *Political Theologies: Public Religions in a Post-Secular World*. H. de Vries and L. E. Sullivan, eds. 494–527. New York: Fordham University Press.

Asad, Talal. 2007. *On Suicide Bombing*. New York: Columbia University Press.

Atran, Scott. 1989. The Surrogate Colonization of Palestine, 1917–1939. *American Ethnologist* 16: 719–744.

Bardenstein, Carol. 1999. Trees, forests, and the shaping of Palestinian and Israeli collective memory. In *Acts of Memory: Cultural recall in the present*. Mieke Bal, Jonathan Crewe, and Leo Spitzer eds. Hanover and London: University Press of New England. Pgs. 148–170

Beinin, Joel. 2006. The Oslo Process and the Limits of a Pax Americana. In *The Struggle for Sovereignty: Palestine and Israel 1993–2005*. J. Beinin and R. Stein, eds. Stanford, CA: Stanford University Press.

Beinin, Joel, and Rebecca Stein. 2006. Histories and Futures of a Failed Peace. In *The Struggle for Sovereignty: Palestine and Israel 1993–2005*. J. Beinin and R. Stein, eds. Stanford, CA: Stanford University Press.

Ben-Amos, Avner, and Ilana Bet-El. 1999. Commemoration and National Identity: Holocaust Day and Memorial Day Ceremonies in Israeli Schools. *Constructing Cultures: Diasporas, Ethnicities, Identities*, Ben Gurion University of the Negev, Be'ersheva, Israel. Paper presented.

Bender, Barbara. 1993. *Landscape: Politics and Perspectives*. Oxford: Berg.

Bender, Barbara, and Margo Winer, eds. 2001. *Contested Landscape: Movement, Exile and Place*. Oxford: Berg.

Benjamin, Walter. 1968 (1940). Theses on the Philosophy of History. *Illuminations*. Trans. Harry Zohn. Hannah Arendt, ed. New York: Schocken Books.

Bhabha, Homi K. 1994. Of Mimicry and Man: The Ambivalence of Colonial Discourse. In *The Location of Culture*. 85–92. London: Routledge.

Bokser, Ben Zion, ed. 1978. *Abraham Isaac Kook: The Lights of Penitence, The Moral Principles, Lights of Holiness, Essays, Letters, and Poems*. Mahwah, NJ: Paulist Press.

Bourdieu, Pierre. 1977. *Outline of a Theory of Practice*. R. Nice, transl. Cambridge: Cambridge University Press.

Bowman, Glen. 2004. About a Wall. *Social Analysis* 48:149–56.

Boyarin, Daniel, and Jonathan Boyarin. 1993. Diaspora: Generation and the Ground of Jewish Identity. *Critical Inquiry* 19(4):693–725.

Boyarin, Jonathan. 1994. Space, Time, and the Politics of Memory. In *Remapping Memory: The Politics of TimeSpace*. J. Boyarin, ed. Minneapolis: University of Minnesota Press.

Brow, James. 1990. Notes on Community, Hegemony, and the Uses of the Past. *Anthropological Quarterly* 63(1):1–6.

Brown, Wendy. 2006a. *Regulating Aversion: Tolerance in the Age of Identity and Empire*. Princeton: Princeton University Press.

Brown, Wendy. 2006b. Subjects of Tolerance: Why We Are Civilized and They Are the Barbarians. In *Political Theologies: Public Religions in a Post-Secular World*. H. de Vries and L. E. Sullivan, eds. 298–317. New York: Fordham University Press.

Butler, Judith. 2008. Sexual Politics, Torture, and Secular Time. *British Journal of Sociology* 59(1):1–23.

Calhoun, Craig, ed. 1992 *Habermas and the Public Sphere*. Cambridge, MA: MIT Press.

Chafets, Ze'ev. 1995. A Nice Jewish Boy. In *The Jerusalem Report*. November 30.

Chakrabarty, Dipesh. 2000. *Provincializing Europe: Postcolonial Thought and Historical Difference*. Princeton, NJ: Princeton University Press.

Chakrabarty, Dipesh. 2002. *Habitations of Modernity: Essays in the Wake of Subaltern Studies*. Chicago: University of Chicago Press.

Chetrit, Sami Shalom. 1997. The Dream and the Nightmare: Some Remarks on the New Discourse in Mizrahi Politics in Israel. *News from Within* 13(1):49–59.

Comaroff, Jean, and John L. Comaroff, eds. 2001. *Millennial Capitalism and the Culture of Neoliberalism*. Durham: Duke University Press.

Connerton, Paul. 1989. *How Societies Remember*. Cambridge: Cambridge University Press.

Cook, Jonathan. 2003. Bedouin in the Negev Face New "Transfer." *Middle East Report Online*. May 10, 2003. Available: http://www.merip.org/mero/mero051003.html.

Crain, Mary. 1990. The Social Construction of National Identity in Highland Ecuador. *Anthropological Quarterly* 63(1):43–59.

Crapanzano, Vincent. 1985. *Waiting: The Whites of South Africa*. New York: Vintage Books.

Dalsheim, Joyce. 2003. Uncertain Past, Uncertain Selves? Israeli History and National Identity in Question. Doctoral Dissertation, Graduate Faculty of Political and Social Sciences of the New School for Social Research.

Dalsheim, Joyce. 2004. Settler Nationalism, Collective Memories of Violence and the "Uncanny Other." *Social Identities* 10(2):151–70.

Dalsheim, Joyce. 2005. Ant/agonizing Settlers in the Colonial Present of Israel-Palestine. *Social Analysis* 49(2):122–43.

Dalsheim, Joyce. 2007. Deconstructing National Myths, Reconstituting Morality: Modernity, Hegemony and the Israeli National Past. *Journal of Historical Sociology* 20(4):521–54.

Dalsheim, Joyce. 2010. On Demonized Muslims and Vilified Jews: Between Theory and Practice. *Comparative Studies in Society and History* 52(3):581–603.

Dalsheim, Joyce and Assaf Harel. 2009. Representing Settlers. *Review of Middle East Studies* 43(2):219–238.

Davies, W. D. 1991 (1982). *The Territorial Dimension of Judaism*. Minneapolis: Fortress.

Dawson, Lorne L. 1999. When Prophecy Fails and Faith Persists; A Theoretical Overview. *Nova Religio* 3:60–82.

Deeb, Lara. 2006. *An Enchanted Modern: Gender and Public Piety in Shi'i Lebanon*. Princeton, NJ: Princeton University Press.

Dein, Simon 2001 What Really Happens When Prophecy Fails: The Case of Lubavitch. *Sociology of Religion* 62(3):383–401.

Derrida, Jacques. (1967)1990. *Writing and Difference*. A. Bass, transl. Chicago: University of Chicago Press.

Derrida, Jacques. 2000. *Of Hospitality: Anne Dufourmantelle invites Jacques Derrida to Respond*. R. Bowlby, transl. Stanford, CA: Stanford University Press.

DeShalit, Avner. 1995. From the political to the objective: the dialectics of Zionism and environment. *Environmental Politics* 4(1):70–87.

Di-Capua, Yoav. 2007. The Intimate History of Collaboration: Arab Citizens and the State of Israel. In *Middle East Report Online*, May. Available: http://merip.org/mero/interventions/di-capua_interv.html.

Dominguez, Virginia. 1989. *People as Subject, People as Object: Selfhood and Peoplehood in Contemporary Israel*. Madison: University of Wisconsin Press.

El-Sana, Morad. 2005. *The Official Data on the Absent-Present Arab Bedouin: Adalah Newsletter* 14, June 2005. Available: www.adalah.org/newsletter/eng/jun05/comi2.pdf.

El-Or, Tamar and Gideon Aran. 1995. Giving Birth to a Settlement: Maternal Thinking and Political Action of Jewish Women on the West Bank. *Gender and Society* 9(1): 60–78.

Emmet, Ayala. 1996. *Our Sister's Promised Land*. Ann Arbor: University of Michigan Press.

Euben, Roxanne L. 1999. *Enemy in the Mirror: Islamic Fundamentalism and the Limits of Modern Rationalism*. Princeton, NJ: Princeton University Press.

Ewing, Katherine Pratt. 1994. Dreams from a Saint: Anthropological Atheism and the Temptation to Believe. *American Anthropologist* 96(3):571–83.

Ewing, Katherine Pratt. 2008. *Being and Belonging: Muslims in the United States since 9/11*. New York: Russell Sage Foundation.

Fabian, Johannes. 1999. Remembering the Other: Knowledge and Recognition in the Exploration of Central Africa. *Critical Inquiry* 26(1):49–69.

Fanon, Franz. 1967. *Black Skins, White Masks*. C. L. Markmann, transl. New York: Grove.

Feige, Michael. 2001. Where Is "Here"? Scientific Practices and Appropriating Space in the Discourse of Israeli Social Movements. In *Israel as Center Stage: A Setting for Social and Religious Enactments*. A. P. Hare and G. M. Kressel, eds. 43–71. Westport, CT: Bergin and Garvey.

Feige, Michael. 2003. *One Space, Two Places: Gush Emunim, Peace Now and the Construction of Israeli Space*. Tel Aviv: Magnes. (Hebrew)

Fendel, Hillel. 2007. A Call to Yesha Residents: Pass through Freely! In *Arutz Sheva*: Israeli National News.com. Available: http://www.frontlineisrael.com/article.php?EntryID=100.

Festinger, Leon, Henry Riecken, and Stanley Schachter. 1956. *When Prophecy Fails: A Social and Psychological Study of a Modern Group That Predicted the Destruction of the World*. New York: Harper.

Fischer, Shlomo. 2004. Fundamentalist or Romantic Nationalist? Israeli Modern Orthodoxy. *Conference on Dynamic of Jewish Belonging*. Van Leer Institute, Jerusalem: Available: http://www.vanleer.org.il/eng/content.asp?id=418.

Foucault, Michel. 2006 (1961). *Madness and Civilization: A History of Insanity in the Age of Reason*. London: Routledge.

Foucault, Michel. 1972. *The Archaeology of Knowledge*. New York: Pantheon.

Foucault, Michel 1991 (1978). Governmentality. In *The Foucault Effect: Studies in Governmentality*. G. Burchell, C. Gordon, and P. Miller, eds. Chicago: University of Chicago Press.

Freud, Sigmund. 1946 (1919). The Uncanny. In *Collected Papers of Sigmund Freud*. 368–407, Vol. 4. London: Hogarth.

Freud, Sigmund. 1957 (1917). The Taboo of Virginity. In *The Standard Edition of the Complete Psychological Works of Sigmund Freud*. 193–206, Vol. 11. London: Hogarth.

Freud, Sigmund. 1961 (1930). *Civilization and Its Discontents*. J. Strachey, transl. New York: W. W. Norton.

Friedman, Jonathan. 1992. The Past in the Future: History and the Politics of Identity. *American Anthropologist* 94(4):837–59.

Friedman, Thomas. 1995. Land or Life? *New York Times*. November 19, Week in Review, Op-ed, pg 15.

Gasteyer, Stephen P., and Cornelia Butler Flora. 2000. Modernizing the Savage: Colonization and the Perceptions of Landscape and Lifescape. *Sociologia Ruralis* 40(1):128–49.

Gellner, Ernest. 1981. Nationalism. *Theory and Society* 10(6):753–76.

Gillis, John R. 1994. Memory and Identity: The History of a Relationship. In *Commemorations: The Politics of National Identity*. J. R. Gillis, ed. Princeton, NJ: Princeton University Press.

Gilor, Dov. 1995. Tragic Results. *Jerusalem Post*. Letters to the Editor. November 10. Pg. 4.

Goldberg, David Theo. 2004. The Space of Multiculturalism. OpenDemocracy.com. Available: http://www.opendemocracy.net/arts-multiculturalism/article_2097.jsp.

Goldstone, Brian. 2007. Violence and the Profane: Islamism, Liberal Democracy, and the Limits of Secular Discipline. *Anthropological Quarterly* 80(1):207–35.

Goodman, Yehuda, and Shlomo Fischer. 2004. Towards Understanding Religiosity and Secularism: The Secularism Thesis and Alternative Conceptualizations. In *Maelstrom of Identities (Ma'arbolet HaZe'uyot)*. Y. Yonah and Y. Goodman, eds. Jerusalem: Kibbutz HaMeuchad and Van Leer. (Hebrew)

Goodman, Yehuda, and Yossi Yonah. 2004. Introduction: Religiousness and Secularity in Israel—Possibilities for Alternative Views. In *Maelstrom of Identities (Ma'arbolet HaZe'uyot)*. Y. Yonah and Y. Goodman, eds. 3–37. Jerusalem: Kibbutz HaMeuhad and Van Leer. (Hebrew)

Gordon, Neve. 2004. The Militarist and Messianic Ideologies. *Middle East Report on Line*. Available: www.merip.org/mero/mero070804.html.

Gorenberg, Gershom. 2008. The Collapse Began Today. *HaAretz*. July 15.

Gramsci, Antonio. 1971. *Selections from the Prison Notebooks of Antonio Gramsci*. Q. Hoare and G. N. Smith, eds. New York: International Publishers.

Greenstein, Ran. 1995. *Genealogies of Conflict: Class, Identity and State in Palestine/ Israel and South Africa*. Hanover, NH: Wesleyan University Press.

Grossberg, Lawrence. 1996. The Space of Culture, the Power of Space. In *The Post-Colonial Question: Common Skies, Divided Horizons*. I. Chambers and L. Curti, eds. 169–88. London: Routledge.

Gupta, Akhil, and James Ferguson, eds. 1997. *Culture, Power, Place: Explorations in Critical Anthropology*. Durham: Duke University Press.

Halbwachs, Maurice, and Lewis Coser. 1992. *On Collective Memory*. L. Coser, transl. Chicago: University of Chicago Press.

Halevi, Ilan. 1987. *A History of the Jews: Ancient and Modern*. London: Zed.

Handelman, Don. 2004. *Nationalism and the Israeli State: Bureaucratic Logic in Public Events*. Oxford: Berg.

Hansen, Thomas Blom, and Finn Stepputat, eds. 2001. *States of Imagination: Ethnographic Explorations of the Postcolonial State*. Durham, NC: Duke University Press.

Harding, Susan. 1991. Representing Fundamentalism: The Problem of the Repugnant Cultural Other. *Social Research* 58(2):373–93.

Harrison, Simon. 2002. The Politics of Resemblance: Ethnicity, Trademarks, Head-Hunting. *Journal of the Royal Anthropological Institute* 8(2):211–32.

Hertzberg, Arthur, ed. 1959. *The Zionist Idea: A Historical Analysis and Reader*. New York: Harper & Row.

Herzfeld, Michael. 1997. *Cultural Intimacy: Social Poetics in the Nation-State*. New York: Routledge.

Hirschkind, Charles. 2001. Civic Virtue and Religious Reason: An Islamic Counter-public. *Cultural Anthropology* 16(1):3–34.

Hirschkind, Charles, and Saba Mahmood. 2002. Feminism, the Taliban, and Politics of Counter-Insurgency. *Anthropological Quarterly* 75(2):339–54.

Horovitz, David. 1995. Israel Fights for Its Soul. *The Jerusalem Report*. November 30, 1995: 14–20.

Ilan, Shahar. 2006. Our Trauma Is Greater Than Yours. *HaAretz*. November 2. http://www.haaretz.com/print-edition/opinion/our-trauma-is-greater-than-yours-1.204091

Johnston, Anna, and Alan Lawson. 2000. Settler Colonies. In *A Companion to Postcolonial Studies*. H. Schwarz and S. Ray, eds. 360–76. Oxford: Blackwell.

Juergensmeyer, Mark. 2000a. *Terror in the Mind of God: The Global Rise of Religious Violence*. Berkeley: University of California Press.

Juergensmeyer, Mark. 2000b. Zion Betrayed. In *Terror in the Mind of God: The Global Rise of Religious Violence*. 44–60. Berkeley: University of California Press.

Katriel, Tamar. 1997. *Performing the Past: A Study of Israeli Settlement Museums*. London: Lawrence Erlbaum Associates.

Keane, Webb. 2007. *Christian Moderns: Freedom and Fetish in the Mission Encounter*. Berkeley: University of California Press.

Keinon, Herb. 1995. Right-Wing Protesters Are Now on the Ropes. *Jerusalem Post*. November 10.

Khalidi, Walid, ed. 1992. *All that Remains: The Palestinian Villages Occupied and Depopulated by Israel in 1948*. Washington, DC: Institute for Palestine Studies.

Khazzoom, Aziza. 2005. Did the Israeli State Engineer Segregation? On the Placement of Jewish Immigrants in Development Towns in the 1950s. *Social Forces* 84(1): 115–34.

Kifner, John, Carey Goldberg, and Joel Greenberg. 1995. With a Handshake, Rabin's Fate Was Sealed. *New York Times*. November 19, front page.

Kimmerling, Baruch. 1995. Academic History Caught in the Cross-Fire: The Case of Israeli-Jewish Historiography. *History and Memory* 7(1):41–65.

Lavie, Smadar. 1990. *The Poetics of Military Occupation: Mzeina Allegories of Bedouin Identity under Israeli and Egyptian Rule*. Berkeley: University of California Press.

Lavie, Smadar. 1992. Blow-ups in the Borderzones: Third World Israeli Authors' Gropings for Home. *New Formations* 17:24–43.

Lavie, Smadar and Ted Swedenberg. 1996. Introduction: Displacement, Diaspora and Geographies of Identity. In *Displacement, Diaspora and Geographies of Identity*, Smadar Lavie and Ted Swedenberg eds., pgs 1–26. Durham: Duke University Press.

Levy, Gideon. 2005. From Khan Yunis, You Can't See the Settlers. *HaAretz*. Available: http://www.haaretz.com/hasen/pages/ShArt.jhtml?itemNo=524506.

Lowenthal, David. 1985. *The Past Is a Foreign Country*. New York: Cambridge University Press.

Lustick, Ian. 1980. *Arabs in the Jewish State: Israel's Control of a National Minority*. Austin: University of Texas Press.

Lustick, Ian. 1988. *For the Land and the Lord: Jewish Fundamentalism in Israel*. New York: Council on Foreign Relations.

Lustick, Ian. 1993. Jewish Fundamentalism and the Israeli-Palestinian Impasse. In *Jewish Fundamentalism in Comparative Perspective: Religion, Ideology, and the Crisis of Modernity*. L. J. Silberstein, ed. 104–16. New York: New York University Press.

Mahmood, Saba. 2001. Feminist Theory, Embodiment, and the Docile Agent: Some Reflections on the Egyptian Islamic Revival. *Cultural Anthropology* 16(2):202–237.

Mahmood, Saba. 2005. *Politics of Piety: The Islamic Revival and the Feminist Subject*. Princeton, NJ: Princeton University Press.

Mahmood, Saba. 2006. Secularism, Hermeneutics, and Empire: The Politics of Islamic Reformation. *Public Culture* 18(2):323–47.

Malkki, Liisa H. 1997. National Geographic: The Rooting of Peoples and the Territori-alization of National Identity among Scholars and Refugees. In *Culture, Power,*

Place: Explorations in Critical Anthropology. A. Gupta and J. Ferguson, eds. Durham, NC: Duke University Press.

Malley, Robert, and Hussein Agha. 2001. Camp David: The Tragedy of Errors. *New York Review of Books*, August 9.

Marty, Martin E. 2003. Our Religio-Secular World. *Daedalus* 132(3):42–48.

Masalha, Nur. 2000. *Imperial Israel and the Palestinians: The Politics of Expansion*. London: Pluto Press.

Mazar, Eilat. 2005. Searching for Jewish Roots in Gush Katif. *Katif.net*, July 28. Available: english.katif.net/.

McAlister, Melani. 2003. Prophecy, Politics, and the Popular: The Left Behind Series and Christian Fundamentalism's New World Order. *South Atlantic Quarterly* 102(4):773–95.

Memmi, Albert. 1967. *The Colonizer and the Colonized*. Boston: Beacon.

Mitchell, W.J.T. 2000. Holy Landscape: Israel, Palestine and the American Wilderness. *Critical Inquiry* 26(2):193–233.

Moran, Anthony. 2002. As Australia Decolonizes: Indigenizing Settler Nationalism and the Challenges of Settler/Indigenous Relations. *Ethnic and Racial Studies* 25(6):1013–42.

Morris, Benny. 1987. *The Birth of the Palestinian Refugee Problem*. Cambridge: Cambridge University Press.

Morris, Benny. 1994. *1948 and After: Israel and the Palestinians*. Oxford: Clarendon Press.

Motzafi-Haller, Pnina. 2001. Scholarship, Identity, and Power: Mizrahi Women in Israel. *Signs: Journal of Women in Culture and Society* 26(3):697–734.

Mouffe, Chantal. 2006. Religion, Liberal Democracy, and Citizenship. In *Political Theologies: Public Religions in a Post-Secular World*. H. de Vries and L. E. Sullivan, eds. 318–26. New York: Fordham University Press.

Moughrabi, Fouad. 1989. The Birth of Israel: The New Revisionism. *Radical History Review* 45:62–85.

Nagata, Judith. 2001. Beyond Theology: Toward an Anthropology of "Fundamentalism." *American Anthropologist* 103(2):481–98.

Naipaul, V. S. 2004 *Magic Seeds*. New York: Vintage.

Nandy, Ashis. 2007. Closing the Debate on Secularism: A Personal Statement. In *The Crisis of Secularism in India*. A. D. Needham and R. S. Rajan, eds. Durham, NC: Duke University Press.

Neslen, Arthur. 2006. *Occupied Minds: A Journey into the Israeli Psyche*. London: Pluto Press.

Neuman, Tamara. 2004. Maternal "Anti-Politics" in the Formation of Hebron's Jewish Enclave. *Journal of Palestine Studies* 33(2):51–71.

Newman, David, and Uri Ram. 2004. Introduction. In *Israelis in Conflict*. A. Kemp, D. Newman, U. Ram, and O. Yiftachel, eds. Brighton, England: Sussex University Press.

Nimni, Ephraim, ed. 2003. *The Challenge of Post-Zionism: Alternatives to Israeli Fundamentalist Politics*. London: Zed.

Nora, Piere. 1989. Between History and Memory. *Representations* 26:7–25. Transl. Marc Roudenbush.

Nordstrom, Carolyn, and Antonius C. G. M. Robben, eds. 1995. *Fieldwork under Fire: Contemporary Studies of Violence and Survival.* Berkeley: University of California Press.

Pappé, Ilan. 1995. Critique and Agenda: The Post-Zionist Scholars in Israel. *History and Memory* 7(1):66–90.

Pappé, Ilan. 1997. Post-Zionist Critique on Israel and the Palestinians Part I: The Academic Debate. *Journal of Palestine Studies* 26(2):29–41.

Pels, Peter. 1997. The Anthropology of Colonialism: Culture, History, and the Emergence of Western Governmentality. *Annual Review of Anthropology* 26:163–83.

Povinelli, Elizabeth. 2001. Radical Worlds: The Anthropology of Incommensurability and Inconceivability. *Annual Review of Anthropology* 30:319–34.

Purdy, Mathew. 1995. Shaken by Rabin Death, Orthodox Jews Look Within. *New York Times.* November 19 41, 49.

Rabinowitz, Dan. 2000. Postnational Palestine/Israel? Globalization, Diaspora, Transnationalism, and the Israeli-Palestinian Conflict. *Critical Inquiry* 26(4):757–72.

Rabkin, Yakov M. 2006. *A Threat from Within: A Century of Jewish Opposition to Zionism.* F. A. Reed, transl. London: Zed.

Radcliffe, Sarah, and Sallie Westwood. 1996. *Remaking the Nation: Place, Identity and Politics in Latin America.* London: Routledge.

Ram, Uri. 1995a. *The Changing Agenda of Israeli Sociology: Theory, Ideology and Identity.* Albany: State University of New York Press.

Ram, Uri. 1995b. Zionist Historiography and the Invention of Modern Jewish Nationhood: The Case of Ben Zion Dinur. *History and Memory* 7(1):91–124.

Ram, Uri. 1996. Memory and Identity: Sociology of the Historians' Debate in Israel. *Theory and Critique (Te'oria u Bikortet)* 8:9–32. (Hebrew)

Ram, Uri. 1998. Postnationalist Pasts: The Case of Israel. *Social Science History* 22(4):513–45.

Ram, Uri. 1999. Introduction: McWorld with and against Jihad. *Constellations* 6(3): 323–324.

Ram, Uri. 2008. Second Wave Post-Zionism and the Apartheid Backlash. *Tikkun* http://www.tikkun.org/magazine/specials/postzionism.

Raz-Krakotzkin, Amnon. 1994. Exile in the Midst of Sovereignty: A Critique of "Shlilat HaGalut" in Israeli Culture II. *Theory and Criticism* 5:113–32. (Hebrew)

Raz-Krakotzkin, Amnon. 2001. History Textbooks and the Limits of Israeli Consciousness. *Journal of Israeli History* 20(2/3):155–72.

Raz-Krakotzkin, Amnon. 2005. The Zionist Return to the West and the Mizrahi Jewish Perspective. In *Orientalism and the Jews.* I. D. Kalmar and D. J. Penslar, eds. 162–81. Waltham, MA: Brandeis University Press.

Renan, Ernest. 1990. What Is a Nation? In *Nation and Narration.* H. Bhabha, ed. London: Routledge.

Rodinson, Maxime. 1973. *Israel: A Colonial-Settler State?* New York: Monad.

Rogan, Eugene L., and Avi Shlaim, eds. 2001. *The War for Palestine: Rewriting the History of 1948*. Cambridge: Cambridge University Press.

Ron, Amos. 2001. Representational and Symbolic Landscapes of the Early Zionist Rural Settlement in the Kinneret (Sea of Galilee) Valley. Doctoral Dissertation, Hebrew University.

Ron, James. 2003. *Frontiers and Ghettos: State Violence in Serbia and Israel*. Berkeley and Los Angeles: University of California Press.

Said, Edward. 1978. *Orientalism*. New York: Random House.

Schmemann, Serge. 1995. Rabin Slain at Peace Rally in Tel Aviv: Israeli Is Held and Says He Acted Alone. *New York Times*. November 18, Section A, pgs. 1, 16.

Scott, David. 1999. *Refashioning Futures: Criticism after Postcoloniality*. Princeton, NJ: Princeton University Press.

Scott, David, and Charles Hirschkind, eds. 2006. *Powers of the Secular Modern: Talal Asad and His Interlocutors*. Stanford, CA: Stanford University Press.

Scott, Joan W. 2007. *The Politics of the Veil*. Princeton, NJ: Princeton University Press.

Selwyn, Tom. 2001. Landscapes of Separation: Reflections on the Symbolism of By-Pass Roads in Palestine. In *Contested Landscapes: Movement, Exile and Place*. B. Bender and M. Winer, eds. Oxford: Berg.

Seremetakis, C. Nadia. 1994. The Memory of the Senses. In *The Senses Still: Perception and Memory as Material Culture in Modernity*. C. Nadia Seremetakis, ed. Chicago: Westview.

Shafir, Gershon. 1989a. *Land, Labor and the Origins of the Israeli-Palestinian Conflict, 1882–1914*. New York: Cambridge University Press.

Shafir, Gershon. 1989b. The Failed Experiment; "Natural Workers" from Yemen, 1909–1914. In *Land, Labor and the Origins of the Israeli-Palestinian Conflict 1882–1914*. 91–122. Berkeley: University of California Press.

Shafir, Gershon, and Yoav Peled. 2002. *Being Israeli: The Dynamics of Multiple Citizenship*. London: Cambridge University Press.

Shavit, Ari. 2004. Survival of the Fittest: An Interview with Benny Morris. In *HaAretz Friday Magazine*. January 16, pgs. 14–17.

Shenhav, Yehuda. 2001. The Representation of Mizrahim in History Textbooks. Available: http://hakeshet.tripod.com/articles2/history.htm. (Hebrew)

Shenhav, Yehuda. 2003a. *The Arab Jews: Nationalism, Religion, Ethnicity*. Tel Aviv: Am Oved. (Hebrew)

Shenhav, Yehuda. 2003b. The Cloak, the Cage and Fog of Sanctity: The Zionist Mission and the Role of Religion among Arab Jews. *Nations and Nationalism* 9(4):511–31.

Shenhav, Yehuda. 2006. The Occupation Doesn't Stop at the Check Point. *News from Within* 22 (5).

Shohat, Ella. 1988. Sephardim in Israel: Zionism from the Standpoint of Its Jewish Victims. *Social Text* 19(20):1–35.

Shohat, Ella. 2003. Rupture and Return: Zionist Discourse and the Study of Arab Jews. *Social Text* 21(2):49–74.

Shulman, George. 2006. Redemption, Secularization and Politics. In *Powers of the Secular Modern: Talal Asad and His Interlocutors*. D. Scott and C. Hirschkind, eds. Stanford, CA: Stanford University Press.

Siegman, Henry. 2004. Sharon and the Future of Palestine. *New York Review of Books*, (19) 51.

Silberstein, Laurence J. 1999. *The Postzionism Debates: Knowledge and Power in Israeli Culture*. New York: Routledge.

Silberstein, Laurence J., ed. 1993. *Jewish Fundamentalism in Comparative Perspective: Religion, Ideology, and the Crisis of Modernity*. New York: New York University Press.

Sivan, Emmanuel. 1995. The Enclave Culture. In *Fundamentalisms Comprehended*. M. E. Marty and R. S. Appleby, eds. 11–68. Chicago: University of Chicago Press.

Slyomovics, Susan. 1998. *The Object of Memory: Arab and Jew Narrate the Palestinian Village*. Philadelphia: University of Pennsylvania Press.

Sprinzak, Ehud. 1989. The Emergence of the Israeli Radical Right. *Comparative Politics* 21(2):171–192.

Starrett, Gregory. 2003. Violence and the Rhetoric of Images. *Cultural Anthropology* 18(3):398–428.

Stasiulis, Daiva, and Nira Yuval-Davis. 1995. *Unsettling Settler Societies: Articulations of Gender, Race, Ethnicity and Class*. London: Sage.

Swedenburg, Ted. 1995. Scenes of Erasure. In *Memories of Revolt: The 1936–1939 Rebellion and the Palestinian National Past*. 38–75. Minneapolis: University of Minnesota Press.

Tessler, Mark. 1994. *A History of the Israeli-Palestinian Conflict*. Bloomington: Indiana University Press.

Tirosh, Yosef, ed. 1975. *Religious Zionism, an Anthology*. Jerusalem: Ahva Cooperative Press, The World Zionist Organization.

Trouillot, Michel-Rolph. 1995. *Silencing the Past: Power and the Production of History*. Boston: Beacon Press.

Volger, Candace, and Patchen Markell. 2003. Introduction: Violence, Redemption, and the Liberal Imagination. *Public Culture* 15(1):1–10.

Walzer, Michael. 1997. *On Toleration*. New Haven, CT: Yale University Press.

Weber, Eugen. 1976. *Peasants into Frenchmen: The Modernization of Rural France 1870–1914*. Stanford, CA: Stanford University Press.

Weinreich, Max. 1980. *History of the Yiddish Language*. S. Noble, transl. Chicago: University of Chicago Press.

Weisburd, David. 1989. *Jewish Settler Violence: Deviance as Social Reaction*. University Park: Pennsylvania State University Press.

Weizman, Eyal. 2002. Introduction to *The Politics of Verticality*. Available: http://www.opendemocracy.net/conflict-politicsverticality/article_801.jsp

Wertsch, James. 2001. *Voices of Collective Remembering*. New York: Cambridge University Press.

White, Hayden. 1987. *The Content of the Form: Narrative Discourses and Historical Representation*. Baltimore, MD: John Hopkins University Press.

Wolfe, Patrick. 1999. *Settler Colonialism and the Transformation of Anthropology: The Politics and Poetics of an Ethnographic Event*. London: Cassell.

Wood, Davida. 1994. The Boundless Courtyard: Palestinian Israelis and the Politics of Uncertainty. Doctoral Dissertation, Department of Anthropology, Princeton University.

Yiftachel, Oren. 1998. Nation-Building and the Social Division of Space: Ashkenazi Control over Israeli Periphery. *Nationalism and Ethnic Politics* 4(3):33–58.

Yiftachel, Oren. 1999. Ethnocracy: The Politics of Judaizing Israel/Palestine. *Constellations* 6(3):364–90.

Yiftachel, Oren. 2000. "Ethnocracy" and Its Discontents: Minorities, Protests, and the Israeli Polity. *Critical Inquiry* 26:726–56.

Yiftachel, Oren. 2002. The Shrinking Space of Citizenship: Ethnocratic Politics in Israel. *Middle East Report* 223. Available: www.merip.org/mer/mer223/223_yiftachel.html.

Yiftachel, Oren. 2005. Neither Two States Nor One: The Disengagement and "Creeping Apartheid" in Israel/Palestine. *The Arab World Geographer* 8(3):125–129.

Yiftachel, Oren. 2006. *Ethnocracy: Land and Identity Politics in Israel/Palestine*. Philadelphia: University of Pennsylvania Press.

Zertal, Idith. 2005. *Israel's Holocaust and the Politics of Nationhood*. C. Galai, transl. Cambridge: Cambridge University Press.

Zertal, Idith, and Akiva Eldar. 2007. *Lords of the Land: The War for Israel's Settlement in the Occupied Territories 1967–2007*. New York: Nation Books.

Zerubavel, Yael. 1995. *Recovered Roots: Collective Memory and the Making of Israeli National Tradition*. Chicago: The University of Chicago Press.

Zerubavel, Yael. 1996. The Forest as National Icon: Literature, Politics, and the Archeology of Memory. *Israel Studies* 1(1):60–99.

Index

Page numbers followed by "*f*" and "n" indicate figures and notes, respectively.